Naomi Stadlen has unique experience of listening to mothers. For over twenty years she has run weekly discussion groups, Mothers Talking, which meet at the Active Birth Centre, and at the shop Born in London. She is a qualified psychotherapist and the author of the bestselling book *What Mothers Do*. She is also a mother of three and a grandmother. Visit www.naomistadlen.com.

HOW MOTHERS

LOVE

MOTHERS

and how
relationships
are born

NAOMI STADLEN

piatkus

PIATKUS

First published in Great Britain in 2011 by Piatkus
Reprinted 2012 (three times)

A CIP catalogue record for this book
is available from the British Library.

ISBN 978-0-7499-5298-3

Edited by Anne Newman
Typeset in Minion by Palimpsest Book Production Ltd,
Falkirk, Stirlingshire
Printed and bound by CPI Group (UK) Ltd, Croydon, CR0 4YY

Excerpts taken from Sigmund Freud's *Introductory Lectures on Psychoanalysis*
reproduced courtesy of W. W. Norton.

Papers used by Piatkus are from well-managed forests
and other responsible sources.

MIX
Paper from
responsible sources
FSC
www.fsc.org   FSC® C104740

Piatkus
An imprint of
Little, Brown Book Group
100 Victoria Embankment
London EC4Y 0DY

An Hachette UK Company
www.hachette.co.uk

www.piatkus.co.uk

Contents

With thanks   vi
Author's note   vii
Introduction   1

1   Making heartroom   10
2   House-room without heartroom   29
3   'I don't know'   40
4   Keeping in touch   54
5   Shadows of Truby King and Freud   75
6   Keeping in mind   85
7   When the candle burns low   111
8   'Am I holding him back?'   122
9   Learning to take turns   135
10   'I can't do intimacy'   158
11   Turning into parents   189
12   Intimacy with two   218
13   Family relationships   243
14   'Athenian' or 'Spartan'?   267
15   Mothers together   286

Notes   311
Bibliography   327
Index   335

With thanks

My warm thanks to all the mothers who have talked about their experiences, especially at Mothers Talking and La Leche League meetings. Thanks also to everyone who read chapters for me: Ceridwen George, Pem Goldschmidt, Anne Manne, Jennifer Marsh, Rachel Montagu, Lauren Porter, who brought together the 'Meaning of Motherhood' Conference in Auckland on 28 November 2008, my son Shoël, Professor Thomas Szasz (who also helped me to explain the confusion over 'mental health'), Veronica and Richard Veasey, my daughter, Rachel, and her husband Eric Wen. To Tovi Wen, my grandson, for discussing the title for this book when he was just six. To Merrill Carrington for a very helpful conversation in London. To Anne Lawrance and Helen Stanton, for their calm encouragement and clear editing. To Anne Newman, for her understanding, and her sensitive editing and copy-editing. To the memory of Professor Martin Wight, pioneer Dean of the University of Sussex who introduced me to Ancient Greek history and to Dante. To Rabbi Rodney Mariner for twenty years of existential Jewish education. To my beloved family, Rachel, Eric and Tovi; Shoël, Natasha and Anna Kateryna; and Darrel. Especial thanks to Tony, my faithful husband, who read chapters at all hours, with his wonderful understanding.

Author's note

The identities of the mothers quoted in *How Mothers Love* are confidential, so I have adopted the following system of referring to them and their families:

> **B** indicates the name of a boy child.
> **G** indicates the name of a girl child.
> **F** indicates the father's name.
> **M** indicates the mother's name.

Quotations are usually cited in order of the babies' ages. When a mother has two or more babies, the quotation usually uses the age of the youngest baby. Occasionally, it has made sense to change the order, if the mother is remembering something from long ago.

In using pronouns, it is important to make a clear distinction between mother and child. This can be confusing if both are female. So, with apologies to girls, I have used masculine pronouns for general statements about a baby or child.

The term mother usually means the person who bears the baby, gives birth to him, and takes care of him afterwards. But this is not always done by the mother alone. Fathers and grandmothers especially may be the primary daytime carers. If the parents divorce and remarry, there may be step-parents taking turns. There may be adoptive mothers as well as biological ones. When a non-professional person stands in for the mother in this way, or takes turns with her, descriptions of what mothers do or how mothers love may apply to this person also. It would be clumsy to keep repeating: 'Mothers, or other relatives responsible for the child . . . ' So this note is to provide a general reminder that observations about mothers may be equally true of other relatives caring for the child.

Introduction

Only babies know the secret of how mothers love. They gaze steadily into our faces and see the myriad changes in our most intimate expressions. We shall never see our own faces as they do. Strange that each one of us has been a baby, yet few of us can recall what we saw and felt then.

How Mothers Love is an attempt to rediscover some of our early wisdom. It is especially important to do this today. The word 'mother' is fast being replaced by 'parent' and also 'caregiver'. But surely the love that mothers give their babies is unique.

One interesting question is who teaches whom to love? It can seem as though babies inspire us, guide us and are our teachers. But babies might not feel so all-knowing. So perhaps love is a mysterious alchemy that is kindled between mother and baby, and is a shared adventure between the two.

Children need their mothers' love. Most mothers want to give it. Often they are giving it much more than they realise. People sometimes talk as if a mother's love is the same as her *feeling* of love. A mother's feeling of love can be overwhelming. However, much of her time is spent in practical tasks. Then she is in a different mode. She might not be conscious of feeling love when, for example, she wakes herself from her much-needed sleep because her baby is crying and needs her. Fortunately, from her actions, the baby seems to sense his mother's underlying love. That way he *knows* that she loves him.

If a mother isn't always conscious of feeling love, how can she tell if she is acting with underlying love? A mother's love means that she is in a kind of dialogue with her child. Long before her child can speak, there is a 'conversation' of questions and answers going on between the two of them.

How Mothers Love is a study of the dialogues that arise during all those repetitive everyday actions that mothers get to know so well. It's not an exploration of extraordinary communications, as, for example, when mothers seem to be in telepathic contact with their children. There are other publications which discuss these.

So *How Mothers Love* is a tentative study of the loving actions of mothers. I was glad to see that another mother had made a similar point before me. 'Mother-love doesn't amount to much except "in action", wrote Prudence Bradish in 1919 at the end of her book *Mother-Love in Action*.

Although it has been pointed out, for example, in Michel Odent's *The Scientification of Love*, that a new mother is flooded with oxytocin, which helps her to feel love, the hormone has no power to compel her to loving actions. In a similar way, research has shown that the brain of a new mother develops. This is the brain's potential. But our brains cannot compel us to become motherly. Becoming a loving mother is not an inevitable result of having a baby, or being flooded with oxytocin, or having a developing brain. Only we ourselves can make our love happen.

Love takes courage to give because there is no guaranteed return. A mother surely hopes that her love will help her child to realise the best of himself. Perhaps it will. Yet even her love can't make that happen. The kind of person the child will become is his own choice. A mother can't trade her love for a precise return. If a mother takes the courage to give her love, it's because she wants to give her best, and love is it.

We can also see that a mother's love for her child is different from her love for her husband or partner. Adults are experienced and in that sense equally matched. Two adults can have a fierce argument with one another, and then make up. A newborn is inexperienced and extremely sensitive. A different way of loving is needed.

At first, a newborn is like a guest. Whenever a mother treats her baby with kindness, just as when she is hospitable to a guest, she creates a good moment. The moment itself will pass. Yet the good of that moment will last. It becomes a memory that can strengthen the growing relationship between the mother and her child.

The loving relationship which she creates with each child is a vital part of being a mother. Creating these relationships is the miracle that mothers are doing all around us. No mother is perfect. Yet, collectively, mothers are working to initiate a new generation into how to relate to other people. It's a momentous overall achievement. Some are full-time mothers; others are employed, either part- or full-time. Yet the desire to relate to their babies seems to be a common one. Full-time mothers have more opportunity. But many mothers with little time to spare still relate intensely to their children.

Not enough is known about how mothers create these very first relationships. This might sound unbelievable, since so much research has been done to try to find out. Researchers tend to measure behaviours which are simple to quantify. But mother-and-baby couples criteria in complex and intelligent ways. The researcher's criteria may not capture the significant signals between them.

Even when researchers go into mothers' homes, they set up situations which can become artificial. This is what Monika Abels found during an ambitious project to interview Gujarati mothers in India with their babies. The mothers were instructed to 'play with your baby as you usually would'. But they weren't sure what this meant.[1] I wouldn't have known either, if I had been asked. I don't think I used to sit down in official 'play mode' with my babies. Play would arise unexpectedly, during our everyday activities.

However, whenever research summaries are published, mothers seem to be impressed. I have heard some mothers discount their own understanding in favour of research results.

Perhaps mothers feel intimidated because their thinking tends to be dismissed as 'anecdotal' or 'subjective'. Yet, when you listen, they are often scientific, meaning that they keep forming hypotheses which they test to gain information. Mothers are natural phenomenologists, though many would not use this word to describe themselves. Phenomenology is the attempt to understand our experience by looking at it in a fresh and unprejudiced way.

Mothers are phenomenological when they try to understand why their babies behave as they do. They study *themselves* as part of the interaction and ask how much their babies are affected by something they did. You might watch, for example, a mother first cuddling her crying baby, and then later see the mother giving him a bath. You could analyse the responses of the baby. But without the mother's logical thinking you could not explain them.

At first, the mother would have started a private brainstorm of questions to herself. Why was her baby crying? Was he ill? In pain? She would run through a range of possibilities. Then she might wonder if she had put him through an over-stimulating day. Yes, that possibility would match the level of crying that she could hear.

(This in itself is based on much experience.) She could then create an informal hypothesis: 'I'll try giving you [*her baby*] a bath. If you are over-stimulated, you'll be able to relax and calm down. Then I'll know you aren't ill.' Isn't this thought process a form of scientific reasoning? Though the mother would probably doubt herself, I believe a radical scientist such as Einstein would have validated her hypothesis and her way of testing it. Einstein said how important it was to ask simple, childlike questions and to take nothing for granted.

Mothers are in a privileged position. Outsiders cannot see all the subtle communications which they exchange with their babies. Mothers have stores of information that they are hardly aware of. They could teach researchers a great deal about how they love.

When researchers set up a project, they usually want to ask particular questions. However, mothers can be approached differently. It is possible to *listen* to them without a specific agenda. It's true that such a listener will create her own particular ambiance, which will affect what mothers say. This is unavoidable. Allowing for this, there is a wealth of data for a listener to learn.

What happens when a listener, using a discipline which has not yet been named, is not doing research but facilitating discussions between mothers? At first, the sheer breadth and also the fragmentary nature of motherly experience can be overwhelming. Mothers communicate both verbally and through their actions. The listener may try to link first impressions to the usual explanations. But, in time, it becomes possible to risk being puzzled or even lost for an explanation. After that, if the listener perseveres, he or she will learn – and this learning will be new.

Since 1991, I have been running weekly discussion meetings for mothers. They are called Mothers Talking. I often have two groups running at different locations. We sit in a circle with toys and toddlers in the middle (babies are welcome up to the age when they can understand what mothers are saying). I ask each mother:

5

'What kind of a week have you just had?' Discussion emerges immediately, because mothers have so much on their minds.

These discussions are for mothers to share experience. My goal is *not* research. My attention is taken up with dividing the time fairly between them, and making sure the questions they raise are opened out for group discussion. I have never made an audio- or video-recording of a meeting, nor field notes afterwards. That would change the purpose and the whole feeling of the discussion.

I look forward to these meetings myself as precious moments in my week, and this probably contributes to a certain excitement in the conversation. It's only afterwards that I can appreciate how much I have heard. As I pick up cups afterwards, or wait for a bus, a few comments come back to me. They may seem quite trivial, but I can hardly wait to write them down while I can still remember the exact words. Mothers make observations that remind me of tiny pieces of a jigsaw. They sound significant, like fragments of a very large picture. But in this case, there is no jigsaw box with a finished picture on its lid. There may never be a finished picture. However, after a good deal of listening, one can recognise fragments which connect together to make a small pattern. In this way, a shadowy larger picture starts to emerge.

For a long time, this picture had no frame. The idea of centring it on an exploration of how mothers love is recent. Now it seems obvious. It has enabled me to reflect on my own experience as mother to my three children and as grandmother to my two grandchildren. I've also had over twenty years of taking La Leche League and Mothers Talking meetings. I see mothers individually or as couples in my practice as a psychotherapist. I also read widely. There's a great deal to think over on such a fundamental subject. Everything in *How Mothers Love* has been through a lengthy questioning process.

For example, mothers on maternity leave often say how tired they are. Many people attribute this to broken nights and lack of sleep. But I don't think this is the whole explanation. Once we notice how actively mothers are responding to their babies, night and day, we may be astonished that they aren't even *more* tired.

Is there any way to discover whether the small patterns I have observed are valid for more than the tiny sample of mothers that I meet? A good test is whether mothers in different parts of the world recognise my tentative 'picture'. In the case of my first book, they did. Mothers have contacted one another on many blogs, not intended for my eyes. Others have emailed me, from many parts of the world. They say that much of their own experience corresponds exactly to that of mothers quoted in *What Mothers Do*. One telling example came from an experienced Mexican doula, Joni Nichols, who wrote in a review: 'As I read the women quoted in the book [*What Mothers Do*] I *heard* them express their confusion, uncertainty, wonderment, pain and insights spoken with the lilting accent of the hundreds of Mexican and Latin American women I work with . . .'[2]

It will be interesting to see whether these books will stand the 'test of time'. I hope that *What Mothers Do* and now *How Mothers Love* will continue to 'speak' to mothers. I also hope they will encourage more mothers to trust their own experience and to write about it.

I have been asked in what way *How Mothers Love* is different from *What Mothers Do*. Both books arose out of my discussions with mothers. But after publishing *What Mothers Do*, I realised that there was more to say. Both books are self-contained, and can be read separately. For example, I shall not repeat my discussion of ambivalent motherly love here, as it can be found in Chapter Nine of *What Mothers Do*: 'What is motherly love?'

Neither book is intended as a 'must-do' manual. *What Mothers Do* does not tell any mother what she 'should' do, nor does *How Mothers Love* tell any mother how she 'should' love. In *What Mothers*

Do, I invited readers to contact me if they could detect any advice on mothering. No reader did. In this book, although I have given no advice on how mothers 'should' love, I have used the last chapter to suggest a way in which mothers might co-operate to find a stronger maternal voice.

How Mothers Love is an exploratory general picture. None of us matches this picture exactly, but I think it is useful to have it. As far as we know, few features of the picture are new. For millennia, mothers seem to have had the task of listening and responding to their children. Individually, each of us is only too fallible. But our collective ability to create loving relationships with our children is essential to the continuing survival of civilised life.

It troubles me to hear people use terms like 'emotional health' or 'mental health' when they are talking about how a mother relates to her baby. When people discuss a mother's 'emotional health' or 'mental health', they are usually conveying value judgments about her behaviour. They are asking whether her behaviour helps or hinders her baby's personal development. The problem is that this language tends to mystify and mislead mothers into assuming that they have been given a genuine medical diagnosis and need medical help to become 'healthy'. I know that terms like 'mental health' are much used, but I want to use simple language here in writing about mothers and babies.

How Mothers Love has been divided into fifteen chapters showing several aspects of a mother's love. I chose them because they cover themes that recurred when mothers talked. There is a great deal to consider; the position of mothers is in continual flux and there is far more to say than can fit into a single book.

I am steeped in the conversations of mothers. I have used extracts from discussions to illustrate my understanding. At first, my chosen extracts might sound arbitrary. However, I want to make it clear that I have only selected statements that seem typical. They are not usually dramatic stories or accounts of exceptional situations.

I am not looking for those. I am listening for statements that are utterly ordinary and characteristic.

I'll start at the beginning, which is also the very core of being a mother. You might expect love to be evident from the outset. But instead mothers seem to start by making an 'empty space'.

CHAPTER ONE

Making heartroom

Even mothers themselves don't realise how much they are doing.

> I've been feeling low on energy, as if I ought to be doing more with
> my time than just being B's mother. And I've been feeling reluctant
> to meet other people, as if I've got nothing worth saying to any of
> my friends. [B, 8 months]

Did she really say, '*just* being my son's mother'? Her son was
busy trying to stand up. He was flushed with excitement, clutching
on to a large beanbag. His mother was talking to a circle of other
mothers and seemed absorbed in conversation. But suddenly, she
put out her hand to steady her son. Sure enough, he was just about
to topple forward on to the carpet. She waited until he had regained
his balance, and then let go her hand.

This describes about one minute of her day. She was being
sensitive to her son, giving him the exact amount of help he
needed. She was also conveying to him that, while she was talking,
she was still looking after him. Yet this is barely noticed by any
of us. Even I only realised what she had said several moments
later. No wonder she thought she 'ought to be doing more with
my time'.

Why is this tiny action important? It was part of an ongoing dialogue of the kind that many mothers and children build up. The son wouldn't have dared to be so adventurous without an understanding that his mother was keeping him safe. This kind of understanding doesn't need to be perfect. Both of them might sometimes misread the signals of the other. But on the whole it would work. Their signals might not be visible to outsiders. Yet, to the child, his mother's understanding may have lifelong importance as his first experience of a human relationship.

One hears elderly people talking about their mothers – not as long-ago memories, but as if they were still in a kind of dialogue, even now. 'My mother wouldn't have approved of this,' people say; or, 'Mum brought me up always to think of others.' In this way, a mother's relationship with her child seems to outlive her.

If we study how these understandings get started, perhaps it will be easier for all of us to appreciate how much mothers are doing. For example, how do mothers begin? Do they all start in the same way? Are there several equally good ways? And what about having regrets about choices? Could a mother make changes now if she didn't start her relationship well and has realised since that it could be better?

At what point does a mother start her understanding, or her relationship, with each child? I used to take it for granted that the relationship started at birth, when a mother could first see her newborn. But then I attended a talk given by two mothers in Auckland, New Zealand. Their first babies had both died before or during birth. So both mothers had returned from hospital alone, without their babies. 'Am I Still a Mother?' was the title of their joint presentation.[3]

After listening to them, I could see that the answer had to be: 'Yes. *Of course* you are both still mothers.' The relationship of mother and child cannot start at birth. It begins at conception. From the start, the mother opens up a tiny involuntary space in her womb to accommodate her child. Gradually, she also opens out a corresponding emotional space. This beginning seems to be something that many mothers do, without being taught.

An expectant mother might not think she has made *any* emotional space. However, it is poignantly evident if it was in vain. If the baby did not survive, as happened to the two mothers just mentioned, or if the baby was taken away for adoption soon after birth, mothers say they feel devastated. 'My life will never be the same again,' said one mother who was compelled to give up her baby for adoption at birth. 'You can't explain the psychological effects of something like that. It's beyond words. It's beyond anything.'[4]

Another mother remembered:

> When I was six weeks pregnant, I went for a scan, and they could see no sign of a foetus. They told me I had probably lost her, but to come back in two weeks, and they'd see what had happened. That was a terrible time for me. I came back in two weeks, and it was a different sonographer – and there was G, perfectly normal. It was only *then* that I allowed myself to feel just how terrible it had been. The sonographer must have wondered what was the matter with us. I was all over the shop. I just fell apart. I realised how much the baby meant to me. [G, 8 months]

Alice Meynell, the English writer and suffragist, took ten years to write a two-verse poem about her first baby who had died at birth. She went on to have eight more children. Her poem ended:

> But oh, ten years ago, in vain,
> A mother, a mother was born.[5]

The simplicity of her words, and their emotional cadences convey the pain that a woman feels when her motherly development is suddenly cut short. (The poem is quoted in full on page 311, together with an additional note.)

Motherhood might sound cosy – but for none of us is it entirely cosy. Motherhood can include times of great joy, as well as anxiety, terror and tragedy. It can be hard to bear all these times. But they are all part of being a mother.

From conception on, we start to change. This change is unique to mothers. Fathers do not change in the same way. Many men today say they are determined to become active fathers. They too are changing. But there isn't an inescapable physical reminder of pregnancy for them, as there is for mothers.

One can link fathers and mothers by using the word 'parent'. Yet the two roles diverge from the start. It's not the father who is suddenly shaking with exhaustion, or ravenously hungry, or who feels queasy after a single coffee. He doesn't become breathless in late pregnancy, or eat some delicious food and then stay awake all night with heartburn, or need to empty his bladder hourly. The interchangeable word 'parent' is inadequate to convey the experience of mothers. Like emigrants, newly pregnant mothers have already left a familiar country and have started a journey towards somewhere new.

> When I was pregnant, I used to say, 'It's time for our nap now.' My partner would look at me in amazement. He'd say, 'Who are you going to nap with?' I meant me and the baby. [G, 10 months]

A host preparing for a long-stay guest will have some idea of the preparations of an expectant mother. Such a host was the poet, Samuel Taylor Coleridge. In May 1800, he wrote a letter offering hospitality to a friend, William Godwin, who had been married to the brilliant early feminist Mary Wollstonecraft. She had died suddenly in 1797, after giving birth to their daughter, also called Mary.[6] So Godwin was a widower and single father, looking after two small girls: Mary Wollstonecraft's older daughter Fanny, by a different father, together with little Mary.

Coleridge obviously felt concerned for his friend. He wanted to offer hospitality to Godwin and to the two girls, even though he hadn't yet decided which of two homes he would be in: 'But whether I continue here [*Nether Stowey*] or migrate thither [*to a house in Keswick*], I shall be in a beautiful country, and have house-room . . . ' he wrote. We can imagine Coleridge pausing to dip his quill pen into his inkpot while he considered what to say next. Perhaps he thought 'house-room' sounded a bit practical and impersonal. He added: 'and heartroom for you, and you must come and write your next work at my house.'[7] It sounds especially warm because he wrote 'house-room' with a hyphen, while 'heartroom' is one whole word.

Surely both these words describe how mothers start their relationships. Having a baby is a major event. Our first need is to create both enough house-room *and* heartroom for the coming baby. Whatever our individual circumstances, this seems to be a common starting route for most mothers. Nor does it usually mean that we are going to order a new room. Both house-room and heartroom are available, though more than likely densely cluttered with our immediate concerns. By 'making room', we usually mean that we shall need to clear and tidy what we already have. We can't start the relationship by crowding it into the minimal space left over from all our other relationships. It will be a major concern, and we need to create a special space for it.[8]

Everything creative seems to start with a moment of empty space. A writer will sit in front of an empty sheet of paper or a blank screen and with, perhaps, a blank mind too, wondering what to say. A concert begins with a silent moment of expectancy, just after the players have tuned their instruments. A race begins with the starting pistol, but there is a moment before the shot when the competitors are lined up, concentrating, ready to begin. I know, as a psychotherapist, that there is a moment of stillness at the start of every session. In all these 'empty' moments, people set aside extraneous concerns to make room for something new.

Just as a host tidies the guest room and gets out some fresh bedding and towels, so an expectant mother tidies away some of her work commitments, and starts to ask herself how she will manage with a baby. This last may not be a comfortable question. All the same, it opens up space. Even worrying about whether the baby will be entirely healthy prepares a mother for several possibilities. Many mothers now have tests, learn their child's gender and minimise the surprise factor, while some decide not to make many preparations until after the birth. It might sound like a paradox, yet even if a mother has chosen *not* to prepare much beforehand, this can still turn out to be an adequate form of preparation.

Making house-room is obvious and visible. Making heartroom is a metaphor which describes a subtle process. However, the physical house-room preparations seem to lead to the more subtle heartroom ones. A grandmother told me: 'My mother, and also my grandmother, would have had – what's the word? – *layettes*. They had complete sets of clothes for each baby. Hand-sewn clothes, hand-knitted woollies, everything. I think it was a good way for them to prepare beforehand.' She meant that these practical preparations would have helped the mother to feel 'in the mood'.

Today, mothers don't always turn to their own mothers and grandmothers for hand-made baby clothes. Instead, they turn to their friends and to what can be bought. From the States, we have the concept of a 'baby shower'. This is a gathering of the friends of the expectant mother, who bring gifts for the unborn baby. Like the slower business of knitting and sewing for the layette, a baby shower seems to help the mother get into the mood for her baby, and to make it all feel more real.

When birth is imminent, there can be such a receptive

atmosphere that other people may feel this special 'heartroom' space too. Tolstoy has given us a description in *War and Peace*. He relates how a princess went into labour, while the entire nineteenth-century Russian aristocratic household experienced 'a common anxiety, a softening of the heart'. Tolstoy was in a good position to know about this, having fathered at least thirteen children, who were all born at home. He continued his account of the household where the princess was in labour: 'Evening passed, night came, and the feeling of suspense and softening of the heart in the presence of the unfathomable did not lessen but increased. No one slept.'[9] The connection which Tolstoy observed between childbirth and our hearts is surely significant. It seems a spontaneous untaught response.

During the early stages of giving birth, some mothers keep a sense of connection to their babies. If the birth is difficult, a mother may find that the connection diminishes and gives way to anxiety for herself. As her cervix widens in the immense process of giving birth, her whole body is making an involuntary space for the baby to emerge. I am not sure how much heartroom a mother has for the child at the moment of birth. 'I am not pushing, I am being pushed!' wrote Sheila Kitzinger, woman-centred childbirth educator, in a poem about birth.[10] Perhaps mother and baby are connected and together in the midst of the action.

After a mother has created an inner hiatus during pregnancy, however tentative, it seems possible for her love to flow into the empty space after the birth. The early act of making heartroom seems to prepare for the act of loving. Making heartroom is expansive. It's like a pair of arms stretching out to welcome a variety of possible babies. When a mother feels the huge opening and melting of her heart towards her particular baby, her feelings seem to close around him, loving him, and him alone, for being exactly the baby that he is. (Mothers of multiples seem to go through this process with each baby individually.)

When I was pregnant, I kept wondering about the chance of that particular sperm and that particular egg, in that particular month, or year. Suppose it had been a mistake? Suppose the baby and I didn't get on? But as soon as I saw B I knew he was ours. I haven't had any of those doubts since then. B is part of our family. I can't imagine life without him. [B, 4 months]

Not all mothers experience love immediately. Mothers seem to expect to fall in love with their babies on sight, and many feel distressed if they don't. The reality is that mothers respond in their own time.

I never wanted children. It didn't go with my lifestyle. G was a mistake. And the first two weeks were very hard when all you do is [*breast*]feed them all day. But now . . . she's an easy baby. She's a very nice baby. She's absolutely my *favourite* baby. I'm still very emotional about it. [G, 6 weeks]

In the first days, I was ready to protect her, but I didn't love her. The trouble was, I didn't know her. I kept crying with worry that . . . [*crying again*] I'd failed her because I didn't love her enough. Now we've both got to know each other. [G, 2 months]

I always knew he'd be a boy, but somehow I expected him to be blond. When he was born, a nurse handed me this dark-haired baby with a squashed-up nose. I was gobsmacked then. He didn't seem mine. He seemed . . . But that's all gone now. I *love* who he is, I love him so much. I love all his independent ideas about things. [B, 2 years]

This mother still managed to find her way to finding heartroom to love her son. It would have been difficult if she had spent all her time wishing he had been blond. I asked her how she had changed, but she couldn't remember. I imagine she slowly let go of her image of a blond baby, and began to see that the colour of his hair wasn't as important as she had thought. This then freed her to warm to her baby as the person he was, rather than grieving for the person he definitely wasn't.

Just after birth, a baby doesn't need much house-room. A four-poster bed in a glamorous bedroom isn't necessary. But what about heartroom? How much heartroom does a baby need? Should mothers provide a *tiny* amount for a tiny baby? How can she know if she is giving the 'right' amount?

Heartroom can't be measured. But it's certainly not tiny. Small though the baby is, he needs a great deal of maternal attention. Most young babies insist on getting it. In the rush of daily life, mothers can get distracted by answering telephone calls, organising meals, worrying about unpaid bills . . . If babies didn't keep crying for attention, many of them would get squeezed out of all the other activities which the mother was hoping to achieve. As babies get older, the intervals *between* moments of attention may grow longer – but babies still need the heartroom quality of the atten-tion, which is tender, warm and welcoming. Even as adults, however long the intervals may have been, children may suddenly turn to their mothers in a crisis and insist that their mothers re-open that generous space.

In other words, heartroom is not something a mother creates just for the birth. Nor is it for the next few weeks, nor until this time next year. 'Once you are a mother, there is no way back,' one mother remarked. If a mother opens up real heartroom for her child, it does not seem possible to fold it away again. The commit-ment will be lifelong. Understandably, some mothers are alarmed at such commitment, and need time to get used to it. But I think that if making heartroom became socially recognised, this would help mothers to feel much more supported.

Nor is making heartroom a one-way process.

Me: What's B like?

M: Oh, he's lovely. He's got a *big* heart. [B, 7 months]

Many mothers say that they had not known that they could love so passionately until they saw the tender and open expressions of their babies. They usually use the words 'love' and 'heart' to describe it.

When I hear G laugh, my whole heart melts, and I feel I would easily *die* for her. [G, 7 months]

Mothers discover that their love is unconditional.

What people don't understand is that they might pick out this or that flaw in a child. But, if it's *your* child, you accept all of that child in a way that no one else would do. [*Loud chorus of agreement from the circle of listening mothers.*] [B, 4 years; B, 11 months]

Mothers sometimes say that their babies teach them about love. I know I found that. Yet we have all been babies ourselves. Perhaps each new baby has the power to *remind* his mother of a love she herself once knew.

Some mothers oppose this kind of love:

My mother-in-law said the other day: 'You know, M, you'll have to harden your heart one day, and leave B to cry. You can't pick him up every time.' But I don't want to leave B to cry. [B, 6 months]

It does sound strange that a mother, of all people, should be advised to harden her heart.

How do mothers cope with these overwhelming feelings in daily living? There comes a stage when a mother realises that her adjustment needs to be ongoing. There is no way back to the way it was before conception. Yet heartroom is not like a door that can be propped open, night and day. It's dynamic and emotional. Mothers find that their moods fluctuate, and that they close off when they feel 'down' and tired.

19

When I'm happy, I can see that B is a lovely boy and he wants to communicate with me, and he has a really great sense of humour. He's got a real personality. Whereas when I'm *not* happy I lose all of that. Then B seems very demanding, and I can't do it, and then I feel guilty, and he picks it up and starts whining. Then I can't see his special personality at all. [B, 7 months]

There are times when you can really *see* your baby. But on other days – do you know what I mean? – you're not so sure. [G, 9 months]

It isn't only mothers who feel moody. Their children may feel irritable too. A mother may feel her child must be irritated with *her*, and protect herself by closing herself a little.

M: There's the shadow side of mothering, the dark side. You don't hear people talk about it much.

Me: What is it?

M: All those times when you are bored. Or you try and try, but nothing you do is right, and you just want to go to *bed*. Or your child does something that you realise you don't like him for. It's usually when you're tired, and have run out of energy. When I've got energy, everything is easier. [B, 3 years]

If the mother was previously a person who was used to spending time in her own company, doing whatever she chose, then sharing the entire day with her baby can be quite a challenge.

First mother: I can't give B enough space from inside myself. He wakes up at five in the morning, and then it's all go till he goes down, around six to nine at night. My helper can give him the space that I can't. She says, 'I can look after B all day. I love him so much.' B screams for joy when he sees her. He doesn't do that for me. I find that hard, very hard. I must admit I feel jealous of her. [B, 10 months]

Second mother: But they go home at night. It's completely different. My mum takes G all day, and she loves it. But you can see the look of *relief* on her face when it's time to go home. [G, 2 years; B, 8 weeks]

The helper's role is contractual. The mother has opened up a lifelong commitment. Her child is unlikely to relate to anyone else as he does to her.

What happens when a second child is born? Can a mother keep open two heartrooms at once? What happens to the first child when the second is born? The novelist Anne Enright wrote about her second baby:

It's exciting having him around. The most surprising thing is the way that the love repeats as much as the pain – you would think there could not be enough space for it, and then, *creak,* another room opens in your heart, huge, full of interest and light. My beautiful boy.[11]

'Heart' is the word that many mothers use when describing how they can love more than one child.

I was so happy with B. He was the apple of my eye. Before G was born, I didn't see how I could love another child as much, and I worried about that. But my friend told me: 'You get a new heart for each child.' And it's true. I love G just as much. [B, 2 years; G, 7 weeks]

When B and G interact with each other, it's so lovely, my heart feels like bursting. [B, 23 months; G, 5 months]

I remember panicking when I was pregnant with my second child because I was afraid I'd used up my quota of devotion on my daughter. Luckily, one of the many surprises of becoming a mother, or father, is how wide your heart can stretch.[12]

The Danish philosopher Søren Kierkegaard was impressed by the way mothers could love many children. In order to explain what mothers did, he had to invent the Danish equivalent to 'heartroom'. He must have thought of the word independently, as he could hardly have known about Coleridge's private letter. In *Works of Love* (1843), Kierkegaard was describing something he called an 'upbuilding' kind of love. By 'upbuilding' he meant a love that was inspiring. As an example of 'upbuilding' love, he mentioned a mother's ability to love many children: ' . . . there really is room where there is heartroom [*"Hjerterum"*],' he wrote.[13]

Not all mothers find adjusting to two children straightforward though; this is discussed in more detail in Chapter Twelve.

As a baby develops and eventually grows into a toddler, his mother finds she needs to adjust her understanding and expectations, to keep open her heartroom space. Her toddler is now experimenting and making independent discoveries about life. Many of his experiments can be extremely inconvenient. He is not the cuddly dependent baby that he once was.

> It was easier when B was smaller. Now his wishes keep coming into conflict with mine. This morning, I turned round and found he was busy squashing a tomato on the kitchen table. I don't like bits of tomato squirted everywhere. [B, 13 months]

There is a widespread idea that a child can be 'adorable' as a baby – but just wait until the 'terrible twos'. A mother who believes this may find she can be quite tolerant with her newborn, but she gets irritable when her child takes steps towards independence. However, I am not at all convinced by the 'terrible twos'. I think the two-year-old is more likely to be reacting, in turn, to a less tolerant reaction from his mother. It must be frustrating for the toddler to find that he is stopped from doing what he sees as adventurous.

Even in the early months, it is not always easy to make space for a person as needy as a young baby. Some mothers fear being overwhelmed. 'The thought of giving myself over to my children was too terrifying,' wrote one.[14] Usually, a mother in this position will complain, 'B's a very demanding baby,' or, 'G is insatiable. After a day with her, I'm right at the end of my tether.' She can sound as though her baby keeps struggling against her. But if we look more closely at the situation, it seems that it is she who is resisting her baby.

> For two weeks B and I had colds, so we couldn't get out. B stopped smiling for a whole day. It was hard; it was very hard for me. I fantasised about going online and buying a ticket and getting on a plane – *anything* just to get away from *him*. I don't like to talk about it because it makes me sound like a bad mother. I want to be a good mother to B. But it can feel very, very hard to stay. [B, 9 months]

> I was in such a state that I held B down in his cot with my arm and I yelled at him: 'GO TO SLEEP!' [*In tears.*] It was a terrible thing to do. Like he'd say, 'Oh, *yes,* Mum, that's a really good idea. I'll try that.' But B looked at me as if he was terrified. [B, 17 months]

Some mothers overrule their children. They are guided by a more authoritarian philosophy, which is described in more detail in Chapter Fourteen. Other mothers discover how to share a laugh with their babies which melts those moments of withdrawal.

> I have health issues, but B is so much fun that it makes the hard bits feel better. He's got a sense of humour. Before I had him, my life was very, very intellectual, and I was very, very serious. But B sees the funny side. *He* can be very serious too, sometimes. But he gets me to laugh, and I haven't laughed this much for years and years. [B, 4 months]

The same mother found it challenging to remain open to her son as he grew:

I find it hard to create the spaciousness that I need to be B's mother. If I think about it too much, then I lose it. I don't have it any more. But, when I don't think about it, *perhaps* I am doing it. [B, 9 months]

This mother was making a good point. Making space is a dynamic act, and it's easy to confuse a momentary closing down with being a total failure as a mother. Many mothers have times when they feel more closed, but later find ways of opening again.

M: I feel really 'down' at night, worrying about everything. It seems worst when I wake up in the early hours.

Me: Is it very hard to lift yourself out of it?

M: Not really. In the morning, I see B's face, and he's all beamy. It's humbling really. He doesn't need much to make him happy. [B, 6 months]

I get so stressed that I forget B could be helping me. So, the other day, I stacked two stools by the sink and invited B to hop up and help me wash up. You should have seen his little face when I said it. [*She demonstrated wide eyes and a huge smile.*] He was: 'Do you mean *me*? Can I really *help* you?' And it didn't matter if he got his clothes wet doing it. He loved it, and it was really nice. [B, 15 months]

It's very difficult when they won't go to sleep – but it's *normal*. It's difficult to explain what I do. Instead of getting frustrated with G, I let her do whatever she wants to do, without judgment. Whatever she's doing, I try to see it as delightful. And then I can time it. Within five minutes, she'll be asleep. I'm convinced that when they are being 'difficult' they are reacting to us. They are playing our games. So I change the energy. As soon as I change the energy, I see a change in G. [G, 18 months]

We can see from these examples that mothers often withdraw when they feel troubled, and seem to offer too little space. Then it seems to take quite a boost of energy for them to change from withdrawal to seeing a way to engage again. Each mother's solution is personal. None of these ways is intended as a magic prescription to others.

However, would it be possible for a mother to offer her child not too little, but too vast a share of her heart? If a mother feels in despair about her own life, and puts her 'all' into her child, in that sense she could be giving too much. Making heartroom means trying to provide enough space for a new person. A child may feel burdened if he senses that his mother has given up everything for him. Yet a mother might feel very discouraged by all the difficulties she has encountered so far, and find it hard to put fresh 'heart' into her own life.

If I were reading this section as an expectant or new mother, I think I might be starting to feel puzzled and a bit anxious. How much is the right amount of heartroom? If it should neither be too little nor too much, how will I know if I've got it right?

Heartroom is a metaphor, so it can't be quantified. In any case, what we give doesn't need to be perfect. Babies seem to sense our good intentions. Occasionally, we give what feels 'just right'. Usually, we fluctuate, which means that all of us have 'down' times. But shouldn't we do better than this? Isn't our best simply inefficient and incompetent?

Fortunately, the whole process of mothering describes something deeper than competence. Mothering has more to do with responding to our children than with demonstrating what good mothers we can be. In this, mothering may be completely unlike a job. A job has a job description, defining an area within which the job-holder has to be competent. A woman who has the job of looking after another woman's baby would need to demonstrate her competence. But if she is mothering her own baby, something special comes into play. Babies are sensitive. They connect to their mothers in feeling, which is primary, and more vital than competence.

I'd like to give one example of this, to show a mother changing from feeling surprised by her child to giving him more heartroom. I remember that while this mother was talking, her little boy skidded over on the floor. She picked him up and was bouncing him up and down on her hip to comfort him, at the same time as speaking. Her story took at least five minutes to tell. I rushed down the parts I could remember, about an hour later. But I must have forgotten a lot of detail.

> On Monday, I took B swimming again. I had hoped that he had learned [*not to be afraid of the pool*] from the first time, but he obviously hadn't because as soon as he saw the water he started screaming and crying. I wondered whether to give up and take him home. If he had been completely hysterical, I would have gone back home with him, no problem. But he didn't seem to be that bad. So we stayed and sat down at the side. I put my arm round him and I could feel how tense he was. After a while, I could feel him getting a tiny bit more relaxed, but it took quite a time, maybe half an hour. I don't know. Anyway, he started watching the big children diving and pointing to them. Then he looked at me and pointed to the water, but we didn't go in right away. When we had sat there for a long time, I could feel that he was really relaxed, so I took his hand and we went to the first step where the water started. He was really *happy*. I felt so *proud* of him. My *heart* expanded. [B, 12 months]

What had the mother done? She had started, as parents usually do, with an expectation. She expected that she could take her son swimming, and that he would be ready to enjoy the water straight away. When he didn't, she felt disconcerted. She considered going home, but decided to stay. 'So we stayed and sat down . . .', she said.

At that stage, she made a shift from being a surprised parent to becoming a 'we' in partnership with her son. She had let go her expectation and instead created room for her son's authentic feelings. Because she was neither stating that they go home nor dragging him to the edge of the water, she could create a quiet moment of togetherness during which she seemed to put her trust in her son. She did not try to calm him, which would have been like contradicting his feelings. Instead, she noticed that he did eventually calm down. Once he was calmer, he became curious, as children usually are. It was he who noticed the diving children and pointed to them. By pointing, he showed he was making sense of what was happening, in what he had probably first experienced as the ear-splitting noise and chaos of the swimming pool. His mother waited until she could feel that he was really calm. It was she who judged the moment and took his hand. But they must have been sufficiently 'together' for her to have judged right.

When she realised that her son had overcome his fear and was able to relax and enjoy the pool, she said that she felt that her heart had expanded. I think this must have been when the whole sequence made sense to her. She might well have worried that there was something wrong with her son for being frightened of the pool on his second visit, and something wrong with her because he'd had this reaction. This expansion of her heart shows how dynamic these motherly sensations really are.

Heartroom is a metaphor for a generous and subtle adjustment that many mothers make for their children. It can't be measured, and it would be absurd to set up a test with a tick box to find out if a mother had 'got' it. If a mother doesn't want to make heartroom, there are usually others who do, such as the child's father (many fathers offer heartroom, whatever the circumstances), grandparents or a professional helper. Mothers who want to give it, but find it difficult, will be discussed in the next chapter.

Fortunately, many mothers seem to find their way to heartroom. As far as I am aware, no familiar word has existed up till now to represent this process, certainly not in English.

This means that mothers are giving their children something they have never named. For millennia, mothers seem to have quietly transmitted heartroom from one generation to the next.

CHAPTER TWO

House-room without heartroom

'Heart' is the word that mothers use spontaneously when they describe their feelings for their babies. But mothers differ, and not all feel able to provide heartroom. How much does it matter if a mother gives her baby house-room – but not *heart*room?

> I don't feel like myself any more. I don't recognise myself. I never used to look like this and I want *me* back. It's been so long, I'm desperate. I could wear nice clothes. I could dress myself to look very nice, but it's not the same. I'm different inside. My *soul* has changed. I need to do something – to travel – to get myself back again. But when, when, *when?* When G's three, when she's five, when she's *fifteen?* I've been without myself for eighteen months. I do all the physical things for G, oh God, yes, all the time. But I've never let G into my core. I don't know if anyone here understands me. I know some mothers let their children in here [*patting the top left side of her chest*], but I never have. [G, 18 months]

'Core' is the word people sometimes use instead of 'heart'. '*Cor*' is the Latin word for heart, though the two have different etymological roots. This mother felt she could do practical things for her daughter, but noticed that other mothers had closer relationships with their children than she had with hers. It's significant that her thoughts kept returning to her earlier lifestyle. She felt depleted in the present. She longed to recover her 'old self'. She didn't consider moving forward to find a 'new self'.

Many new mothers fear that they will become *less*, as mothers. A baby can feel like an intruder, diverting the mother's attention, and perhaps also her heart, from her career. 'We [*mothers*] fear becoming one-dimensional,' wrote one reporter in a British newspaper.[15] Most women have created identities for themselves at work. Being a mother, by contrast, can seem unglamorous and mundane.

> I don't know who I *am* any more [*tears*]. [B, 5 months]

> How can you be a mother without losing yourself? I look in the mirror, and I don't know who I am any more. I don't look like I used to look. I feel *lost*. [B, 9 months]

The current ideal of a beautiful woman seems to be someone cool, groomed, elegant, and looking as if she has never set eyes on a baby in her life. No wonder so many new mothers feel lost.

Some mothers recount very painful feelings. The writer Stephanie Merritt has written a book on her experience of 'postnatal depression'. When her baby was born, she changed her entire pleasure-seeking London journalist's way of life. She became a single mother and went to live in the village where she had grown up. Even though it was her choice, the reality must have been a shock. Like the mother quoted at the beginning of this chapter, she said that she would rush around doing practical tasks for her baby, but that she knew something essential was missing. She wrote:

Only I knew the dark motivations behind my earnest care, only I knew that I was overcompensating out of guilt, because in my heart I knew that I was a bad mother. I must be a bad mother because I didn't feel what I was meant to feel. In truth, I didn't feel anything at all. I was simply empty, scoured, a flimsy wicker framework built around a void. At my core, where a well of fierce maternal love was supposed to be, there was only absence, and to disguise this absence I put on a fervent show of motherhood.[16]

This is precise writing. Like the mother at the start of the chapter, she refers to her 'core'. Her words 'void', 'empty', 'scoured' and 'absence' build up a picture of an empty space – but very different from the heartroom kind of space. Heartroom opens up a warm and hospitable space. The 'void' instead of 'the well of fierce maternal love' shows that Stephanie Merritt could identify what was missing. But she had no idea what to do about it.

Other new mothers describe phenomena such as loss of appetite, inability to sleep, frequent crying and feelings of worthlessness. Health professionals interpret these as symptoms of the 'mental illness' of 'postnatal depression'. A mother can ask her doctor for medications, and these can help her to feel more like her previous self. But successful medication is not conclusive evidence that she was ill. The assumption of illness remains unproven.

The difficulty with assuming that these mothers are suffering from a 'mental illness' is that the phenomena that they describe (loss of appetite, for example) are then defined as 'symptoms'. This means that we see the phenomena, or the mothers' behaviours, as bizarre and irrational. However, might these very inconvenient behaviours be meaningful? If we understood the life situations of mothers better, might each behaviour start to make sense? Perhaps mothers are responding, not to a mysterious illness, but to a life difficulty.

One way in which a mother can start to feel anxious is by trying to ignore her difficulties, telling herself instead that 'there is nothing wrong' and that she 'ought to be happy'. Sometimes, in retrospect, a mother can see her situation more clearly. The next mother could see, years later, an obvious difficulty that she didn't recognise at the time:

> When my first baby was born, I literally cried every day for about six months . . . I felt that I had 'nothing to be upset about' and I know that my health visitor and others suspected that I had postnatal depression. It was only when I looked back that I understood that this might have been quite a reasonable response to the huge changes in my life. It was the first time I had ever had responsibility for a baby, I had stopped work, had no family near by, had had to find a whole new circle of friends as none of mine had babies and were at work all day . . . I felt wholly out of control.[17]

But what about other mothers who have a great deal of support from family and friends? Is there any justification for their feelings of distress? Mothers often tell themselves: 'I've got a beautiful baby. I shouldn't feel like this,' 'I know I should be positive,' 'I should be over this by now.' They often compare themselves critically to an 'ideal' mother who is completely calm and happy. This means that a mother can feel she has failed to be a good mother if she thinks that she might have any issues that she might be upset *about.*

These mothers describe feeling distraught. They can see that they have wonderful babies. They want to love their babies, yet they feel estranged from them. 'It wasn't that I didn't love the baby,' explained Stephanie Merritt. 'I knew that I loved him, but I knew it only at a conceptual level.'[18] It's interesting that mothers who define themselves as 'being useless with babies' or not enjoying the baby stage, don't describe this dilemma. These mothers aren't expecting to feel warm love, so it's not a conflict for them that they don't. But that means their babies experience a more remote and tepid relationship. Surely it is reasonable of the conflicted mothers to feel so troubled.

If a mother expresses her suffering, online for example, postings come pouring back, reassuring her that it is normal to feel as she does. But the mother does not *feel* normal. Often she fears she is going insane. Besides, when she looks around, she can see other mothers who seem happy. Harriet Lane, who, like Stephanie Merritt, wrote a memoir on her postnatal distress, was astonished to hear a friend describe the first year with her baby as the best year in her life. For Harriet Lane, it was anything but.[19]

Feeling at war with herself, the mother cannot relax for a moment. She feels guilty that she can hardly focus on her baby because she feels so anxious for herself. The poet Gerard Manley Hopkins put into words this level of anxiety:

> O, the mind, mind has mountains; cliffs of fall
> Frightful, sheer, no-man-fathomed. Hold them cheap
> May who ne'er hung there.[20]

'Hold them cheap' is exactly what so many well-intentioned people do when they tell the mother she is doing well, and assure her that they can see how much she loves her baby really. I'm capable of voicing these platitudes myself. It's hard to listen to someone who keeps saying she is a bad mother.

Surely the extent of the mother's distress confirms that she herself knows that something is very wrong. Blaming herself for being a bad mother is an attempt to articulate it. It can feel a relief to start by expressing black thoughts, because it frees the mother from the high idealism about motherhood which is so far from her reality. What right have we to urge her to look on the positive side? She would if she could. She knows that her baby needs her love, but that's easier thought than done. She is quite clear that she cannot yet feel love towards her baby.

However, mothers in this predicament do find ways through. I have asked many mothers how, but they aren't always sure. Listening to their accounts, it seems that a first step is to accept how they feel. The support of a friend can help. So can comparing notes with similar mothers and discovering that 'I am not the only one'. When mothers feel safe enough to talk about their feelings, they often discover that these feelings were *about* something.

In a very simple published case study, a health visitor said she had listened to a mother whose baby wasn't sleeping well. The mother also said she was anxious about the attitude of her partner. The health visitor commented that it was the first time anyone had helped the mother 'to think about what was happening and to put her feelings into words'. She arranged to meet the mother again, but the mother telephoned before the appointment to say that 'she had talked to her partner' and also that her baby 'had been sleeping through the night'. The two authors who used this case study comment: 'Instead of simply providing advice about sleeping diffi-culties early in the interaction, the health visitor made *space* [*my italics*] to listen.'[21] This seemed to enable the mother to articulate and solve her problems herself.

Sometimes, the difficulty can be the birth itself. A mother might have been told that she should be grateful for the birth that she had. Yet her experience might have been disappointing. Giving birth evokes some of our deepest feelings. It would be strange if we were not profoundly affected. 'The birth had a very bad effect on me,' said one mother. 'It upset me every day for months, and made it very difficult to bond with my baby. Phys-ically, it was about six months before the pain had gone completely.'[22]

A television documentary gave examples of mothers who

described their feelings to psychotherapists. The title of the documentary was 'Help Me Love My Baby'. One mother 'realised that she had never come to terms with her miscarriage, and this, at least partly, explained her extremes of anxiety, OCD and depression'.[23] Another mother recalled how she had 'gone to live with her grandmother at the age of twelve, because of her mother's drinking. "I'd never had a positive relationship with my own mother," says [the mother]. "I'd had to look after myself. I realised that I was terrified of anyone being dependent on me as a result."'[24]

It isn't always easy to admit to feelings such as anger at failures of a partner; or hurt feelings towards one or both of the mother's own parents. Often the partners and parents are the very people on whom the mother depends on for daily support.

To make everything worse, if a mother has been used to being criticised by her close family members, it can seem natural to assume that her baby, when he cries, is fault-finding too.

> Every time my son cried, I thought he was criticising me. My breakthrough came when he was nearly one year old and I suddenly realised: he's crying because that's his *only* way of telling me something. Of course I always knew this rationally, but it took me a long time to feel it. [B, 5 years]

Once a mother has a breakthrough like this, and can identify some of her anger, terrors or hurt feelings, she can connect to herself better as a coherent person. Her genuine feelings give her reasons for behaviour that had previously seemed bizarre. She can recognise herself as human again. The most terrible fears are shapeless. But talking about fears gives them shape, and, once they have shape, it is possible to see choices in how to deal with them. In the same way, if a mother can recognise that she feels angry, she can start to make sense of her own actions. Her terror for herself eases. This frees up some energy, and enables her to feel stronger. It is then much easier to love her baby.

Many mothers need time before they feel ready for this. A mother can't rush this process and force herself to reflect. Fortunately, it seems that, from what mothers say, we don't have to do everything perfectly from the start. We seem to get second chances later on, when we can do a lot to lessen the effects of our early shortcomings.

> Nothing prepared me for the life change of becoming a mother. I found it hard. I was depressed, so I got help. What emerged was to do with my childhood. My mother didn't have a lot of emotional space for me. So when 2B was born, I was able to *be* there for him, instead of feeling I had to keep doing things. But last year, 1B had appendicitis. I went to hospital with him and stayed there for a week. And I was able to be there for *him*. I really think it healed our relationship. I feel that I made it up to him. [1B, 6 years; 2B, 3 years]

Another mother reflected:

> My first child was very needy. I couldn't be the mother he needed and the mother I wanted to be. I feel ashamed that I got angry and shouted at him. But now I look at him and see there is a special bond between us. We are *war* buddies. My second child is quite different. He is very calm. I have a special bond with him too. [B, 4 years; B, 14 months]

Some fathers describe similar painful feelings after the births of their babies. These are mentioned briefly on pages 191–2. They, too, might value the opportunity of discussing these feelings.

Sometimes a mother can feel angry for a different reason. It may be with an older child, and the relationship between them can appear on the verge of breaking down. Mother and child are barely on speaking terms. The mother complains that her child has withdrawn and avoids conversation. Every time the mother resolves to be nicer and to give her child one more chance, he does something dismissive or sneering that re-ignites her anger.

It can be very tempting to blame the child for problems in the relationship. There are countless ways of doing this, but none of them is justifiable. As mothers, we are the stronger party. If a child is withdrawn and unfriendly, this is a *result* of his interaction with us. A mother cannot truthfully protest that she is his victim or that he 'makes' her react in particular ways. She is a responsible agent, and her child cannot compel her to do his will.

What may have happened in a painful relationship like this is that the mother is not offering heartroom, but has focused on a kind of template of a child, which she would like her own child to match. If only he did the 'right' things, she keeps thinking, which would be closer to her 'child template', she would feel better towards him and their relationship would improve. What she may find difficult is to see her real child. He is a unique person who can never be like an ideal template.

One mother who was diagnosed as having postnatal depression said she was ' . . . in love with the *idea* [*my italics*] of having a child'.[25] But of course her real child was different from her 'idea' of one. Then why couldn't she simply fall in love with the real child?

I think you need to be open to your child, to understand what he needs. But if you are too full of your own thoughts, you don't hear him. [G, 3 years; B, 5 months]

I think the first six weeks were hard. After that, it was like coming out of the darkness. It was like B was a lot of tasks. I hardly took time to look at him. I felt numb inside. I was just washing clothes, feeding and getting to sleep. B was what they call 'very high need'. I hadn't expected that. Almost as soon as he was born, he let me know that he didn't want to be left and he didn't want me to put him down. Other mothers seemed to have more docile babies, who didn't mind being put down. Now I love B so much that I wouldn't want him to be one of the more docile ones. [B, 11 months]

My head used to be full of 'should's of how a family situation 'should' be. It made me strident. Having children has softened me more than I ever dreamed possible. [B, 7 years; G, 4 years]

Many mothers seem to have found ways to move from acute distress to the discovery that they can accept and love their babies. The next mother sounded so joyful, it was hard to believe that, for several months before and after the birth, she had been flat on her back, in pain whenever she moved. The baby's father withdrew and left her. For months, her little daughter then clung to her mother constantly throughout the day.

G has made me the mother I am. If she had been an easier baby, I'd *never* have become the mother I am now. [*Holding her daughter close and stroking her hair.*] I'm very grateful to her for being so demanding, because I *like* the mother I have become. [G, 16 months]

On the final page of Stephanie Merritt's book, she indicates how much she has changed:

When I was younger and more dogmatic about what I wanted from life, I prized the idea of independence so highly that I failed to understand the value of *inter*dependence; illness has forced this recognition on me, against my natural inclination to live as an island, and it has been an important lesson to have learned.[26]

It sounds a very important lesson to have learned – or perhaps re-learned. We are born '*inter*dependent'. No one has a 'natural inclination to live as an island'. John Donne used the same image when he wrote in 1624: 'No man is an *Iland*, intire of itselfe.'[27] Turning oneself into an 'island' is a very human way of protecting oneself when other people are hurtful. It sounds as though Stephanie Merritt's realisation that she could not feel love for her baby had stirred her to address an old interpersonal dilemma of how to love without getting hurt.

Having a baby may intensify a mother's problems over how to love. But it can also be a great incentive to change. Babies have not learned defensive ways to avoid getting hurt. A new baby may be one of the safest people with whom a mother could try out a tender and loving way to relate.

CHAPTER THREE

'I don't know'

People often say that 'mothers know best'. I sometimes say it myself. But, like nearly every statement about mothers, it's only partly true. It's certainly not the way most mothers start out.

> I thought I'd prepared myself and read a lot about babies, but after the birth I found I knew nothing, *nothing*. I kept thinking, What is going on? [B, 2 months]

> I have so many questions I can't answer. They are all about tiny details. There's such a lot that I don't know. [G, 3 months]

> *First mother*: F went back to work this morning. I'm on my own. And I've come to the end of the stretch of motherhood that I'd prepared for. I don't know what comes next. I don't know what to expect. [G, 2 weeks]

> *Second mother*: Well, but you know what? I *still* feel like that. [B, 7 months]

It takes time to learn about a baby. It's an extraordinary process. Mothers are learning about hitherto unknown persons. The earliest discoveries they make are often small and imperceptible. A mother might not realise that she is making any progress.

> It's odd being a mother. I haven't got five minutes to put on the wash, but I *have* got half an hour to stand in the street watching a robin. [G, 7 weeks]

This mother was speaking to several other mothers, and they immediately laughed. They understood how odd it sounded. They didn't need her to explain how useful the washing machine had become. However, putting dirty washing into a machine can be difficult to do while holding the baby, whereas watching a robin could be combined with baby-holding. Young babies, they seemed to agree, often wanted their mothers to hold them.

And yet there was a rueful sound to the laughter. Watching a robin – what good does that do? Doesn't that just prove that mothers are doing ridiculous things, unworthy of their time? What is the point of a mother looking at a robin with her baby?

What are mothers *supposed* to be doing? Mothers have the task of introducing their newborns to social life. They do this by relating to their babies and beginning to communicate with them. At first, babies don't know how to communicate – nor do they realise that they can. They express how they feel by crying, or by becoming contented. But it doesn't occur to a newborn to look round and check whether he is getting any response.

A to/fro of 'dialogue' seems an enormous change from life in the womb. Human civilisation depends on generation after generation being able to understand and communicate with one another. We aren't born knowing how. We learn it. Becoming a mother must mean doing some of the oldest work there is. But the mother's responsibility to help her baby to communicate is not widely recognised. Mothers themselves may not even realise that this is what they are doing.

This helps us to understand the 'robin' mother. She had begun to notice moments when her baby seemed contented, and was thankful for them. When her daughter seemed relaxed while she was holding her and they were watching the robin, her response must have been: 'Thank goodness I've found something that you like! Let's watch a bit longer.' It's a good example of how *small* the first steps of communication can be and how insignificant they can seem at the time. Yet these small steps are crucial.

Before the birth, a mother may have read up on babycare and planned how she would manage her life with her baby. But there may be a surprise ahead of her. A newborn cannot simply be 'managed'. He is capable of expressing his own strong views about the details of his care. His views may not always coincide with hers. This means that 'babycare' is more subtle than it looks. It's not a matter of applying this method or that. It's a conversation. It can turn into a battle.[28] Or it can become a series of negotiations and agreements between two people.

But how can one possibly 'negotiate' with a newborn? Books rarely describe this. But can mothers learn how to do it from one another? Do experienced mothers teach new mothers what to do, or at least how to get started? This is a very interesting question. You might think that maternal experience could easily be handed on. Experienced mothers certainly *want* to help bewildered new mothers. So why don't they?

> Listening to my friend who gave birth four days ago and who *never* asks *anyone* for help, I could hear over the phone how she was all over the place and tearful. I'm trying to remember how I was then. It's so different now. Compared to *then*, today's a breeze. [G, 9 months]

One experienced mother remembered how she used to feel:

> The questions new mothers ask aren't the ones to which there are obvious answers. I remember, when I was a new mother myself, I'd

ask experienced mothers how they would deal with a situation. They used to answer, 'I don't know,' which I found frustrating. I was sure they had a *proper* answer that they weren't telling me. But now I say it myself. My sister-in-law's baby is four months old, and she has just asked me if I know how to get a baby to sleep more. But I really *don't* know. I've learned, as a mother, to accept things, not to solve them. [G, 4 years; B, 12 months]

Mothers develop in different ways, and these responses may not represent all of us. The important point here is that these mothers had moved on from how they were at the start. But in what way? How could they change so much that they could hardly recall those intense early weeks?

One mother, rocking her toddler on her hip, tried to explain:

As soon as the baby's born, you get all this advice. It's very confusing. You keep trying to follow the advice and you think there's something wrong with you and your baby if the advice doesn't work. And then, at some stage, you realise you've got a little *person* there, not . . . not some *object* that has to be fed and pacified. [G, 15 months]

It might sound obvious that a baby is a little person, but it seems easy for new mothers to lose sight of it. As the mother pointed out, there is a great deal of professional advice on how to manage everyday life with a baby. This advice can appear helpful. But it's confusing. Advice-givers can't describe a mother's particular baby. Instead, they speak or write, not only as if all babies are similar (as in some ways they are), but as if all babies *ought* to be similar.

Each mother and each baby is unique. This might sound obvious too, but again, a mother may lose sight of it. It makes a great deal of difference. For example, one mother may have seen others lay their babies down in their cots. But her unique baby screams each time she tries to lay him down. She has no idea why. However, she doesn't want to cause him distress, so she 'negotiates' terms such as: 'You seem happy when I'm holding you upright. But I need something to eat. We'll have to find a way to do this together.'

At first, the negotiations have to be one-sided, because the baby can have no idea of alternative options. However, mothers seem to have these conversations *as if* their babies were able to reply. Perhaps this makes it easier for a baby to join in when he is old enough.

Not all mothers realise that they could do this. The mother who was so sure that her toddler was a little person had experienced a crisis of confidence, much earlier:

> Last week, G and I seemed to be 'going backwards'. She wouldn't sleep. I lost my nerve, so I started reading one of those books, you know, that tell you how to put your baby into a routine. I wrapped her up, like it said, and G just *stared* at me. Then I started patting her back. At that point, the routine of back-patting seemed to stretch endlessly ahead of me. It looked unremitting and grey. All the joy went – it felt joyless. Where was all my mothering – those tiny little details I was starting to recognise in G? I had been starting to learn. But all that seemed to have turned to *nothing*. [G, 5 weeks]

'Those tiny little details' were the early signs of communication between mother and baby. Like the 'robin' mother on p. 41, this mother was getting to know her baby. She hadn't realised, until that moment, how much she had already begun to learn.

The beginning can feel overwhelming. At birth, a baby's feelings, like his skin, are very tender. He needs his sensitivity to enable him to learn. Yet this same sensitivity means he is susceptible to pain. He can cry in agony, despite his mother's best efforts to comfort him. New mothers often become tearful when their babies cry. These tears help them to stay tender and soft to their babies, even when they do not know why their babies are upset. Looking back, one mother remembered:

I wasn't prepared for how much you love them. You feel so terrible if you have to do something to upset them. The lower lip starts to wobble, and . . . Words can't explain it. You feel a terrible mother. [B, 5 months]

Usually, there isn't much time for a mother to reflect on the newborn stage until it is over.

At first, I was dancing on hot coals, trying to do everything G needed. But she's not a newborn now. She seems much more confident. And I've got very tired. [G, 2 months]

Although this mother felt she was 'dancing on hot coals', it will have been her own dance – not quite the same as your dance, if you are a mother, or mine. She was trying to do what her daughter needed. However, she is as unique as her baby. So she had to find her own way of being her daughter's mother. This particular mother realised that the newborn phase was over when her daughter was 'much more confident'. Without thinking about it, the mother knew it was safe to relax – a little. And as soon as she relaxed, she realised how tired she was. There is no word for this very significant stage of tiredness. Mothers often mention it. It means that they have achieved a level of understanding with their babies and can afford to be a shade more aware of their separate needs again. It's a landmark.

But how do mothers learn to 'dance'? Each new child is an unknown person. Not knowing this person who is so dependent can feel alarming. Nor is it a new dilemma. For example, this was exactly how the novelist Mrs Gaskell felt when she confided to her diary, one Tuesday evening in August 1836, when her first child was eleven months old:

How all a woman's life, at least so it seems to me now, ought to have a reference to the period when she will be fulfilling one of her greatest and highest duties, those of a mother. I feel myself so unknowing, so doubtful about many things . . . [29]

Many mothers today feel 'so unknowing, so doubtful'. After all, babycare is rarely on the school curriculum now. Many women only acquire quite basic information during pregnancy. This isn't ideal, but with resources such as the Internet and health professionals, it may not turn into a disaster. Some details of babycare would make valuable additions to the school science syllabus. Updated information about breastfeeding and vaccinations, for example, would be invaluable.

But mothering is more than babycare. It covers the need to relate to an unknown new person. Not-knowing a pre-verbal person can feel a challenge. However, is it a handicap? Perhaps admitting to *not*-knowing can be an advantage. This was the great insight of Socrates, the fifth-century BC Athenian philosopher.

Socrates was told that the Delphic Oracle had stated there was no man wiser than himself. With his characteristic logic, Socrates set about seeing if he could disprove this. He decided to interview several men whom he considered much wiser than he was. But he found that when he questioned the 'wise' men, the attribution of wisdom turned out to be groundless. Socrates commented after questioning one 'wise' man: 'He knows nothing, and thinks that he knows; I neither know nor think that I know. In this one small point, then, I seem to have the advantage of him.'[30]

This was a revolutionary discovery. It still is. Then, as now, most people admire anyone with claims to knowledge. Socrates boldly asserted that it was wise to know when one did not know.

This discovery by Socrates is useful for mothers. Many reach the position of not-knowing almost at once. Most mothers learn some methods of basic babycare from books, hospital classes or from one another. These usually make babycare appear universal and simple. But, with her own unique new baby, a mother discovers that she has reached the edge of what is known. And even after she has started to know her baby, the two of them find they reach new phases when the mother feels lost all over again.

I don't know where I'm going. [G, 11 months]

I feel I don't know B any more. When he was younger, I always understood exactly what he meant. Now he does things I really don't understand, though I keep trying to. [B, 16 months]

We are in uncharted territory. [G, 18 months]

These mothers have all read books on babycare. But the books are about babies in general. It is different when a mother considers her own baby together with her own ideals and aspirations. She is alone on her unique path. It can feel frightening to admit that she does not know the way ahead. Yet this seems a valuable beginning to being a mother. It enables her to start from a position of humility. From humility, it is easier to learn.

This turns mothering into an adventure. We are not stuck with pre-ordained answers. We are free to learn how to be our own kind of mother. In this era of training and certificates, it can feel liberating to discover that here is something we can work out for ourselves.

I used to think that you had to be *made* to learn. But, as a mother, I find I'm learning all the time. [B, 22 months]

Loving usually leads to learning. Many mothers love deeply, so we should expect their learning to be deep too. Love enables them to transform their detailed observations into small stepping-stones of understanding.

B does everything slowly. He stretches slowly and breastfeeds slowly. I can understand why he was born two weeks late, now that I've *met* him. [G, 21 months; B, 13 days]

B resists sleep. If there's anything happening, I can see him straining his eyes to stay awake for it. But when he's really tired he goes quiet. I felt quite liberated when I realised that. [B, 3 months]

First mother: If G rubs her eye, I know she's tired and ready for sleep. But if I miss that sign, she'll cry and get distressed. I think people think I'm neurotic because they'll see me react to my baby for apparently no reason. [G, 3 months]

Second mother: Yes, it's like that for me too. When G is about to sleep, she gives some little howls. People think that's the sign that she *can't* get to sleep, and they want to lift her up. But I know she just needs to give her little howls and then she's away. [G, 5 months]

Mothers often find their love growing together with their understanding.

I loved G when she was born for being my baby. But now I love her whole personality. I'm so in love with G as a person. [G, 8 months]

Yet these early steps can be so small that mothers do not always realise the good start they have made. Even mothers who are beginning to understand their babies sometimes say they have failed. What does this mean? What do 'success' and 'failure' mean, when mothering a baby?

Mothers often start by defining success in terms of bringing their babies into line with widely held views. They make statements such as, 'I feel I've failed because B refuses to take a bottle.' However, a breastfed baby may have his own strong views about feeding from a bottle. He is as human as his mother. In this sense, she had not failed. She was *successful* because she had recognised that her baby had communicated his personal choice.

Mothers say, with a note of panic in their voices: 'But he *has* to eat,' 'He *has* to sleep,' or, 'He *has* to learn to trust other people.' Yes, a baby does need to do all these things. But the panic that mothers describe usually turns out to be about timing. It would be so much easier if babies did the 'right' thing at the 'right' time. However, a baby can have no idea that he needs to sleep at this precise moment, because his mother has decided he should. Yet however exasperated she feels, it does not mean that she has failed as a mother. She has received a clear message from her child. Mothers in this predicament have found that, if they can respect the message, however unwelcome it may be, they can then continue to communicate with their babies as persons.

> A few months ago, I'd have tried to encourage G to have a nap when I thought she needed one. Now, if she doesn't want one, I say, 'All right. You don't want a nap. If you want to be up, we'll be up.' [G, 9 months]

> G has her own way of getting to sleep, and it really seems to work for her. After her bedtime story, she gets up and bounces really hard on her mattress. It seems to use up the last bit of her energy. It's the opposite of what all the books tell you about winding down gradually and quietly. But it obviously works for her. After that, she's ready for sleep. I've learned to trust *her* method. [G, 3 years; B, 6 months]

There is a great deal for us to learn about when to trust our children. It depends on getting to know them as persons. A lot of problems dissolve into non-problems when we can do this.

> With my first child, I was looking for solutions. I'm not solution-based now. There *aren't* those sorts of solutions. [B, 2 years; B, 3 months]

> The really difficult thing about being a parent is, for me anyway, being able to stay in uncertainty. You'd like to *do* something to resolve issues, so you can stop thinking about them. But usually that just makes everything worse. Time will unravel whatever it is. You have to wait, though it's hard to feel so uncertain. [B, 11 years; G, 8 years; B, 8 months]

More often than not, you can't solve whatever it is. Time solves it. You rush around, trying to make things better for your child. But what you learn is that a problem simply passes. I used to be a problem-solver and what I'm learning as a mother is when to accept things as they are. [G, 3 years; B, 8 months]

This is an important discovery. It's not nearly as simple to do as it might sound. Waiting in uncertainty, without knowing what to do, when she feels deeply concerned for her child is one of the harder parts of being a mother.

Obviously, mothers are not eternally accepting and waiting. They intervene and are active on behalf of their children. This is the more visible side of their mothering. But there is also an equally important, less visible, quieter and harmonic side that seems characteristic of experienced mothers.

This quieter 'waiting' side becomes especially important if the child falls ill. Most new mothers are passionately protective of their babies. Yet a baby's health and even life are not always under his mother's control. Here, her ignorance and inexperience can feel frightening. If her baby is seriously ill, there will be technical medical information for a mother to take in. Based on this, she often has to take difficult decisions. It's a heavy responsibility for which it is not possible to be fully prepared.

Frantic moments of seeking out information in order to make decisions usually alternate with slow periods of simply waiting to see how the baby does.

It can be hard to wait. Yet a mother sitting beside her ill baby has something precious to offer. She is not as ignorant or helpless as she might feel, though she might need a lot of encouragement to believe it. A mother starts by not knowing her baby, but soon she discovers the minutiae of his preferences. If her child is in pain or distressed, it helps to listen to his mother. All those loving details that she has collected may make a great difference. Even in extreme situations, and even when there may be little time left, a mother who is warmly supported can use her relationship to help her child. His health may depend on medical expertise. But she might be able to contribute something intimate and personal.[31]

> My struggle was always trying to find a way for G to be a person, not just a label. When people talked as if she was just the label [*of her illness*], I used to think, Don't say *that* about my baby! [1G, died at 2 months; 2G, 4 months]

> B had his vaccination jabs and he was ill after them. I'm always longing for more sleep, but when B was ill I found I didn't put him down all night. I held him and walked with him and rocked him. I didn't *mind* the tiredness; I was feeling so sorry for B. It had a good result because I found it brought us closer together. I realised I'd do *anything* if it made B feel happier. [B, 3 months]

Often, when a child is ill, it reminds his mother how special he is. It is easier to be aware of this at birth, but then she may overlook it in the hurry of everyday life.[32] We often talk as if babies have to climb up a kind of ladder of progress to reach the heights of adulthood, where we are. But this is only partly true. Babies seem wonderful as they are, without climbing a single rung.

Why then do we talk about our babies as if they were recalcitrant mechanisms in urgent need of repair? 'My baby keeps waking up.' 'My child rejects solid food.' 'My child won't share nicely with his friends.' Do we really want 'faultless' babies? Aren't our real babies, with all their personal idiosyncrasies that we have come to know, the people we genuinely love?

> I am not a religious person. But I feel so lucky to have G. When she is happy, her grin stretches from ear to ear. A few weeks ago, I was on a bus, and a man looked at G and said to me, 'You are blessed. You have been truly blessed.' And I agree with him. I do

feel blessed. I know it's a religious word, but it's how I feel. [G, 7 months]

Mothers often find they alternate between the uplifting feeling of being so fortunate as to have their babies, and the down-to-earth feeling of a life awash with practical details.

> You sit down to breastfeed and, almost immediately, you can see a dirty cup over there and piles of papers and clothes that need sorting, and you keep wishing you could stand up to clear it all up. [G, 2 years; B, 2 months]

> When G is nearly falling asleep, I start to make plans. I'm going to do this and then that. But then I think, Don't be silly, she could wake up at any moment. Don't put the wash on before you've been to the toilet. [G, 4 months]

Looking after a baby brings up new self-awareness. Many mothers discover that they enjoy being with their babies, much more than they had anticipated.

> If I'd known more about babies, I'd have taken a year off work. I'm reconciled to going back now, but at one time I thought of picking up G and running away with her. [G, 4 months]

This brings up a larger issue of whether some mothers are being compelled for financial reasons to return to work against their deeper feelings. (This will be taken up in Chapter Fifteen.) Other mothers discover that living with a baby doesn't please them at all, and can't wait to resume their work. A mother may try to predict how she will feel after the birth, but there is no way that she could be sure of her feelings in advance.

It is not easy to start mothering in ignorance and to learn so slowly. All the same, I suspect more mothers would choose this adventurous route if they were better respected and supported as mothers by all of us. Instead, all their work to understand their babies is either unnoticed or taken for granted. This can leave mothers feeling that their contribution to society is negligible.

Every mother who is bringing up a baby with her love is making a wonderful contribution. To an outsider, her love might sound excessive. But it seems to be what mothers choose to give and also what children need. Children don't seem to thrive on moderation. They thrive on the very heat of our love, and they seem to need it immediately, at the start. They seem to glow when we cherish their bodies and their early endeavours to learn and experiment.

A mother's love is not a luxury. It is her way of reaching out to each new child. It starts with the two of them creating a pre-verbal dialogue together. Slowly, this develops into ordinary language. Then the child is linked to the rest of us. Eventually, he will join our adult world. But first his mother has to reach out to him.

Not that a mother ever gets to know her child completely. Even in such an intimate relationship, her child will always be a mystery. We shall see in the next chapter how non-verbal communication both adds to her knowledge – and enhances the mystery.

CHAPTER FOUR

Keeping in touch

Mothers communicate their love through their actions more than they might think.

> B can be very naughty. He doesn't nap in the day. He just wears me down. My husband works long hours and my family live abroad. It's so hard [*tears*]. What is on my mind is the worry that I cannot love B enough. [B, 8 weeks]

I recognise that worry. In my early days as a mother, I used to sit holding my sleeping baby, and my thoughts would drift far away. Like the mother above, I asked myself if I was loving my baby enough. It was a revelation to sit opposite this mother and see how much she was expressing her love through the tender way she held her small son. She was surely communicating to him that, even though she might feel worn down, she was still 'in touch' with him. She was giving him one of the most vital lessons he has to learn. He won't make it on his own. But most babies don't have to. They can feel the reassuring warmth of their mothers' touch.

Touch is a language we learn before we can speak. From the start, it's the *continuity* of touching which seems to be important to us. A quick pat on the head seems too brief for a newborn. The need for continuous touch is reflected in our language, although, as we grow older, we don't mean it literally. 'Keep in touch', we say, as adults. We usually mean through telephone or electronic means. Still, these keep something precious alive for us. Although we have five senses, we don't use the other ones in the same way. We don't frequently say: 'Keep in earshot', or, 'Keep where I can smell you'. Touch seems to be special.

When did we first learn the language of touch, and who taught us? Before we were born, *we* initiated touch, and no one taught us. Each one of us must have discovered it. With our tongues, our hands and our feet we learned to touch our own bodies, the umbilical cord, placenta and our mothers, from the inside, long before we were born and, therefore, long before our mothers could touch us.

Expectant mothers can feel their babies moving in the womb, and can guess what they are doing. Many mothers today have regular scans. These enable them to see their unborn babies. Professor of Child Neuropsychiatry at the University of Milan Alessandra Piontelli quotes an obstetrician looking at a screen showing ultrasound pictures of a baby aged twenty-five weeks. We can sense the obstetrician's excitement:

> Now the cord is there . . . he seems to be pulling it . . . he is hanging on to it . . . like a rope! . . . now back with his hand over his head . . . he always seems to be looking for something to hold on to . . . his cord . . . or his head . . . [33]

Does a baby's touch feel pleasant? How do mothers respond? One mother, thirty-seven weeks pregnant, was the only expectant mother at a meeting. The other mothers were complaining how wakeful their babies were at night. When it was her turn to speak, she said:

My baby doesn't sleep through the night either. As soon as I lie down, he gets very lively. It's his *dancing* time.

But not all mothers feel so positive. At one antenatal class, the teacher asked:

Antenatal teacher: Have any of you started to have feelings about your baby?

M: I don't know about *my* feelings. But my baby doesn't seem to like me very much.

Antenatal teacher: Oh? How can you know that?

M: He has already started kicking me very hard. He *must* be angry with me to kick like that.

So whether positive, negative or, very likely, a mixture, mother and baby have begun to get the feel of one another long before they see one another. This seems a superb preparation for the more intentional communication which will start after birth.

Once the baby is born, he is no longer held tightly inside his mother's womb. The muscles of his arms and hands seem lax and far less under his control than they were before. However, the muscles that have a new importance are those of his mouth that enable him to suck and swallow. A breastfeeding mother, or anyone who puts a finger into the baby's mouth, may be astounded to discover how strong those muscles feel. For at least the first half year, these muscles are a baby's most reliable way of connecting to his environment.

Once he is born, the baby's mother is able to hold him, and a whole language based on mutual skin-to-skin sensation begins. Mothers seem to need this as much as their babies. Quicker than thought, their hands relay back to them all kinds of impressions of their babies: warm, smooth, soft, sweaty, flaccid, taut, silky, vibrant . . . Perhaps their babies discover reciprocal information.

Fortunately, no one has thought of teaching babies how to learn it, so each baby continues to be self-taught. Perhaps we discover by accident how effective our touch can be, as a means of communication.

> One night, I was feeling fed up because breastfeeding was hurting and my nipples felt very sore. I let out a sort of exclamation. Then G put her hand up on to my arm. It was probably just coincidence. But it felt ever so sweet. [G, 9 days]

As mothers, we are not beginners, because we have learned the basic language of touch, however imperfectly, as babies ourselves. There may be useful techniques to learn as adults, such as how to support the baby's head or how to hold his body safely while we clean him. Fortunately, however, mothers are usually left to blunder through the early weeks, rediscovering for themselves how to communicate through the pre-verbal language of touch.

Touch is a very honest language. But one obstacle to understanding it is all the desensitisation that a woman has probably taught herself at work before having children. Anyone who has spent several years in employment will have learned to suppress physical sensations. Hunger and thirst need to be deferred until a break, while sometimes a woman is required to eat and drink at a business lunch, however un-hungry she might feel. It is often necessary to appear interested when a more genuine response is straightforward boredom. At other times, it is politic to feign disinterest when she feels deeply concerned. It's not always easy to keep alert in the afternoon, when her whole body craves to lie down and sleep. It may pay to laugh at unfunny jokes, or to keep poker-faced at the ridiculous. Other bodily reactions, such as weeping, stiffening with anger or startling in fear, all need to be under a degree of control.

After years of this control, it can be difficult to sense the signals from a person as uncontrolled as a baby. The signals may not be difficult to decode in themselves. But mothers often need to get back to the simplicity of them.

Communication through touch is different from verbal conversation. If you are talking, I must be silent in order to hear you. If you keep talking, you won't have an opportunity to hear what I'm saying. Talking depends on alternating. But touch is simultaneous and our responses are often quicker than conscious thought. A mother holding her baby may feel him sink more heavily in her arms. She may not think, Oh, he's dropped off to sleep. But her arms will probably have responded to the heavier sensation by holding him more securely.

Unlike verbal communication, the language of touch seems to continue even when the mother is asleep as well. It's not only the baby who is reassured by keeping in touch.

> *First mother*: F and I decided this week to put B into his cot to sleep. [*Before that, he had slept in their bed with them.*] B sleeps quite well there. But I miss him. I used to breastfeed him in our bed and he'd fall asleep in my arms. I'd sleep too. I never sleep so well when B is in his cot. [B, 8 months]

> *Second mother* [*very quickly*]: I second that. [G, 3 years; B, 6 months]

Our babies know us well too. Sometimes, the mother's conscious communication may be at variance with her more embodied feelings. Her baby will *invariably* pick up the embodied feelings. They must be obvious to him. Perhaps a mother takes her baby to a family gathering, determined to enjoy the occasion. However, she may also anticipate critical comments on her mothering from her relatives and be unaware of how tense she feels. Her baby responds to her tension and cries with distress right through the family gathering. He grows calm the moment he can feel her relax after she has said goodbye and they are out of the front door.

This kind of experience must give babies some very useful data to process. As adults, we may hardly be conscious of how sensitive we are to non-verbal signals. A research study on the subject of intimate relationships between adults concludes: 'In fact, when there is a discrepancy between verbal and nonverbal messages, people tend to believe the nonverbal ones.'[34] But this article does not ask at what stage we learn all this. It seems likely that if we tend to put more trust in non-verbal messages, it is because we learned that language first.

Mothers register non-verbal signals too. Only if a signal seems surprising (such as, 'I wonder why G feels so hot'), does a mother become conscious of it. There seems to be an active sensing of impressions, exchanged very quickly between the two.

Perhaps the sheer speed of the exchange, and perhaps because it cannot be seen, may convey a false impression. Some people describe mother and baby as 'one'. It's true that, from the outside, they might look and behave like one. Some mothers even say that they experience their babies as extensions of themselves. But this can't really be the case, because mothers and babies often astonish one another by responding independently of one another. They are separate people. If mother and baby look like one unit, it is because their tactile sensitivity enables them to sort out one another's signals very quickly.

This kind of communication is intimate. A mother may be trying to keep up verbal conversations with other adults at the same time. Typically, there are two levels of conversations which she juggles simultaneously.

I was telling the story of the birth at my antenatal class, because that's what I'd agreed to do. But my words sounded rehearsed, as if I was talking on automatic. The *real* conversation was *here* [*indicating the baby in her arms*], and I was thinking: Now it's feeding time. Now it's burp time. Now it's the other breast. That was inside a bubble where I really was. [G, 5 weeks]

59

Mothers discover that, with many young babies, only continuous bodily contact will relax and calm them. Calm babies from what? When we think about it, it must feel extraordinary to be born into a life in which they are no longer continuously in touch with the warm walls of the uterus. Touch, in the womb, must have felt integral to being alive. It seems to take months before we learn to be confident when we are not touching anyone.

It annoys me when my friends don't understand. Like they say: 'Why do you say you can't have a shower? Just put G down for ten minutes. *What's* the problem?' As if G would let me put her down! [G 4 months]

The poet Samuel Taylor Coleridge, who invented the word 'heartroom' (see p. 14), described an experience which he said was common:

Many a parent heard the three-years child that has awoke during the dark night in the little crib by the mother's bed entreat in piteous tones, 'Touch me, only touch me with your finger.' A child of that age, under the same circumstances, I myself heard using these very words in answer to the mother's enquiries, half hushing and half chiding, 'I am not here, touch me, Mother, that I may be here!'[35]

It would be interesting to know if other people have noticed this. Perhaps many of us need the frequent reassurance of warm touch to feel 'here' for the early years of our lives.

I am always holding B. He cries if I put him down. He cries if I even *start* lowering him into his cot. [B, 3 months]

Today many babies receive professional daycare, individual or institutional, while their mothers work. Does this ruin the communication? Life isn't perfect. Many mothers work hard in their free time to sustain the relationship, however tired they are. (This situation is discussed in more detail in Chapter Fifteen.) However, many mothers dread returning to work because they will no longer be able to hold their babies. The importance of their feelings needs to be recognised.

People see how tired I am and they offer to take G for me. I know it's kindly meant. But people don't realise how I *feel* about G. It's almost as if I've grown a new organ, an organ of love, that means I am happiest if G and I are together. [G, 2 months]

I booked a massage for myself, and I left G with F and some friends. When I arrived, I found I'd got the time wrong. There was an hour to wait. I was *hysterical*. I phoned F, and my friends assured me that they'd got plenty of baby food – they had a baby themselves – and not to *worry*! I knew it was irrational, but I couldn't help it, I was very upset at being so long away from G, and I didn't enjoy my massage. I *hated* it. [G, 11 months]

So much is written about mothers feeling trapped by motherhood. We need to realise that not all mothers feel this.

When I leave G to go out, I think, This is great. I'm so enjoying this. It's wonderful to get out sometimes. But later, as soon as I've decided it's time to get back to G, I want her *immediately*. And whatever way I'm getting back to her is always too long. I want to rush back. I want her right away. [G, 7 months]

I thought I'd join a gym, so I found one with a crèche, and I put B in it. But he clung to me so tightly you couldn't get a credit card between us. So I changed my mind and stayed with him. [B, 17 months]

In parts of our culture, this basic primate clinging response may hardly have had any opportunity to develop. For example, in the West, there has been a long tradition of laying babies down in cradles, cots and prams rather than holding them. Many new mothers, brought up in this tradition themselves, are disorientated when they listen to their newborns crying with distress as soon as they are laid down alone. It is confusing for these mothers because, in their experience, being put down alone in a cot is normal.

> When I was a baby, I was left to sleep at the bottom of the garden. No one heard if I cried. Now my instinct is not to do it that way. I carry B in a sling. He hates lying flat, so I have to keep him upright. But I'm in a conflict about being so needed. I can hear a loud voice in my head telling me I'm doing it all wrong. [B, 3 weeks]

Some babies need this contact for longer than their mothers expect.

> I've always picked B up when he cries. But I should have thought I'd see more of a result by now. You'd think I'd be able to put him down on the rug, and he'd be all right if I was sitting beside him. But he won't be put down. He wants to be carried the whole time. I'm afraid we've spoiled him and he won't learn independence. [B, 5 months]

Are there babies who like to be held more than others? Some babies protest vehemently if they are laid flat, especially those suffering reflux. Yet, even without this problem, most babies do seem to enjoy being held. John Bowlby wrote a footnote, in his forthright manner, in the middle of his book, *Attachment*: 'My assistants and I have made a special point of picking up tiny babies who their mothers say are not cuddly. With us they are cuddly. The fact is that the mother does not like to cuddle a baby. Later on, we find these babies become non-cuddlers and squirm when held. Of course,' he adds, 'some brain-damaged babies are hypertonic and may be non-cuddlers from the beginning.'[36]

This is a very interesting observation. Very few characteristics are common to all young babies. It would be interesting to know whether further observations by mothers would bear Bowlby out.

In simple, traditional societies, babies used to be carried in slings or shawls, which solved the problem of how a mother was to get on with her life and still stay in touch with her baby. The recent proliferation of baby carriers and slings has encouraged a revival of this simple idea. Slings continue to be improved and many varieties are now available. A wide range of slings is important because mothers, and also fathers, have different builds. A sling which feels ideal for one person might be uncomfortable for another.

The variety of slings also communicates a message: new mothers are now more aware that their babies might want to be carried. But I can remember how amazed I was to see a sling for the first time. Just before my daughter was born, in 1971, an American woman showed me her 'baby carrier', and it looked so exciting that I asked how I could get one. I remember ordering it from California, where there seemed to be only one style available. I was warned not to use it before my baby was three months old, and I couldn't wait to start. When I did, people in the street kept stopping me to ask: 'Is that a little puppy you're holding to your chest?' Everyone assumed that a baby would be transported in a pram.

The recent popularity of baby slings indicates a change of expectation. Mothers now recognise that their babies might want to be carried not just outside but around the home by their warm-bodied parents. Most slings also enable mothers to see and talk to their babies very easily. Words come more comfortably when the mother's and baby's bodies are touching, and their heads are close to one another.

M: I don't feel so frightened [*of being a mother*] any more.

Me: What has changed?

M: I think I've just become a good mother.

Me: [*I was amazed. M had seemed so underconfident, just a few weeks earlier.*] How can you tell that you've become a good mother?

M: Well, I was at the doctor's for B's second lot of injections. There were mothers there just holding their babies like . . . [*She gestured holding a baby horizontally, well away from her body.*] I held B up against my shoulder and I stroked his back and I whispered in his ear that he was going to be all right. And he hardly cried. [B, 3 months]

This mother saw that even though her son was getting injections from the doctor, she herself had an important part in the process by preparing him.

If you see a circle of mothers who have met in a café or playground to talk, you are likely to find at least one of them standing, bouncing up and down, soothing and comforting the baby in her arms. It is an awesome thought that most of us are so uncomfortable after our births that untold hours of mother-time may have been spent in holding us to calm us.

If no one comforts us, in any way whatsoever, the sense of feeling distressed without bodily comfort seems completely intolerable. Babies rock themselves, bang the backs of their heads, or withdraw. These behaviours are well known in some orphanages. Patreascu Peberdy was taken from a Romanian orphanage and adopted by a British couple. He was brought up in England. This is how he described his orphanage after he revisited it as a young adult: 'For many of the [*babies and small children*] still in [*a Romanian Home for Incurables*], there is nothing for them; their lives are spent sitting in stinking conditions, in dark corners, simply rocking backwards and forwards.'[37]

Why does holding make so much difference? Partly, the pressure of the mother's arms seems to restore a womb-like, safe feeling of containment. How mothers find the 'right' amount of pressure for each baby might be a chapter in itself. But holding

64

provides more than that. There is also the temperature of the mother's skin. It seems to communicate a profound sense of heat. Mere warmth doesn't seem sufficient for a baby. Babies seem to need *heat*. This heat doesn't only reach the baby's skin surface, where the mother's arms are holding him. It seems to penetrate deep within. Babies seem to experience this as feeling filled and satisfied. Not being held seems to communicate the opposite – a terrible sense of chill and deep inner emptiness. These descriptions occur in literature and autobiographies, usually in vivid language because the sense of loss is so painful. For example, Virginia Ironside wrote:

> It would be glib to say that I longed for a mother's love, a mother's arms around me. I knew I felt empty, but I had no idea of what would fill me up.[38]

Fortunately, many babies have mothers or perhaps carers who are willing to hold them. Sometimes holding will comfort a crying baby. Even if it doesn't, mothers often sense that continuing to hold their babies is better than putting them down uncomforted. A mother may be holding her baby in desperate faith that she is doing him some good. There may not be an obvious change to confirm that she has made a difference.

> I can't bear it when he's in pain. There's nothing I can do. I hold him, but it doesn't help him, and he just goes on crying until he falls asleep. [B, 6 weeks]

> G is teething, and last night I really didn't feel like picking her up. It had been a long day and I'd run out of energy. I wanted my dinner, and picking G up felt just too much. She cried, and I just sat there, wondering what to do. In the end, I did pick her up, and I'm *so* glad I did. She really needed me. I got my dinner in the end, much later. [G, 4 months]

G always used to cry in the evening when she was little. I didn't know what was wrong. I used to hold her, but I couldn't calm her. F used to say, 'Put her down in her cot. If she's crying anyway, she might as well cry in her cot, and you could get some sleep.' Perhaps I was being irrational, but I *couldn't* do that. If G was crying, I felt I wanted to hold her. I couldn't have gone to sleep if G was crying, anyway. [G, 5 months]

This surely communicates a profound message to an impressionable small baby. If his mother stays with him through difficult times and doesn't give up on him, it surely leaves him with a sense that his troubles are not too much for other people. People will be there for him.

However, not all mothers do this. Some mothers find it extremely difficult to stay with a distressed and suffering baby. It seems wrong to tell them that they 'should'. If a mother can't cope with this kind of distress, there must be alternative ways for her to communicate her support.

'Holding', observed psychoanalyst Donald Winnicott, 'includes especially the physical holding of the infant, which is a form of loving. It is perhaps the only way in which a mother can show the infant her love.'[39] Surely he was right about holding being a form of loving. But is it 'the only way'? Some mothers, as Bowlby has pointed out in his book *Attachment*, don't like to cuddle. Others may be physically ill and unable to lift their babies. But that doesn't mean they have no other way to show their love. Motherly love is strong and mothers are resourceful.

I went to see my physio this morning, and she gave me some bad news about myself. She also said it was bad for me to pick B up and hold him. I wasn't sure what to do because I always hold him when he cries. I came home and then B started crying. It was completely different crying from anything he'd done before. I didn't have any strength left. I couldn't pick him up. What could I do? He cried and I cried. We both cried. But I'm an adult, so I absorbed most of his crying. I knew I'd have to deal with my crying later, when I was alone. I tried to show B that in no way was he responsible for my crying. Finally, I found a way to calm him. I *blew* on his forehead, and he liked that. He fell asleep. [B, 4 months]

Another mother, disabled years earlier in a car accident which she narrowly survived, tried her utmost to be a 'normal' mother to her son. But, one afternoon, her positive attitude deserted her, and she wept.

First mother: I wish I could bend down. I can't play on the floor with B. I've always had to ask other people to pick him up for me. There are so many things I wish I could do. [B, 14 months]

[*One mother in the circle offered her a tissue, and stroked her shoulder very gently. As soon as she had recovered enough to listen, mothers observed*:]

Second mother: But B looks completely happy. You are giving him everything he needs. [G, 14 months]

Third mother: That's what I was going to say. You give him so much. Not many children get so much attention. [G, 15 months]

Second mother: B has learned to be patient. He's much more patient than any of *our* babies. He knows you can't pick him up, and he just waits till someone else lifts him up for you.

This made sense as we had all seen B patiently waiting. Able-bodied mothers sometimes say they feel frustrated when their babies ask to be carried all the time. But mothers who are physically unable to carry their babies sound as though *not* being able to carry one's baby feels even worse.

For the first three months, I was unable to lift G. So I found a really lovely woman to come in to help me. But I *hated* her. I didn't care how lovely she was. *I* wanted to be the one to carry G, and give her baths, and look after her. [G, 13 months]

Some mothers were daughters of mothers who didn't enjoy cuddling.

I think all babies are tactile. But my mother was adopted as a child. She never cuddled us. She always kept a distance. [G, 12 months]

My mother was adopted. I don't think her adoptive mother was very warm to her. She was never hugged as a child, so I think she just withdrew. You can see it in her now. It's had a long-lasting effect. [*Cuddles her own son.*] She said she used to force herself to cuddle myself and my brother, because she knew she ought to. [B, 2 years]

Often, it takes more than one generation to heal a particular loss.

Nor does everyone with a cuddly mother hold a passport to a good life, although it surely helps. However, many books make most important claims for the benefit of touch, with dire predictions if the mother fails to touch her baby often enough and in the 'right' way. There are books on 'attachment parenting'; about Jean Liedlof's 'continuum concept'; and books on 'baby-wearing', all promising wonderful results if mothers follow their instructions, and predicting poor results if they don't. But this is confusing. It's not the *amount* of touch that makes the difference, but whether mother and baby enjoy it in the first place. If one of them doesn't enjoy it, then it is not a communication of their love.

I had a nice moment yesterday. G has her own room, and I was sitting beside her in the evening. She was crying and wriggling, and I kept thinking maybe I was being a bad mother because I wasn't picking her up and taking her to bed with me. I felt really *bad*. And then this thought came to me: *No.* I'm the mother she's got. She hasn't got a different sort of mother. It's me. Then I put my hand on G's tummy, and I felt a real warm flow of love go from me to her, and it was a really *lovely* feeling. [G, 7 months]

Sometimes it's the baby who doesn't want too close contact.

I've been reading a lot of books on attachment parenting recently. I like their views very much, and I want B to feel secure in the way they explain. The only thing is that B doesn't always want to be attached to me. I assumed that he did, but I found out by accident. One day, I laid him down by himself, and I could see that he really liked it. He likes to play, or to fall asleep. [B, 4 months]

Clearly, there can be no rules for how mothers and babies should connect. What matters is that they find ways to suit both of them.

It was Winnicott who not only recognised the importance of the mother's holding, but also saw that, if a mother was holding her baby, she must have begun by picking him up. I have never seen a description of picking up a baby in as much detail as his. 'Here is a mother with her baby girl,' he said, originally aloud as part of a radio broadcast. 'What does she do when she picks her up? Does she catch hold of her foot and drag her out of the pram and swing her up? Does she hold a cigarette with one hand and grab her with the other? No. She has quite a different way of going at it. I think she tends to give the infant warning of her approach, she puts her hands round her to gather her together before she moves her; in fact, she gains the baby's co-operation before she lifts her.'[40]

This is beautifully observed. Newborns startle when they are picked up suddenly, throwing out their arms and legs in what looks like a shock of distress. Many mothers discover that picking up their babies slowly, putting their hands under their babies exactly as Winnicott recorded, and then pausing before lifting them, means that they avoid startling them. I think it was brilliant of Winnicott to perceive that picking up a baby is an art in itself.

I haven't found a comparable detailed description of putting a baby down. This, too, is surely an art, and must partly depend on a mother being sensitive to her baby's readiness. For some mothers, putting the baby down is a simple action, whereas others complain that 'he will never let me put him down'.

> G seems to save her screaming fits for me. When other people are around, she's entertained and happy. But when it's just us, she won't let me put her down, not even for a minute. And yet there's stuff I have to finish. I don't know what to do. I've lost my temper – I've always had a very quick temper, and that's one reason I used to say I didn't want a kid. I shouted at her, 'Don't *do* that!' and I felt I was on the slippery slope – and she's only eight months. [G, 8 months]

Many mothers get locked into this kind of tussle. It usually starts when a mother says she knows how her baby 'ought' to behave. For example, after a feed, her baby 'ought' to let her put him down to sleep. Yet her baby is giving her completely different signals, suggesting that he would prefer to relax in her arms. Her belief in what he 'ought' to want is stronger than her ability to accept what he actually does want. When this happens, she can easily lose confidence in her child, and then in herself as a viable mother.

'The tender touch of a mother' is almost a cliché. But mothers do not always touch tenderly. What about physical chastisement, which is also a form of touching? This covers a range of actions from an occasional light tap on the hand to regular thrashings of older children. These actions have in common the intention of a bigger and stronger person to inflict punitive pain on a small and sensitive person. The idea is to 'teach him a lesson' or 'show him who is in control'.

Typically, the mother has no idea *why* her child is doing the action that appears to her so 'naughty' or 'out of control'. She instantly *assumes* a bad reason for it, which she doesn't stop to question. She has 'lost touch' with her child. Her violent solution is to subjugate her child, rather than to understand him and continue their communication. Her child may be cowed superficially, but usually smoulders with inward anger. Physical chastisement may appear to be a quick way of dealing with a 'difficult' child. The child may indeed now be doing exactly what his mother wanted. But we seem to be born with a sense of justice and fairness. For the child, being smacked by an angry mother for an action which he thought was reasonable doesn't qualify as just or fair. He seems to withdraw a degree of trust when this happens. If it happens often, the intimacy between mother and child becomes more difficult to restore.

A different problem again arises over seductive and sexual touching. This is discussed on page 181.

A mother's responses to her child aren't always perfect. However, her touch enables her to sense messages from her baby. But what happens if a mother is not 'listening' to her baby in this way? Then it can be hard to notice her baby's signals. Instead of decoding these signals, she can perceive his behaviour as inappropriate or meaningless. She may hold him for hours, yet she is not really 'in touch' with him.

Julia Hollander gave this very honest and vivid account of trying to connect to her second daughter, who had cerebral palsy:

Constantly ravenous and uncomfortable, she [*the baby*] slept fitfully and started to miss milestones – no eye contact; no fixing and following; no smile. I tried to hold on in there, accept that after such a traumatic birth her development would be slow. As each day passed, my yearning grew – when would she respond to my kisses, my soothing songs and my constant embrace? How long would it take for her to show that she loved me as I loved her?[41]

It must have been heartbreaking to hold her baby in 'constant embrace'. Yet Mrs Hollander was painfully aware of what her baby was *not* doing. She was also conscious of her own unrequited overtures, which were perhaps at a more advanced level than her baby could manage. She had an older daughter, and surely the comparison between the two girls made it especially painful for her to accept just how undeveloped her younger daughter still was. Because of this negative focus, the contact between mother and baby seemed stuck.

A foster carer took over, and sensed the more basic needs of this baby: 'She [*the baby*] is determined. She will not be ignored. I have a cloth sling, and this becomes [*her*] home. She lies over my heart, sucking on my finger. For the next few months, I wear [*her*] whenever I am awake.'[42]

Both the mother and the foster mother spent long periods holding the baby continuously. But the foster mother had a more positive view of her, based on the signals she was picking up, rather than mourning what she couldn't do yet. So her way of holding must have been a more 'in-touch' experience for the baby. Before her first birthday, the foster mother recorded that the little girl smiled.

As babies develop, their ability to touch becomes more purposeful. Their ability to grasp seems to be present from birth. A mother can put her finger by a baby's hand, and he will open his hand and grasp it with a soft, warm and relaxed grip. Yet it is amazingly strong. Gradually, the baby starts to reach out to new things, beyond his mother. His mother then realises that she needs to learn a new vigilance to keep him safe.

> I sit down with B at a table, and I quickly sweep out of reach with my arm anything I think he might grab that I think he shouldn't have. [B, 6 months]

G's curiosity fascinates me. There's a space between the bath and the wall where the hot-water pipe goes. G touched it, it was hot, and she cried. But when the hot-water tap isn't on, it's cold. She keeps going to touch it because she can't work it out. [G, 11 months]

As children start to develop speech, it becomes a quicker mode of communication. Speech can cover distance. A child can shout, 'Mummy, I *want* you!' even if he isn't sure where his mother has gone. Older children learn to speak more, and touch less. Words can be more explicit than touch. All kinds of details can now be shared with many other people. Through speech, a child is in a better position to be understood by others. This means that, by degrees, he can manage more distance between himself and his mother.

Difficulties can then arise. Sometimes a child clings to his mother and fears distance. At other times, a mother may cling to her child. It can take time for the two of them to discover how to move from closeness to a comfortable distance from one another.

After that, touch becomes a more abstract concept. 'I'm deeply touched,' we say, which we don't mean literally. But there are those intimate confessions that are best said between two people who can touch one another. They are more difficult to shout across a distance. 'I love you', 'I'm so sorry' and other such admissions are easier to confide when two people are physically close.

Touch is also important once we start our adult sexual lives. Women who missed out on being touched lovingly when they were small girls seem to crave it later. Here is their chance to experience wonderful feelings of tender touching with a sexual partner for the first time. It's interesting that most of us only become mothers after we have enjoyed a 'revision course' with our partners in the language of touch.

The wish for touch also occurs at difficult times in our lives, when we feel small, frightened, helpless, or when we are in great pain or dying. Our intellectual abilities can feel inadequate to these powerful experiences. Perhaps these times reactivate our pre-verbal memories of being small, new and helpless in a loud and confusing world. But, by this time, many of us have experienced the comfort of our connection to other people. Our ancient sensitivity to touch can be a great help to us.

What about the expression, 'left holding the baby'? People use it to convey a negative sense of being burdened. But when we hold our babies, we are engaged in a most positive act. It gives us an opportunity to express a message of welcome that a baby can feel. It can last each person for a lifetime.

CHAPTER FIVE

Shadows of Truby King and Freud

This chapter is theoretical. At first, it was part of the previous chapter on keeping in touch. Now I've separated it, thinking that a tired mother might prefer to save it for later reading. This is for readers who are not too tired.

Most mothers and babies discover for themselves how to communicate through touch. So do they need to be taught how? The unfortunate truth is that just about *everything* that mothers would do independently with their babies has been challenged. People keep coming up with 'improvements'. These people are then perceived as 'experts' and their ideas spread.

Two particular 'experts' have had a strong influence on our ideas about how mothers and babies should touch one another. The ideas of both of them are said to be outdated now. But this doesn't seem to be true. Ideas have long lives, and both these particular sets of ideas seem very much alive today.

Frederic Truby King (1858–1938) was born in New Zealand. He went on to study medicine in Edinburgh, and was horrified by the poverty of mothers he observed there. In 1904, he visited Japan

75

and was impressed to see how well breastfeeding benefited both mother and baby. He resolved to revive breastfeeding because, he said: 'The natural food direct from the mother's breast is the child's birthright.'[43]

Truby King published his bestselling book, *Feeding and Care of Baby* in Britain in 1913. It contains 260 pages devoted to the minutiae of practical childcare. He laid special emphasis on hygiene and clock-regulated timetables for breastfeeding and sleeping. (His four-hourly breastfeeding schedule is discussed on page 268.)

In the middle of this lengthy practical regimen is one short section with a more motherly heading: 'Mothering and Management'. It covers the need of babies to be held.

MOTHERING AND MANAGEMENT

Babies who are allowed to lie passively in their cots and who do not get sufficient 'mothering', tend to be pale, torpid, flabby and inert. An infant should never remain in its cot continuously in one position. Not only should the position in the cot be changed from time to time, but the baby should be picked up at intervals and carried about. The stimulation afforded by natural handling is beneficial and necessary, but much harm is done by excessive and meddlesome interference and undue stimulation.[44]

The wording of Truby King's paragraph is fascinating. He wrote it in the passive voice. This meant that he could avoid the word 'mother'. Although the paragraph is headed 'mothering', it appears to refer to actions, rather than to the person of the mother.

In other words, 'mothering' is presented as a series of necessary, utilitarian actions, to prevent babies becoming 'pale, torpid, flabby and inert'. There is no suggestion here that mother and baby might have feelings about touching one another, and use touch to express their love for one another. And what exactly did Truby King mean by 'meddlesome interference and undue stimulation'? Could he have meant *cuddling?* Was he claiming that a mother's cuddles were harmful for her baby?

Truby King travelled around the world, setting up schools to train mothers. His ideas spread. Countless mothers thought that they weren't 'allowed' to cuddle their babies. At the Truby King Mothercraft Training Centre in Highgate, north London, the director, Mabel Liddiard, was so impressed by Truby King's regimen of fresh air that every night, babies were put out in their cots on to the balcony of Cromwell House at the top of Highgate Hill, where it is breezy in the mildest weather. There was no relenting on the fresh-air-at-night regime during the freezing winter of 1951, so the poor babies must have developed a high level of stamina.

Fortunately, not everyone was so impressed by this regime. I talked to a woman who had worked at Cromwell House in 1950. She admitted: 'We always had to pick the babies up. We had to turn them from one side to the other in their cots by the clock. I used to cuddle them if no one was looking. You got told off if you were seen doing that.'[45]

Today, we have the concepts of 'kangaroo care' and 'attachment parenting' which make the opposite claim – that maternal holding and cuddling are beneficial for babies. But these ideas haven't killed off Truby King's theories. You can still hear mothers being warned not to handle their newborns 'too much', and being taught that babies 'need' to sleep in cots by themselves.

Truby King had almost an exact contemporary, who is the second major 'expert'. It is interesting to find how much the two men had in common. Both came from large families and both were devoted to their mothers. Both visited the famous neurologist, Professor Jean-Martin Charcot, in Paris (in 1880 and 1885–6 respectively), before they married. Each married a devoted wife, and each had a daughter who continued his work. Each believed his views were scientific and had the utmost confidence in his own findings. But they weren't in competition because neither seemed to know about the other.

Unlike Truby King, Sigmund Freud (1856–1939) thought that maternal touching was not just functional but 'a source of pleasure'.[46] The mother of a baby, he wrote, 'strokes him, kisses him, rocks him . . . '[47], and he concluded, in his final work: 'By her care of the child's body she [*the mother*] becomes its first seducer.'[48] He commented: 'A mother would probably be horrified if she were made aware that all her marks of affection were rousing her child's sexual instinct and preparing for its later intensity.'[49] But, he believed, such a mother had no need for self-reproach. 'She is only fulfilling her task in teaching the child to love.'[50]

Freud, like Truby King, was concerned about parents who 'display excessive affection' to their babies.[51] But he didn't explain how parents could distinguish what he considered to be excessive from what he thought was normal.

The most innovative part of Freud's thinking was to claim that we have sexual feelings from the start. What exactly did he mean? It's important to have Freud's exact words in front of us. Too many people refer to him as a psychiatrist, which he wasn't, and attribute to him beliefs which he never held. It is only fair to consider his *own* words about the early contact of a baby with his mother.

Both Freud and Truby King thought breastfeeding was vital, but for completely different reasons. Truby King was thinking of the nutrition. Freud was fascinated by the sucking it required: 'If an infant could speak, he would no doubt pronounce the act of sucking at his mother's breast by far the most important in his life.'[52] Why? Because, Freud tells us, the baby wasn't just sucking for food. He identified two stages of sucking:

> The baby's obstinate persistence in sucking gives evidence at an early stage of a need for satisfaction which, though it originates from and is instigated by the taking of nourishment, nevertheless

78

strives to obtain pleasure independently of nourishment and for that reason may and should be termed *sexual*.[53]

It is interesting to notice that he describes two stages of breast-feeding: ' . . . when children fall asleep after being sated at the breast, they show an expression of blissful satisfaction which will be repeated in later life after the experience of a sexual orgasm.'[54] He went on:

> But we observe how an infant will repeat the action of taking in nourishment without making a demand for further food; here, then, he is not actuated by hunger. We describe this as sensual sucking, and the fact that in doing this he falls asleep once more with a blissful expression shows us that the act of sensual sucking has in itself alone brought him satisfaction.[55]

He observed: 'We can only refer this pleasure to an excitation of the areas of the mouth and lips; we call those parts of the body "erotogenic zones" and describe the pleasure derived from sucking as a sexual one.'[56]

This is a very interesting observation. Although mothers and wet nurses must have observed how babies like to continue sucking even after they have finished feeding, they don't appear to have written about it as a sexual action. Freud's point is an original one.

How much could Freud have learned from his own personal observation of babies? He was the father of six children. 'In the case of my own children, who followed each other in rapid succession,' he recalled, 'I neglected the opportunity of carrying out observations of this kind; but I am now making up for this neglect by observing a small nephew . . . '[57]

In the 'Little Hans' case, Freud wrote: ' . . . I have for many years been urging my pupils and friends to collect observations on the sexual life of children – the existence of which has as a rule been cleverly overlooked or deliberately denied.'[58] It sounds as though his opportunities for direct and close observation of breastfeeding might have been limited.[59]

Freud doesn't define what he meant by 'sexual', nor explain how he could be so certain that breastfeeding infants were experiencing not just pleasure but sexual pleasure. However, he provides a detailed visual account of the two-stage breastfeeding process which very few people had bothered to spell out before. First, there is the hungry sucking, which then turns into the second stage and becomes what we now call 'comfort sucking'. In the second stage, the baby is making sucking movements but is not continuing to swallow milk. Freud is right to point out that this second process requires explanation. Despite his emphasis, mothers today are often told that comfort sucking isn't important. The baby has finished feeding, so he is said to be 'just messing about'. Mothers are often advised to take the baby off the breast at this point. But comfort sucking is not 'messing about'. Here, Freud has at least recognised the importance of this stage.

However, Freud's conclusion – that the baby must be experiencing sexual pleasure during the second stage of breastfeeding – is not self-evident. A sexual orgasm is often called a 'climax' because it represents the greatest intensity of our feelings. Sexual sensation increases until the person is burning with need for satisfaction. But the process of eating occurs differently. The sensation of being hungry *before* eating is when the baby's feelings are most urgent. A baby can't reach a climax in the instant of starting to breastfeed because it requires time to be satisfied by enough food.

As a baby starts to feel more full, he becomes calmer, relaxed and then sleepy. He has now received the main protein and fat content of the feed, after which the breast milk, as we now know, becomes more watery. He is thoroughly satisfied, because his mother's milk is perfectly attuned to his needs. He can now relax because he is no longer hungry. Slowly, the whole nature of his sucking changes.

How far is this second kind of sucking the intensely pleasurable sucking that Freud described? I'm responding to this question not only as a woman who has helped mothers to breastfeed for thirty years – I have also spent years breastfeeding my own three babies. The children are adults, but the sensations of breastfeeding are unforgettable. The non-eating sucking feels a much lighter movement, a mere fluttering of the baby's lips. It seems that the *feeding*-sucking, rather than the second kind of sucking, has provided the more intense sensation. The final sucking feels like the winding down of the last vestiges of wakeful tension so that the baby can gently glide into sleep. This allows him to 'sleep like a baby' because he is completely relaxed. After that, Freud's description of the blissful expression of the sleeping baby is a good one.

But Freud was adamant that it wasn't the food that had given the baby satisfaction: '. . . the fact that he falls asleep once more with a blissful expression shows us that the act of sensual sucking has in itself alone brought him satisfaction.'[60] Freud's conviction is interesting. He himself seems to have had his own personal experience of non-nutritional oral pleasure. He smoked cigars daily and said they were essential to his creative work. He described a miserable time, when he was trying to give up smoking, as not having 'anything warm between my lips'.[61] This is an interesting statement because Martha Freud made sure that her husband always had regular and punctual warm meals. So, in his own life, he had separated nutrition from the pleasures of cigar smoking. Perhaps, for him, the sensation of having something 'warm between my lips' gave him an experience of sexual pleasure. Could Freud have been extrapolating from his own pleasure at an after-dinner cigar to making a generalisation about how babies feel during the second stage of breastfeeding?

Although Freud describes a breastfed baby's expression as blissful, his actual account of breastfeeding sounds as if he thought it left the baby unsatisfied. A baby, he thought, would get more pleasure sucking something *other* than the breast.

> But at first the infant, in his sucking activity, gives up this object [*his mother's breast, presumably*] and replaces it by a part of his own body. He begins to suck his thumbs or his own tongue. In this way he makes himself independent of the consent of the external world as regards gaining pleasure . . . [62]

But do babies gain a special pleasure by sucking their own thumbs or tongue? I have seen some babies suck their fists, but usually it is because they are desperate to feed before their mothers have finished undoing their clothes. I have never seen a baby come off the breast and suck his hand in preference, except when mother and baby haven't got the position quite right. Also, what is the meaning of the reference to 'consent of the external world'? It sounds as though Freud believed that 'the external world', which presumably refers to a mother or wet nurse, didn't 'consent' to a baby gaining independent pleasure. This seems an odd statement, yet Freud makes it without explanation.

There is also Freud's revealing comment: 'And for however long it is fed at its mother's breast, it will always be left with a conviction after it has been weaned that its feeding was too short and too little.'[63] Moreover: 'It seems, rather, that the child's avidity for its early nourishment is altogether insatiable, that it never gets over the pain of losing its mother's breast.'[64] This is certainly not a universal truth. It seems to depend very much on whether the mother has helped her baby to wean in a sensitive way. There is ample evidence, for example, from the range of mothers' accounts in the book *How Weaning Happens*, that babies and children are not insatiable, and can end up very satisfied with their breastfeeding experiences.[65]

Freud made strong assertions about what babies feel. He was writing as the authoritative figure of a doctor in his time and as the founder of psychoanalysis. However, it is difficult to be sure what babies feel. He didn't seem to have discussed his sexual theory with his wife. It is interesting to discover that very few mothers have commented as *mothers* on Freud's work. Freud's theory that breastfeeding babies experience sexual feelings has neither been sufficiently defined nor proven. Mothers who are currently breast-feeding would be in a good position to comment.

I have wondered about Freud's statement (see p. 78) saying that a mother is 'only fulfilling her task in teaching the child to love'. But what kind of love would a baby learn from Freud's descrip-tions? He would learn to be sexually aroused without his mother realising, because his mother would be horrified if she was 'aware'. He would learn to make himself 'independent of the consent of the external world as regards gaining pleasure'. Presumably, his mother would be part of 'the external world'. He would always feel that breastfeeding, which had given him such blissful pleasure, had been ended too soon. Freud's version of love sounds a lonely experience for both mother and baby.

The idea that babies' sucking is sexual has affected the way people think of it. Breast-sucking is widely regarded in the West as an adult sexual act, which can be tolerated in small babies, but is considered inappropriate as the child grows older. The age at which it becomes inappropriate is usually clearly stated in babycare literature. The stipulated age differs, usually to accord with social convenience. However, most babies are not ready to stop breast-feeding when they reach an arbitrary date in the calendar. They develop at individual rates. A minority of mothers continue breast-feeding their children until the children spontaneously stop. The majority of breastfed babies are forced, coaxed or seduced into stopping breastfeeding before they are ready. They have to forgo all the comfort and security they could have enjoyed.

Truby King and Freud held very different theories on what babies needed. But in one respect they were similar. Both stated that the mother was a very important figure. Strangely, both saw her role in an impersonal way, as a kind of service-provider. What mattered was what she provided, not who she was or how she felt about her child. For both men, a mother seemed to be a potentially dangerous figure – someone who could touch her baby too much. The solution, for both of them, was to encourage babies to be independent of their mothers. 'Truby King babies' were only to be picked up at the correct times for eating or for turning about. 'Freud babies' were supposed to teach themselves how to get pleasure from sucking their own tongues and thumbs.

However, if babies are to learn to relate to other people, it might be very important that they are *not* learning to be self-sufficient in their cots, or sucking their thumbs. A baby's attention needs to be outgoing to enable him to exchange signals with his mother. And it is this theme which links the previous chapter to the next one.

CHAPTER SIX

Keeping in mind

'How can you expect a man who's warm to understand one who's cold?' This was the question Solzhenitsyn asked near the beginning of his novella, *One Day in the Life of Ivan Denisovich*. And again, near the end: 'A man who's warm can't understand a man who's freezing.'[66]

That same challenge to understand another person is exactly the one that mothers face. In Solzhenitsyn's story, a medical orderly was sending a prisoner out of the relatively warm prison hospital into the sub-zero temperatures of a Siberian winter. The medical orderly might find it extremely hard to understand just how cold the prisoner would feel. In exactly the same way, mothers are confronted by sharp contrasts. It is not easy for an adult, who has learned how to think in words, and to communicate, to imagine how it feels to be a new person who has not yet experienced either possibility. Perhaps this is why we can barely remember how we felt, just after we had made the irreversible transition to life outside the womb.

I try to put myself in G's place. It must be like arriving on another planet. Suddenly she's expected to find her own food and [*breast*] feed herself. She used to be fed by the umbilical cord. [G, 5 months]

Can a mother really attain anywhere near enough understanding? Solzhenitsyn was right to question whether real understanding could ever be possible. However, he was describing people in prison camps who might not survive unless they mainly looked out for themselves. Fortunately, few mothers are in this degraded position. They are responsible for babies whom they are learning to love. Once a woman becomes a mother, she cannot afford to think primarily about herself. Slowly, she learns to be a 'couple' with her baby, and to think about the two of them. Her thinking is an invisible base which enables her to formulate ideas and to make decisions. All these activities are expressions of her love.

Perhaps in every culture, there are accounts of how much mothers think about their babies. One verse by the biblical prophet Isaiah, from the eighth century BC, gives a good example of how this attentive kind of thinking must have seemed like a 'trademark' of mothers. Isaiah was writing to reassure the Jewish people that God had not forgotten them. He chose two images to bring his message home: a shepherd remembering his sheep, and a mother remembering her baby. Isaiah's words about the mother were:

> Can a woman forget her sucking child?
> Should she not have compassion on the son of her womb?
> Yea, these [*mothers*] may forget,
> Yet I [*God*] will not forget you [*the Jewish people*].[67]

The interesting point about this image is its context. Its success depended on its sounding true. If it were normal to look around and see that most mothers were visibly looking after their babies, then the Jewish people would feel reassured. If it were very unusual to see such mothers, then the image would fail and people would continue to despair that God had forgotten them. Isaiah needed to use safe images. This means that we can logically conclude that, in his time, it was very likely that people were used to seeing vigilant shepherds, and mothers who were (with rare exceptions) visibly remembering their sucking babies.

Isaiah's words are nearly three millennia old. Yet even now, there still seems to be a popular expectation that a mother might be absent-minded because she is thinking about her baby.

> I drove to the supermarket yesterday, put B in a trolley, got all my shopping done, and lined it up at the checkout counter. I thought I'd been very efficient. Then I discovered I'd left my wallet at home. The woman in front of me was packing up her shopping, and she said: 'Ah, well. You've got a baby, haven't you?' [B, 2 months]

So the woman in front clearly expected mothers of small babies to be forgetful. The sight of a young baby in the shopping trolley meant that no further explanation for doing all one's shopping without a wallet was needed.

Mothers try to stay in control of everyday details, but even so:

> Oh dear, I've just noticed that I'm walking out of the door [*with G*] without putting my shoes on! [G, 13 months]

How can mothers focus on their babies so much that they forget essentials like wallets and shoes? Have their brains gone mushy? Besides, it's one thing to focus on something for a couple of hours. But many mothers say they are thinking about their babies all day and night. Are they being honest?

Many mothers describe how intensely they think about their newborns. They hold them, gaze at them and wonder about them. But such intense observation comes at the price of screening out a good deal of ordinary life.

How many times have I been in the middle of a room and asked myself: '*What* was I about to do?' [B, 3 weeks]

My life revolves around B. Who I am, I don't remember any more. A few days ago, my husband and I were talking about B. Then my husband said, 'Do you mind if we talk about something else?' And we were both silent. Neither of us could think of anything to say! [B, 8 weeks]

I use the word 'thing' a lot. I say: 'Pass me that red . . . thing', 'Where is my yellow . . . thing?' I can never think of the words. [G, 9 months]

The mother whose husband wanted them to talk about something else was one of three first-time mothers who talked to me, one afternoon. Each had a boy and, by chance, each boy was eight weeks old. One mother was English, one French and one from an Asian family. Yet each described being a mother in a similar way. Each said she was *very* tired:

I have no energy.

I have no memory any more.

I don't listen to what people tell me. I *look* as if I am listening. But I'm not taking anything in.

I asked: 'Well, where *is* your attention then? If you're not listening, is your attention wandering to something else?' They replied:

I'm thinking about *him*. *All* the time.

I'm thinking about what he wants and what to do next.

I'm trying to understand what he needs.

I could see the results of all this thinking as we talked. First one baby cried, then another. All three mothers were brilliant at recognising what their babies wanted. It sounded simple once they had explained it. But, as an outsider, *I* wouldn't have realised. In each case, the mother responded, the baby stopped crying and looked very peaceful, and so the mother's understanding was validated.

He wants a feed.

He's telling me that he wants to be in his sling.

Me: How did an eight-week-old baby tell you that?

[*The mother gave me an exhausted look.*] I don't know. I just *know*.

He needs to burp and then he'll be hungry again.

All three mothers felt that their relationship had only just begun to feel manageable:

I think I'm over the worst.

It's getting easier now.

It's better than it was.

I asked: 'What has changed? What makes it easier?'

He's more of a person. He recognises me now.

He smiles at me.

We went to visit my husband's family. My husband held B, and he told me that B's eyes kept following me right round the room. I feel he knew I was his mother.

Why is being a mother so difficult? Why are new mothers so tired? If they spend a lot of time thinking about their babies, how can merely *thinking* about a baby be so tiring?

From what mothers describe, one primary reason for finding it tiring is that a mother is responsible for a new person who does not at first communicate intentionally with her. But he depends on her. So she has very little leisure to focus on her own personal thoughts. She has to select from her own thoughts only those which are essential. She keeps switching from brief moments of thinking about herself to intense times of thinking about her baby. She has to keep asking herself what he needs from her. He may not know the answer either. This means that she has to make detailed observations which won't yet connect up. She has to keep a great deal of disconnected data at the ready. Understanding brings relaxation, when several observations fall into place. So not-understanding-yet leaves her puzzled and unable to relax.

Slowly, over many months, the intense times of maternal attention pay off. The mother finds that she can recognise her baby's actions and see short sequences of meaningful behaviour. One can hear her excitement when she does this. These moments of understanding bring renewed energy. As one mother put it:

> I suppose every time I understand B it's like little grains of sand. Nothing much in itself. It's only in time that it grows and it'll make a big sand castle. It grows in tiny amounts. Each grain adds to it. [B, 14 months]

What 'little grains of sand' do mothers discover? Often they are minuscule details. But they confirm that the mother really has started to understand her child.

> People talk about babies being angry. But how do you *know* if your baby feels angry? He can *look* angry. He can go red in the face and do things that might seem angry. But then it turns out he's *hungry*. [B, 3 weeks]

> I think when a baby cries, you look for just one thing that's the matter. But what I've learned is: it starts off as one thing and then it changes. Like one moment he *doesn't* want the breast and he screams if I offer it, and the next moment he *does* want it. [B, 7 weeks]

G knows that she exists. She knows it in a physical sense. It's a huge change, and I don't know how else to explain it. I can see that the penny has just dropped and she knows that if she kicks a ball and it moves, she knows that it's because *she* has kicked it. [G, 8 months]

B invents things. He woke up one morning saying, 'Doth'. I thought, 'Doth'? What can that be? But B's two words are 'Daddy' and 'moth', and I realised that he had combined them. [B, 20 months]

Some very useful 'grains of sand' are when mothers realise how much their children are learning from studying themselves.

G has learned to nod when she means 'Yes'. At first I thought she must have some kind of a tic. But now she's got good at it. She must have observed us and realised that we do it. [*I counted myself nodding four times while the mother was telling me this! I'd never noticed before how often this particular mother and I nodded at one another.*] [B, 4 years; G, 12 months]

B keeps patting his cheeks, and I knew he must have learned something, but I didn't know what it was. Then, the other morning, I was stroking moisturiser into my face, and I looked down at B and he was patting his cheeks. And I suddenly realised that *that's* what he'd learned. [B, 13 months]

These observations require a lot of motherly patience. It can be tempting to dismiss babies' actions because they take a long time to understand.

For several nights, G was sleeping badly and I was like: 'Be quiet, G, and go to sleep.' People said it was teething, but I wasn't sure. Then I thought: Adults toss and turn when they've got things on their minds. G is processing so many new things. I expect she's got a lot on her mind. After thinking that, I could be much calmer, and we've had some peaceful nights now. [G, 4 months]

B gets very cross when I don't give him what he wants. This morning,
I offered him banana for breakfast. He started shaking the tray of
his high chair. He wanted *peas*! As soon as I gave him peas, he was
all right. When I've got energy, I can work out what he's trying to
tell me. But, when I'm tired, I think, You are making a fuss over
nothing. [B, 10 months]

A mother might not realise how much she has learned about
her child. But when she offers to take care of another mother's
child, it can bring home to her how well she now understands her
own:

A friend asked me to look after her baby, and I really had to
work at it. It made me realise how well I know G, because I kept
looking at my friend's baby and thinking, What do you want?
Whereas with G it's so easy. I *know* what she's likely to want.
[G, 10 months]

However, even the most attentive mother can never understand
her child perfectly nor know exactly how he feels. But perhaps
these shortcomings are beneficial. Her child might feel 'crowded'
if she knew him too well. The psychoanalyst Peter Fonagy made
this point in discussing the process of 'mentalisation'. By this,
he meant our ability to be aware of other people's thoughts and
feelings as well as our own. We learn this from infancy on, when
we observe that our caretakers can 'reflect' our feelings, 'accu-
rately but not overwhelmingly'. [68] Fonagy clearly recognised that
a mother's understanding didn't need to be perfect.

Maternal thinking is hard enough as it is. Mothers need to
update their data as their children develop, outgrowing a phase
that the mothers had got used to.

It's the unpredictability that I find hard. You spend ages creating a
soothing atmosphere with a story and a [*breast*]feed. A few months
ago, B would have gone to sleep. But now, suddenly, *bingo*, he's

awake. He gets up and toddles off to do something. He's not tired. But I haven't had dinner, or done anything. [B, 16 months]

Mothers have to keep noticing changes, and adapting.

G is mobile now, so I keep having to think of all the dangers. She is completely fearless, and I'm so proud of her not being frightened. So I'm thinking, What is she doing now? Should I rescue her or should I let her find out for herself? How badly could she get hurt? It's exhausting. I'm *very* tired. [G, 10 months]

Your mind goes in all directions, thinking of all the possibilities. You have to be about twenty steps ahead. [G, 20 months]

From the slow process of keeping a mental list of potential dangers, a mother may suddenly have to react at lightning speed. Inevitably, babies learn to move quicker than anyone anticipated.

B has learned to roll over, this week, both ways. He's getting more independent. But now he can roll, the only safe place for him is on the floor. [B, 4 months]

Once, I had my back turned and G climbed up five stairs. Five! I didn't know she could climb up *one*. She fills me with awe. [G, 13 months]

I put my mug of coffee near my laptop, and then I had to rush away because I could hear 2B crying. And when I got back 1B said, 'Mummy, coffee, floor, sorry, *sorry*, Mummy.' My coffee had gone all over the laptop and onto the floor. It wasn't 1B's fault, and I couldn't get cross with him. It was *my* fault. I should have thought where I was putting my coffee down. I was tired, and I just wasn't thinking. [1B, 2 years; 2B, 3 months]

As children grow, they themselves notice that their mothers, or mother substitutes, *do* keep them in mind, and try to protect them.

M: I can remember falling down my grandmother's stairs when I was less than two. I knew how to fall by then, so I wasn't hurt. I remember I was doing up my shoe and I leaned forward too far – and down I went.

Me: How much do you remember?

M: My grandmother's *face*.

Clearly the panic or concern on the grandmother's face on behalf of her granddaughter had made a stronger impression than any fear or pain at falling.

It's surprising to discover how inexperienced a small child can be. A mother might assume that her child knows the consequences of an action, when, for example, he is banging a glass on the table. To her, it is obvious that a bang or two will break the glass. Yet her child seems unaware of that and is simply banging away to find out what will happen next.

A baby seems to live primarily in the present, with no sense of the future. So this is what preoccupies his mother. She has to keep calculating and timing when her baby is likely to be tired, when he will be hungry, when he might feel cold, and so on. She tries to factor all this into her plans for the day. She is thinking on behalf of two people, and constantly making decisions to try to create a good day for her child as well as herself.

Strangely, as a mother gets good at keeping her child in mind, the results can look so effortless and so harmonious that to other people – and even to the mother herself – it can seem as if her hard-won understanding of her child just happened of itself. Only her tiredness indicates how much mental work it really required.

I laugh when people ask if I'm tired. *That's* not the problem. It would be nice if just a proper sleep would take it all away. No, the real problem is all that *mental* work. Wondering if you're doing the right thing. [B, 3 weeks]

The tiring thing about being a mother isn't the physical side. It isn't the tasks. It's *mental*. It's all those little decisions that are going on in your head, like: Should I do *this*? Is it time to do *that*? All decisions. I spend all day making these minute decisions and by the end of it I'm exhausted. Yesterday, my boyfriend asked me, 'Do we need more bacon?' I said, 'Oh, *you* decide.' I feel I can't make one more decision, not even if it's for myself. [B, 11 months]

At the same time, no one can focus so intently on one person without needing some kind of break. Many mothers describe moments when they simply blank out. For quite a while, they don't think about *anything*, or they relax and think about something completely different. It's an essential way of recovering from hard *mental* work.

I can really trust my sister with my baby. She's the calmest mother I know. So I gave her G to hold, and I was talking to my niece, when I suddenly caught sight of G in my sister's arms. It was like: Oh! I've got a *baby*. I'd only been talking for ten minutes to my niece but it was as if I'd been away for a long holiday. [G, 3 months]

I must have been pushing the buggy with my eyes shut. I suddenly came to. Where was I? *God!* I think. I'm a mother in London responsible for two small children. [G, 2 years; G, 3 months]

M: If B has a nap, I like to relax and watch something mindless on television.

Me: Is that because you keep using your mind as a mother?

M: Yes. [B, 4 months]

Mothers often create attention breaks for themselves. Some mention sewing, knitting and cooking, especially baking. They say this helps them to recover not only from responding to babies, but also toddlers and older children.

Mariella Doumanis gives a fine example in her book, *Mothering in Greece*:

> I cannot help thinking back . . . to the many cakes I have baked for my children, giving all my attention to the details in the recipe, striving for quality in the end product, and while focusing on the task ignoring, or trying to, the very people it was supposed to serve.[69]

A self-contained task, such as making cakes, can be calming after trying to keep pace with a family of lively, adventurous children.

It's when a mother has a break from keeping her child in mind that she can catch a glimpse of how much she is usually doing.

> About two months ago, I was invited to a party. F looked after G, so I went. There was a champagne reception first, and I can clearly remember standing there, with a champagne glass in my hand, thinking, This is *all* I have to do. Just stand here and talk to these people. It's so easy. I don't have to keep turning my head to see if G is all right. [G, 5 months]

Is so much intense thinking really a good idea? Perhaps a mother could think about her baby *too* much. She might then be thinking about her baby to such an extent that it could become an obsession rather than a learning process. However, can an outsider really judge which it is?

> A friend came to play with G, with his mother. At first, I thought his mother was making too much fuss. I thought she kept hovering over him, wherever he went. But then I noticed that her little boy had poor eyesight and kept bumping into things. So after a bit I decided that his mother was probably worrying the right amount. [G, 3 years; B, 4 months]

Mothers are frequently reprimanded for thinking too much about their babies; they may be called neurotic, worrying, or 'a

96

helicopter parent'.[70] Friends may tell them, 'It's not healthy to be too wrapped up in the baby.' But people who pass these judgments tend to be hasty. Certainly, with a dependent baby, there is a great deal for a mother to worry about. If she isn't sure, it makes sense to worry rather than not to. She may have previously had fertility problems, miscarried, gone through a difficult birth, or her baby may have recently had a sudden illness or accident. These kinds of experiences can leave mothers feeling jumpy for months. Obviously, it is possible to worry to an unjustified degree. But people with responsible jobs often receive respect from the rest of us when they say they are preoccupied with the concerns of their work. Wouldn't it be fairer then to regard a mother as 'innocent until proved guilty' in this respect? We could then regard her concern as justified, unless we have definite evidence that it isn't.

> When G was new, I used to have to keep checking her breathing to make sure she was all right. And if ever I walked upstairs, thinking that today I had become confident and had learned not to worry, I'd think, Ah, but that's *exactly* the time when something will go wrong, just the one day that I've become overconfident and I don't check. So I'd run downstairs to check again. [G, 12 months]

> When 1G was nine months old, she had gastroenteritis for ten days. It was a terrifying time for me. I remember how, when she was much better, I was walking down the street and asking myself the question: how old does she have to be before I stop getting so worried? Just then, a car stopped beside me. A mother got out with a boy of about seven. She said to him, 'Are you all *right*?' And I saw on her face the same amount of worry that I had just been through. Then I knew the answer was: never. As a mother, you *never* stop worrying. [1G, 3 years; B, 2 years; 2G, 10 days]

When mothers describe how they keep their babies in mind, they are obviously talking about a voluntary act. But to an outsider it can look involuntary, as if a mother has been 'taken over' by her baby. 'The organising concept of an autonomous individual pursuing personal satisfaction is not applicable to motherhood,' wrote Lyn Craig in the conclusion to her book, *Contemporary Motherhood: The Impact of Children on Adult Time*. 'After children are born, love, attachment and responsibility kick in, and women will provide care even to their own detriment. It has been suggested that becoming a mother more closely approximates being afflicted with an addiction than exercising a free and ongoing choice.'[71]

To the outsider, mothering might well look like 'being afflicted with an addiction'. Mothers might care for their babies at the cost of their own *physical* wellbeing. They themselves sometimes complain that they are not exercising choice. I've heard many mothers say: 'When B cries, I have no choice but to pick him up.' But of course they do have choices. They are exercising their free will. They have balanced their child's distress against their own need for sleep, and decided that the child's distress is more urgent. They hope to catch up on sleep eventually. This is a moving decision. Many mothers defer their own needs several times a night. It seems a great pity to see this moral choice misunderstood and written off as an 'addiction' that is beyond their control.

Keeping her child in mind becomes more complicated when the mother is simultaneously trying to communicate with other people.

People see you having coffee with a friend. But they don't see that you hardly have time to look at each other. Both of you are looking after your babies. [G, 6 months]

When you're on the phone, you're listening to different things with your two ears. You're listening to *him*, and you're also trying to listen to the conversation. [B, 16 months]

M: I have G with me at my work, and I'm hoping it can be fun for her.

Me: Can you concentrate?

M: Well. Sometimes I feel as if my head . . . [*She put both fists to her forehead and made them fly outwards in opposite directions, to show how her attention was completely divided.*] [G, 13 months]

So far, the idea of keeping a baby in mind has been about mothers who observed their babies in a positive way. However, a mother might think about her child all the time – but in a very negative way. I found a good example on the first page of the *Memoirs of Field-Marshal Montgomery*. He was the fourth child out of nine. He wrote: 'Certainly I can say that my own childhood was unhappy. This was due to a clash of wills between my mother and myself . . . If I could not be seen anywhere, she [*his mother*] would say – "Go and find out what Bernard is doing and tell him to stop it."' He comments: 'I . . . gradually withdrew into my own shell.'[72]

It is impressive that the mother of nine children *did* keep him in mind. But her negative attention seemed to have hurt him deeply. It is interesting to discover that he later gave this same kind of negative attention to his enemies in World War II. He suggested that a commander-in-chief 'has got to strive to read the mind of his opponent, to anticipate enemy reactions to his own moves, and to take quick steps to prevent enemy interference with his own plans'.[73] Almost, he sounds like his mother trying to curtail his own childhood movements, although he was using a negative way of thinking to gain, ultimately, a most positive military result in the Battle of El Alamein.

However, not every child might grow up to find such a positive use for negative attention. Many children might withdraw into their shells – and stay there.

There always seem to be some people who will attribute very negative motives to everything that children do. A mother can absorb this kind of attitude, and get annoyed with her child, attributing to him a negative motive he is unlikely to have learned yet. More experienced mothers can be helpful in suggesting other likely explanations:

> *First mother*: G pretends to cough. I can tell it's not real coughing. It's false. When she coughs, I hold her and pat her back. But I know this is false. And I'm thinking, How has G learned to be false, to be manipulative, at only *four* months old? [G, 4 months]
>
> *Second mother*: Perhaps she's playing. [B, 15 months]
>
> *Third mother*: Perhaps she's practising. [G, 17 months]
>
> *Fourth mother*: Or perhaps she just likes the sound it makes. [G, 13 months]

These mothers were unanimous in challenging the idea that a four-month-old would be manipulating her mother. With sympathetic tact, they didn't argue with her reasoning. They simply offered alternative explanations.

What happens when a mother does *not* keep her child in mind? It's only when a mother *doesn't* do something that we can become aware of what a huge difference it makes. A woman, orphaned as a child and sent to live with her strict grandmother, observed that loving mothers 'keep their children in mind'. She used this phrase three times in an essay she wrote for a course I was teaching. It was years before I myself saw the importance of this, so I didn't notice her words until I reread her essay years later.[74] Then I was moved to see how painfully she felt what she had missed.

When a mother has started to get to know her child, but then dies before her child becomes an adult, the child is suddenly no longer in his mother's mind. 'Your mother creates your life story and weaves it into the vast web of life stories of human existence,' wrote Dorothy Rowe in her preface to the book, *Death of a Mother*,

Daughters' stories.[75] When our mother dies, this story is left in our hands. Not only do we have to tell the end of *her* story, but our own story remains with us. We can no longer tell her all the highlights, so that she can add them to her special mental 'database' devoted to us. No matter how old we are, once she has died, it can feel strange not to have a living mother to hear the next episode.

Rosa Ainley described this well. Her mother had died when she was eight, and the book, *Death of a Mother, Daughters' stories*, was her idea. She wrote about her mother:

> I wanted her to be there, but I've also wanted her to know me, who I am and what I do and what I like . . . Her death, and the changes that followed, left me feeling always out of place, outside, out of focus, out on a limb, out out out; and is it in spite of her death or because of it that I'm also ferociously, and, I'm told, formidably certain of who I am and what I want to be . . . as well as lost, vulnerable, uncertain?[76]

Without a mother, or other adult to take charge of the child's developing life story, the child can feel incomplete and adrift. The mother seems to hold her child together when she links one part of her child's life to another. Only she knows the very beginning, the inception, pregnancy and birth, which they both shared.

Children can also feel adrift if they have a living mother who does not keep them in mind. Camila Batmanghelidjh founded Kids Company, a play centre for disadvantaged children in London. In her book, *Shattered Lives*, she describes how she visited the parents of some of the children who came to her play centres, and had this to say about the mothers that she observed:

> Many children are, sadly, exposed to chronic failures in care giving. At the milder end, this is represented by a preoccupied, depressed or substance-addicted mother whose capacity to hold her baby's needs in mind is impaired. The mother is too absorbed in her own

survival or impoverishment. She has no emotional resources to meet the child's needs appropriately. The baby feels catastrophically dropped out of the mother's caring mind. The mother's mindfulness, which should have held mother and infant in a diad [*sic*] is no longer holding the baby safe. The infant experiences distress which is not relieved.[77]

Ms Batmanghelidjh had visited many of the children's parents. Her conclusion is a sensitive and intuitive collation of a great deal of experience. To her, it was clear that the mother holding her child in mind would be keeping that child safe.

If the mother is alive and present, she must be keeping her child at least partly in mind. Still, the part might feel too small or too part-time. Her child might then feel forgotten. Not to matter enough to be remembered seems a dread that many people have. However, a child may discover that he can be remembered in a negative way, provided he becomes anti-social. This seems to be preferable to being forgotten.

I found an interesting example of this dilemma in a report and a tape-recorded conversation of a group of adult prisoners. The prisoners were attending a special meeting within their prison, and talking about where they hoped to live when they were released. Two of them confessed to a terror of being sent to a *new* place where no one would recognise them. One said, 'I'm getting out of here soon. What do you think I am most afraid of? Losing my image. I'm going from who I was, where everybody knew me, to going to X where nobody knows me. No one's going to know anything about me. And that's my biggest fear. I used to love the fact that everyone I saw *knew* me . . . They were *scared* of me, scared I might kill them or something. And that's my biggest fear, of *losing* that image, and just being an ordinary everyday person that people *don't see*.'[78]

This prisoner is talking about how he imagines other people

keep *him* in mind. His aspiration is to be remembered as fear-some, because he has noticed that frightened people have indeed kept him in mind. This is greatly preferable to the alternative of being 'out of sight, out of mind'. Being kept in mind as a *good* person seems to be outside his experience. Decca Aitkenhead, the reporter, didn't ask whether this prisoner had a mother who had felt unable to keep him in mind. However, it certainly sounds likely.

From all this, we can see how important it is for mothers to *continue* to keep their small children in mind. What does it mean, to keep someone in mind? It's not like keeping something valuable in a box. Once you've put the valuable thing in the box, the box will take care of it, and you only need to remember where you put it. Keeping a baby in mind is different. A baby is a live and tangible being, whereas a mind is a metaphor.[79] We haven't really got a cavity inside us that we call 'mind'. So how can we keep a tangible baby in our intangible minds?

In a literal sense, we can't keep a baby within a mind. Instead, we are describing the complex way that a mother remembers her child often enough for whatever stage her child has reached. This is not to say that mothers do this perfectly. Nor does it mean that mothers are mysteriously born less self-centred than other people. Mothers have to teach themselves to think in this sensitive way and to keep making small adjustments as their children develop. It is impressive to see how many of them do.

Over time, the mother can see that her child is learning to trust her, and she doesn't have to react quite so quickly. She may not consciously put it this way to herself, but she feels more relaxed, and finds that she has time to think about herself again.

I looked in the mirror this morning and saw my own face, and I thought, Good. I'm still there. If you think how often you normally look in a mirror – on the way to the loo, before you go out, all the time – I don't think I've had time to look in the mirror for *weeks*, since becoming a mother. [B, 2 months]

What happens when another baby is born? We cannot think so intensely about two different children simultaneously. Mothers seem to seek out reasons to justify how they prioritise, and this is described in Chapter Twelve.

Can't this way of thinking be shared? After all, many children have two parents. What about fathers? Don't they keep their babies in mind equally well? At one meeting, several mothers said how much more *relaxed* they felt when their husbands and partners were present. I asked: 'How relaxed do you feel? Can you turn your mothering alertness right off?' I was startled by a loud 'NO!' from all of them: 'I just let my partner do the practical things'; 'The responsibility is always there.'

> F doesn't share the responsibility. It's just *you*. You for today, for tomorrow, for the next five years, for the next ten years. [G, 7 months]

> If F is not with G, he doesn't *think* about her. He loves her a lot, and loves being with her. But I'm always *thinking* about her. Even if F has her, I'm thinking [*pretending to check her watch*], Are they all right? Is it all right to phone, or should I leave them to get on with it? I hope they aren't getting in the car. No, actually that would be all right. All the time! [G, 11 months]

Fathers may answer differently. However, it sounds as though this detailed way of keeping the child in mind is usually co-ordinated by one person. The mother, who has been relating to her baby since conception, is the most obvious person to do this.

What happens if the mother is the family's main breadwinner? Mothers who soon return to employment *do* have to think about

other things. It is precisely in the area of keeping the baby in mind
that it can become so stressful. During the working day, mothers
report moments of 'checking in' to their babies. It might simply
mean a quick switch of attention, or perhaps a telephone call.
Keeping a baby in mind, even at the *back* of her mind, can help.
Thinking about her child prepares a mother to be more sensitive
when the two get together again.

One mother left her child at home in the care of her husband.
She described the mental change she had to make when she came
home after she had been very absorbed in work:

> Coming home after work is like taking your place in a completely
> different orchestra, playing a different tune. And if you're not in
> tune with it, you get – I can't think of the word that's means not
> playing in harmony. And the way to get harmony is to make your-
> self *stop* before you go in, so you can hear what music G and F are
> playing. I have to remind myself to stop on the doorstep. If I stop
> and *then* go in, it's all right. [G, 12 months]

But is a mother really necessary for a child as old as twelve
months? Isn't a child of that age ready to benefit from professional childcare? Many professional child-carers are hardworking
and dedicated. Some are warm and devoted to the children in
their care. But it is exactly in the area of keeping a particular
child in mind that they may find it difficult to equal what
mothers do.

If a nanny is substituting for the mother, she will keep track of
the development of the child in her care. She might then be in a
position to make the same kinds of detailed observations and
connections that mothers do. But for her, this process might be
much more difficult than for the child's mother.

M: I used to be a nanny.

Me: Is it different?

M: Completely. It's completely different. It's . . . being a mother means you're on a different wavelength. You're thinking with a different part of your brain. As a mother, you are in tune with your child. You know what he wants. There's all that connection. As a nanny, you've got to work at it. And, even when you do, there's things that you'll never understand. [B, 9 months]

One of the skills you learn as a parent, that you are not aware of until you ask someone else to look after your child, is that *you* know what she can manage and what she can't, what's likely to be dangerous for her and what isn't, when to help her and when to leave her to work it out on her own. A person coming to it 'cold' could never understand all that. [G, 17 months]

Eventually, children benefit from *not* being instantly understood. They learn to communicate effectively with people who are not in tune with them. But before a child can do this, his mother's under-standing and her ability to translate his early attempts at conversa-tion are essential. Without her help, trying to explain to an uncomprehending adult might seem too daunting. Some children become subdued and make few demands. They 'save up' their energy for when they are with their mothers, together again.

Why do children benefit if they are kept in mind? It's difficult to be sure, and to correlate one aspect of mothering with how the child appears later on. One can only speculate. It seems to help a baby to feel understood and valued. As his mother begins to connect his responses together into meaningful sequences, her child may start to feel recognised as a person whose actions connect up and make sense. It is possible that this enables the child to feel like a coherent person.[80] 'Even very young children, children who haven't yet learned to read or add two and two, *have* learned profound truths about their own mind and the minds of others,' wrote Alison Gopnik, Andrew Meltzoff and Patricia Kuhl.[81]

Sooner than one might think, babies learn to keep their mothers in mind.

I notice that B used to cry desperately for me, even when I was near him. But now, when he hears me make certain sounds, he *knows* I am coming and his crying stops. [B, 6 months]

G remembers things I say. Like when she climbs on to the table, which isn't allowed, she keeps saying, 'No!' Or she stands up in her high chair and I hear her saying, 'Down!' When she does something I think is wrong, I've been telling her it makes Mummy sad. So now, when she does those things, she points to my face and says, 'Sad'. I ruin it all because I can't help bursting out laughing. [G, 17 months]

B knows me so well. The other day he said to me, 'Mummy, are you angry?' I said, 'No, B, I'm not angry, I'm just feeling frustrated.' Then he leaned forward and stared and *stared* at me, at my face above the eyes. He said, 'No, Mummy, you are *not* frustrated. You've got those two lines on your forehead. You are feeling angry.' [B, 3 years; G, 8 months]

When other people reflect back something that seems true about ourselves, we get a sense of being 'real'. After all, is it only children who like to be kept in mind?
'Pat!'
'*Chris,* hel*lo!*'
'Long time! You're looking very well.'
'I'm fine. How've *you* been?'
'Not too bad. Not bad at all. Are you busy as ever, or can I tempt you to come for a coffee?'
'Love to, but I'm late for work as it is.'
'Ah well. Nice running into you. I thought: I *know* that's Pat.'
'Good seeing you, Chris. Take care. Got to run.'
This imagined dialogue is based on countless observed ones. I

was amused to find that, an hour after writing this, I went to my bank and overheard two people greet one another in *exactly* this way. The exchange can take as little as two minutes, first escalating loudly, then winding down, and ending with no commitments on either side. Yet the encounter seems to give the two people a lift of spirits. Each feels recognised by the other. Each feels important to the other. Each carries away a renewed impression of the other, and a sense that the other person has a renewed impression of themselves. Each looks flushed, smiling and more alive than before.

The English poet John Clare began a sonnet with the line: 'I am, yet what I am none knows nor cares . . . '[82] In ten simple words, he has stated that just to *be* is not enough. It is important that others know and care about him. Surely this is a truth about all of us. We thrive on other people knowing who we are and caring for how we are. There are countless ways of showing that we have remembered the significant others in our lives. It seems that people feel lost and adrift if they do not feel remembered.

Eventually, as children grow up, many mothers discover ways of keeping them in mind that are supportive and tactful without being intrusive. There are increasing times of separation. But, typically, the child goes on a day outing, off to school or whatever it is, while the mother seems to keep her child in mind, as if she is keeping him safe. Some children return with stories of hair-raising escapades. Telling their mothers seems to 'ground' the children. It is the mother who keeps the whole life story together. Our children have a unique ability to cause us times of sleepless anxiety. But our concern seems to help them to feel all of a piece.

Observing other people, keeping them in mind and learning to understand them isn't formally taught, and probably couldn't be. Like so many social interchanges, we learn it best when we ourselves are young. It can then help us to interact with other people for the rest of our lives.

For how long does a mother continue to keep her child in mind?

In 2007, I had an opportunity to speak with Edwina Froehlich, one of the seven founder mothers of La Leche League. She was ninety-two years old, warm and easy to talk to. I asked: 'Do you still feel like a mother? I don't mean to La Leche League. I don't even mean to your grandchildren. I mean, do you feel like a mother to your *own* children?' She replied: 'Well . . . I have three sons in their fifties. I don't tell them what to do any more, or criticise them for anything they do.' She explained: 'All three of my sons live near by. I always feel something here [*touching her heart*] when one of them is walking towards me. I feel a sort of pride that they are my sons. Well, in answer to your question, I don't need to talk to them every *day*. But I talk about . . . once a week. I usually call them once a week and ask them how they are doing. These modern cellphones are very convenient. I like to know how they are.' She described one of her sons and how she had found a weekly time when he would be free, to telephone him.

I said: 'So *you* initiate contact?' She replied: 'I do, yes. I want to know how they are. I feel kinda *funny* not to know how they are.' I asked: 'Can I quote you on that? It sounds important.' She said: 'Of course you can.' So I sat down and wrote up this conversation as soon as I had left her.

The whole conversation was in the simplest language, and yet described the strong feelings of a mother in her nineties. Obviously, not all mothers do this and it might sound strange to a mother who has organised her life differently. But it was moving for me to discover how a mother can keep her children in mind for a lifetime. Edwina Froehlich died about nine months after our conversation.

What then is the answer to Solzhenitsyn's simple question, 'How can you expect a man who's warm to understand one who's cold?' Surely the answer is that you can't expect such understanding without working for it. If the warm man is prepared to work round the clock, as mothers do, to study the cold man, and if he is able to think about and connect together some 'little grains of sand', then even the warmest man would get an idea of the degree of coldness of a prisoner outside in the Gulag.

This extraordinary level of understanding is what many mothers achieve, day after day.

CHAPTER SEVEN

When the candle burns low

It is easy to feel overwhelmed at being a mother. Mothers discover that babies usually like their presence. When a mother is present, she is sharing a great deal of her life. Evenings and weekends are not 'time off', nor are holidays leisure time. Love for her child makes it feel worth doing. But love also makes it harder because of its limitless nature. There is always something more that a loving mother could do. Surely it isn't possible for a mother to sit down and say: 'Good. I've done everything I can.'

First mother: The other day, G fell asleep by herself. She's never done that before. I didn't know what to do, so I just lay down on our bed to think. I felt so different, being a mother.

Me: Different in what way?

First mother: I'm here. I'm in life. Before G, I could always stop whatever I was doing. G is for ever. It's a job I'll never finish. There will never be a time when it's all done. Mothering is . . . *huge*. I haven't taken in how huge it really is. [G, 2 months]

Second mother: It's too huge for *me* to take in, even now. [B, 16 months]

Luckily, some of being a mother is very practical. But the practical tasks depend on the mother's decisions on what to do. There is more than one way of doing just about anything for a baby. It's not easy to keep weighing up decisions on the baby's behalf. Many of them are not trivial. They will affect the child's future. Yet mothers often have to decide 'in the dark' because there isn't time for research or there isn't sufficient information to hand.

I've been reading a book on vaccines and it made me feel sick. I'm so ignorant. I just accepted vaccines for G because I trusted what was on offer. I need a mentor. I need an experienced mentor to discuss difficult questions like this. [G, 16 months]

I'll tell you what it is. It's that all our lives we've had appraisals. In our jobs. At school we had them. Now we are suddenly left in this important work just to get on with it. [B, 18 months]

Without official appraisals – with no mentor or supervisor, no line manager, no reports to write, no departmental meetings where one can share problems – but often making significant decisions, mothers can judge themselves harshly.

I'm not used to failing. Being a mother has faced me with lots of times when I've failed. [B, 3 years; G, 5 months]

I keep comparing myself to other mothers, and I think I'm a bad mother. B keeps waking up at night. I'm very analytic, but I can't get to the bottom of what I'm doing wrong. [B, 6 months]

When I've been angry with G, usually I find it's because of my Judgment Voice. It's been telling me that I'm not a good mother, and that I shouldn't be like this and I should be doing it all better. [G, 9 months]

Everything would be all right if I could only switch off that nagging voice. [G, 20 months]

Why are mothers so self-critical? Surely it's not surprising. Most women receive very little preparation for motherhood. It takes time for a new mother to discover her own preferences. So, at first, she keeps measuring herself by the standards of other people. These standards may be alien to her own values. But she is too 'new' to ignore other people's standards. And by these standards, she may be failing. Usually, when mothers say they are failing, they are taking as the norm values that are not their own.

Fortunately there are many Internet message boards where a mother can share feelings and find companions. Yet, even though these can be so helpful, misunderstandings can arise. I think there is something about typing and clicking away a post that sometimes sounds brusque and snappy to the recipient.

There are very few groups which provide safe places for mothers to meet one another face to face, to discuss their mothering. But face to face is a more sensitive setting. Mothers can pick up visual signals from one another, especially from noticing how other mothers interact with their babies. When mothers feel safe, they can be very warm and receptive to one another.

M: The candle inside me has burned quite low at the moment.

Me: How do you mean?

M: It's hard to find the energy . . . I know it's wonderful with G, but also . . . [*tears*]. There's never time to recover. My partner works long hours. My mum lives far away. I'm giving all the time. I know it's terrible to say this. But I get so *tired*. There's no let-up.

[*Later*:] It helps me to talk about it here. I say what I think, and everyone listens to me, and at the end I go home feeling lighter. [G, 5 months]

A mother turned up at a different meeting looking strained and white. I thought she might be ill. She said:

I'm so tired. I'm just very . . . [*sudden tears*]. I didn't know . . . [*She cried for about three minutes. The other mothers sat in respectful silence.*] I thought I was just tired. I didn't know that I needed to cry. I haven't cried like that, really cried, since G was born. [G, 6 months]

She went on speaking. The colour had returned to her face (as it had to the previous mother after she had cried), and she seemed restored. I think mothers need a safe place where they can feel 'held' if they cry. Neither mother had been conscious of wanting to cry. But being a mother is responsible work, and I wonder whether holding back tears is one reason why mothers so often say they feel irritable.

First mother: I've had a difficult week. It came after two illnesses. B and I were both ill. I just felt stifled. I couldn't remember anything. I'd forget words I know perfectly well. I'd go to a shop and forget what I'd come for. I felt constricted at my throat, as if I was trying to stop myself from crying. I just didn't want to be a mum any more. I was short-tempered with B, though I felt so guilty. B felt it and was even more demanding. Yesterday, I went for a walk with [*second mother*] . . .

Second mother: It was a long, uphill walk. I'm so sorry.

First mother: Oh, no, it was fine. I came home and I ran a bath and put something special in it. And I got in and *all* my tears just flowed out. I just cried and cried. After that, I fell in love with B again. [B, 22 months]

When mothers meet, they don't only cry. They perceive details about their children that no one else sees. Mothers are social and it can feel wonderful to share these moments.

Sometimes your child does something amazing in a public place, and you look around for someone to share it with. You bubble up [*gesturing bubbles rising from belly to throat*], until you feel you will *burst* if you don't share it. [G, 10 months]

I've just taken B to baby gym and you see another kid doing some-thing special, and you catch their mum's eye. She's over the *moon*. [B, 15 months]

Also, a circle of mothers can generate down-to-earth humour. A group laugh is special. It can combine compassion for the speaker with an awareness of how much mothers share. The following had a whole circle of tired mothers laughing:

A few weeks after G was born, a very good friend rang and said, 'I won't offer to visit you yet. You're probably still wrapped in a cocoon of bliss.' I wanted to yell at her: '*Cocoon of bliss?* What planet are you on? I'm going *insane!* I just want someone to talk to.' [G, 2 years; B, 4 months]

Mothers frequently help one another to keep their sense of proportion.

You let your child cry and you think, That's it. I'm the worst mother in the world. And then you come to a meeting and you talk about it and everyone laughs, and you think, B's not going to be ruined by *one* bout of crying. You get your sense of proportion back, and then everything is all right again. [B, 17 months]

Have you guys any suggestions for getting a baby to sleep longer and wake up less often? [*Silence. No one answered.*] Okay. So there's no solution, right? It's normal. It's not something I'm doing wrong. I always feel guilty that I'm doing *everything* wrong. [B, 2 months]

First mother: I have this low-level anxiety all the time. It's not just about G. It's about myself. If my heart starts to palpitate while I'm breastfeeding, I think, What would happen if I died of a heart attack? [G, 4 months]

Second mother: It's not really anxiety about yourself. It's because of the effect on G. I feel anxious too – and I *know* I'm not afraid for myself. [G, 20 months]

The whole circle recognised the first mother's account of anxiety. This immediately lessened the tension. If they were all feeling it, it was obviously an unavoidable part of being a mother.

Often, instead of problem-solving, mothers give encouragement by their understanding of one another.

First mother: With my first baby, I thought I'd be stuck with a crying baby who wanted to be carried everywhere for *ever*. People would say, 'Don't worry, he'll have grown out of it in a few months.' [B, 12 years; B, 8 weeks]

Second mother: But a few months, or even a whole day, with a new baby – they mean nothing. You feel as though you really can't bear even one more *second*. [G, 2 months]

At one meeting, a six-week-old baby kept crying. The problem seemed to be trapped wind. Another mother asked: 'Would you like me to take your baby for a bit?' The first mother agreed, and the second mother held the baby, bouncing and patting her. When she gave the baby back, I asked the first mother how she had felt.

That was very helpful. I kept looking at 2G and I could suddenly see a little person struggling with trapped wind. I really saw *her*. Seeing her like that helped me to see that her crying wasn't all my fault. [1G, 2 years; 2G, 6 weeks]

She held her little daughter in a more relaxed way from then on, and the baby rested her head on her mother's shoulder and fell asleep.

A group can also help for those times of panic when a mother feels sure she is doing everything 'wrong' and ruining her baby. She begs other people to *please* tell her what to do. Yet often what she finds most helpful, if it is available, is the warm compassion of other mothers.

> I can't go on. I can't do it. It's too hard [*tears*]. B can't sleep unless I hold him upright in his sling. I haven't slept properly for weeks. I haven't got a relationship with my boyfriend any more. He's just the other baby-holder. I'm like, 'Hi. *Take* him!' We haven't had a cuddle since B was born. I was all for attachment parenting. But now I feel I've failed as a mother. I've got B dependent on me and the sling and he can't go to sleep any other way. [B, 6 weeks]

Some people would argue that she *has* failed, and that she *ought* to have got her baby to sleep on his own in a cot. So I listened with interest to what other mothers at the meeting said to her. I noticed that no one judged her for her choice of attachment parenting. Nor did anyone give her any advice. Her tears evoked 'fellow-traveller' feelings, and each mother described her own difficulties.

However, to my surprise, at the end of the meeting, the first mother stood up. 'This meeting has restored my belief in myself,' she said. 'I know what I'm doing now. I know *why* I'm doing it.' I gathered that she had realised that being a mother couldn't be easy. The other mothers had all said they were struggling with their own difficulties. Clearly there was nothing wrong with her for experiencing difficulties too.

Also, as they talked, the mothers had redefined their situations. Instead of describing their 'difficulties', they said they had *chosen* to adapt to their babies. They noticed that each mother and baby had found a personal adaptation which suited them. However, they *dreaded* being disapproved of by other people whose priorities were different. Of course, this change of perception didn't change an iota of the mother's physical sleep problem. Yet it seemed exactly what she needed to give her the energy to carry on.

If a mother has more complex problems, a group meeting

might not be enough. An individual conversation might work better. But for everyday 'downs', meeting other mothers can be a tonic.

If they are on their own, mothers find individual ways to recover energy.

> We slept in, this morning. We had a terrible night. G was itchy and kept waking up, to scratch. I've been singing nursery rhymes all *night*. Then G fell into a sound sleep. I got up and made myself some tea. It was *wonderful* tea. Tea! I could feel it going all down me, warm and comforting. [G, 7 months]

> When G sleeps, I make a big decision *not* to catch up on washing-up or laundry. I write up my diary or read my book. That way, I get back in touch with myself. And I really need to, so I can be more present with G. When I've got myself together, it makes a *huge* difference. If I don't make time, I feel misty and grey. [G, 8 months]

> I feel such a failure as a mother. I've got no confidence. So I bought myself a big diary. I put the dates in and wrote down all the things I was doing well as a mother. It's so easy to forget. But now I think, Look at *that!* I *am* doing some of it well. [B, 11 months]

> It's so easy to get stuck in a routine. If I think of something I'd like to do, I think, Oh, *no!* There's so much to do. Simpler to leave it. But every time I forget the routine and do something nice I've been *so* glad I did. [B, 5 years; G, 3 years; G 3 months]

When mothers seem most unsure of themselves, it turns out that they always have several 'back-seat drivers'.

> I feel as if I'm walking a tightrope because a tiny [*negative*] comment can knock me right off. [B, 6 months]

Slowly, mothers learn how to fend off comments.

People keep telling me to do with B whatever they did with their babies. And I'd like to have something to report back, to tick their boxes. Then one day I thought, Fine. You are all doing it *your* way. B is my baby and I'm doing it *mine*. Then I felt much better, and I could really enjoy B for who he was. [B, 7 weeks]

At my baby-massage class, they have 'Tummy Time'. That's when you turn your baby over on to his tummy so that he can push his torso up. But B didn't like that at all. He likes to look at people. He refused to lie on his tummy. Then I was told he'd have flabby muscles and he'd never learn to walk. I was very upset. It took a *lot* of thinking afterwards to convince myself that it was rubbish. [B, 4 months]

People say: 'Do you have to pick G up every time she cries? You could put her in the next room and shut the door. Crying won't damage her, you know.' Then I say, 'Look. I'm not the sort of mother I thought I was going to be. A baby's cry is biologically designed to make the mother feel uncomfortable. So that's how it is for me.' [G, 6 months]

Once a mother can defend herself, it's easier to be more generous to herself.

I feel a confident mum now. It makes it possible to admit how *frightened* I was at first. I didn't like it at all. Things that used to throw me then aren't problems any more. [B, 15 months]

After G was born, I used to think there was a CCTV camera in the house, watching everything I was doing. Then, one day, I realised, no, no one is watching. It's just me. I can do anything I want to. [G, 3 years; B, 13 months]

I have an Invisible Committee that compares me to other people and finds fault with what I'm doing. But, on good days, when I let go and just let myself be with my children, the Invisible

Committee . . . I don't know . . . it's evaporated. [G, 9 years; G, 7 years]

Mothers look to one another for support. But if they don't feel safe, mothers resort to talking as if there were only one 'right way' to care for a baby. Every time this happens, an opportunity to befriend one another has been lost.

When a mother learns to be more confident in how she is mothering, her confidence can sound incomprehensible to other mothers who are still struggling. But the confident mother often sounds especially strong because she feels relieved at coming through such a challenging start.

Last time I was here, I said I was enjoying being a mother. But I worried about saying that. To other mothers, it might sound smug. [B, 2 months]

I find I like myself more. I've always been a self-critical person. I set myself very high standards that I usually can't live up to. But I look at G and I feel pleased about her. So that makes me feel good because F and I helped to produce her. She's *herself*, of course. But I'm feeling quite pleased with myself. [G, 13 months]

A circle of mothers who feel more secure can be very generous to a newer mother.

People tell me B looks very happy. But I think he looks happy because he's a happy baby. He has a happy disposition. I can't see his happiness as the result of anything I've done. [*This aroused an immediate protest from all the mothers listening to her. They pointed out that she interacted very well with her baby. At the end, the mother said, shyly:*] That's good to know. [B, 7 months]

You hear mothers come here and they say how tired they are, and then you look and they still have energy to be nice to their child, and to stroke them and comfort them and be gentle. [B, 15 months]

120

A more experienced mother [*after more than an hour of listening to an entire circle of mothers saying they felt like failures because they couldn't get their babies to sleep in the evenings*]: I've just one thing to say to all of you. Don't EVER think you're a bad mother. [G, 3 years]

Are such mothers just being 'nice'? I don't think so. I think when a circle of mothers look round at one another (provided the whole circle isn't feeling insecure), they can see a great deal of good in each other. They seem to need to reflect it to one another. It's hard for them to recognise such wonderful qualities in themselves.

Listening to one another, mothers can hear that each of them is fallible. They suddenly realise that they have put the mothering benchmark up way too high. This benchmark needs to be lowered to a manageable level. Then they can all reach it. Many times I have heard mothers confess to their failings, and each failure simply gets absorbed by the group as part of being human.

In a group, the harsh judgments a mother may give herself when she is on her own at home are softened. This lightens her burden and makes it easier for her to love her baby. Her tiredness is still there. The responsibility is still there. The unsolved questions are still there. But the sense of failure she felt at home has changed. That changes everything.

CHAPTER EIGHT

'Am I holding him back?'

Some mothers believe their role requires them to fight to give their children every possible advantage. 'Motherhood transforms us into tigresses,' wrote one journalist. 'Like it or not, we're hard-wired into wanting our children to achieve.'[83]

Every day, there are play sessions, story readings, music classes, baby gym and other stimulating activities organised for small children, even for babies. If a mother lives in a city, there are sure to be more events on offer than she could get to. If she doesn't take her baby to them, is she depriving him of his chance to achieve?

> I want to do things right for B, but I'm never sure whether I'm doing enough or too little of it. How much is *over*stimulating and how much is *under*stimulating? [B, 4 months]

At first, this seems like a typical modern dilemma of having too many choices. But there's more to it. The pressure to stimulate their children makes mothers anxious. They wonder whether they are competent to help their children forward (and not hold them back). Many mothers today have only a few months of maternity leave. They are especially concerned to use the time well. However, the pressure to be stimulating seems to interfere with their ability to relax and feel calm enough to love.

> I think if I've bought an educational toy and done some construc-
> tive play with G, I'm achieving something. But if I've just been
> hanging out with her all morning, and there's absolutely nothing
> to show for it, even though we've been having a really lovely time,
> I feel as though I'm failing to be a good mother. [G, 5 months]

This is a very significant statement. Why should an educational toy seem so much better than 'hanging out' together? Mothers often feel under great pressure to introduce their babies to 'educa-tive' experiences. They worry that their babies might find their mothers boring and understimulating. Mothers who have been working in very competitive jobs, less than a year earlier, often describe their panic that their child might lag behind the rest, and lose a desperate race towards some invisible future finishing line.

> G is the only one of the babies we know who can't crawl yet. She
> *nearly* can. And she's absolutely *fine*. But I saw her sitting by herself
> in the middle of all the crawling tots, and I found myself thinking,
> Oh, *no!* She'll be the one at school who is all on her own, without
> any friends. [G, 9 months]

It's hard to feel confident. How can a mother know whether her baby is developing well or not? In many walks of life, hiring a professional is the solution when one is so ignorant. Wouldn't it be better to leave the stimulation of one's child to someone who is trained?

> People often think a professional would do a much better job than
> they themselves would as parents. I've got a friend who says she
> feels bad for not stimulating her child enough. She hasn't got time
> to do creative play, activities with sand and water, basic music,
> reading stories, drama and number work. She's thinking of

employing a helper who would give her child more chances than she could offer. [G, 3 years; B, 7 months]

In contrast, the psychoanalyst René Spitz observed: 'The existence of the mother, her mere presence, acts as a stimulus for the responses of the infant; her least action – be it ever so insignificant – even when it is not related to the infant, acts as a stimulus.'[84]

If this is true, then a little stimulus from the mother must go a long way. But that is not the impression you would get today. Walk into a toyshop and you are confronted with all kinds of 'stimulating' play objects in bright colours, which bleep, sing songs, flash lights and move when touched. These toys promote the view that ordinary life can't be stimulating enough.

> I can remember when G was a baby each day was a huge endless *void* that I had to fill, and I didn't know how to fill it. We used to get dressed and go to the shop. The *shop!* Big part of our day. [G, 23 months; B, 3 weeks]

Although she was ridiculing herself for going to the shop, it sounds a very good way of filling a void. Even for a young baby, as her daughter was then, there would have been plenty to learn. She would probably have sensed the change in her mother's whole manner, how she stopped being attentive to her daughter and became serious about planning, choosing and calculating what she could afford to buy. Her mother might also have a relationship with the staff that showed her daughter how she related to people they met daily. This mother's instinct in getting the two of them to a shop every day sounds sensible, not ridiculous at all.

Of course, this is not a prescription for *all* mothers to take their babies out for daily shopping. There is a tendency today to turn what should be one mother's particular choices into 'necessities'. Suddenly, the whole thing becomes onerous, an endless list of activities, advocated by other people, that a mother *ought* to do. Even having fun can be turned into a task.

Dr Margot Sunderland probably meant to be encouraging when she wrote: 'It all starts with the face-to-face dance in infancy. If you have lots of lovely face-to-face conversations with your infant, pathways will be formed in your child's higher brain which are the key to the art of relating.'[85] According to this way of thinking, it doesn't matter how mother and infant feel about a face-to-face conversation. It is defined as 'lovely', so they are supposed to want it. The implication is that without it, 'vital pathways' in the child's higher brain will *not* be formed.

Fortunately, in reality, 'the art of relating' is much more spontaneous. Mother and child relate, whether face to face, back to back or whichever way, because they are doing something together. What they do might *not* be lovely. It might be necessary. In any case, their relationship is developing all the time, affecting the child's brain, and also his heart and other organs and, indeed, every aspect of himself.

However, the mother isn't responsible for providing all her child's stimulation. Nor is it essential to employ a professional. Babies are capable of generating their own ideas and activities.

M: G was independent from her birth.

Me: How could you tell?

M: Well, after she was born, I'd have her lying on my chest, and she'd insist on lifting up her head. That seemed to be her *project*. She had very strong neck muscles. [G, 15 months]

I look at G on her changing mat, and she's kicking and waving her hands and looking at them. And I think, She's having a different kind of experience. If I was holding her *all* the time, she wouldn't have that. [G, 6 weeks]

What G loves best is for F and me to be doing our own thing near her, while she gets on with hers. [G, 10 months]

It is possible for a mother to overlook the aliveness of her baby and instead perceive him as a sort of empty vessel that she has to keep filling and refilling with entertaining contents. If a mother sees him like this, she will feel compelled to pack her day with busy activities. If she can see how active her baby really is, the two of them can slow down and relax. Psychoanalyst and paediatrician Donald Winnicott described how he watched babies play with a simple spoon, and concluded: 'By allowing your baby time for total experiences, and by taking part in them, you [*the mother*] gradually lay a foundation for the child's ability eventually to enjoy all sorts of experiences without jumpiness.'[86]

I read that if you give a baby of six months a pencil and paper, they learn to use it and can develop into an artist. So I decided I'd try. But what I hadn't taken on board was how much you could do with a pencil and paper that isn't actually drawing. B crumpled the paper and tasted it. And he experimented with the pencil in all kinds of ways. I watched in amazement. [B, 8 months]

It's wonderful to watch a child experimenting like this. At the same time, it is easy to overlook how important the mother's own presence is. 'Because we love babies, they can learn,' states Alison Gopnik simply.[87] In a similar way, Anne Manne wrote: 'Because so much of a child's world is mediated through relationships, [*and*] because their emotional, social and cognitive development are plaited together, it is the sensitivity and responsiveness of the *relationships* which matter most.'[88] I think 'plaited together' is a good image to describe how children integrate their love with their learning.

I thought B needed a stimulating environment. But what I learned was that he only enjoys it if he's with someone who loves him. [B, 13 months]

A child can have relationships with all kinds of people. It does not always have to be the mother. However, the mother knows her child well and can provide a special combination of love and understanding which helps her child to develop, until he is ready to enjoy play with his peers.

Once a mother slows down enough to notice when her baby is interested in his own projects, she is also in a position to notice something else – that even a baby is capable of protesting when he *genuinely* feels bored. *Then* it seems a good time for the mother to think about finding something more stimulating to do.

When G has slept and fed and had her nappy changed, I think she gets bored. She gets absorbed if I show her things. [G, 2 months]

B was very mellow when he was little. But now he makes a tiny noise, and if I don't react immediately it grows into a horrible squealing which I really don't like. He stops if I hand him a toy. And then the penny dropped. He was *bored.* It was as though being bored really *hurt* him. He needs to be exploring and extending his interests the whole time. [B, 4 months]

There is a baby – I expect you have heard of him yourself – who is happy to study his cot mobile (or other educational toy) all morning while his mother does some useful tasks; who will fall asleep in about half a minute after his mother lays him down; who is perfectly happy for her to leave him with someone else; nor does he ever, at a later age, back away in alarm when she is trying to encourage him to be adventurous and try a slide at the playground; and he has no qualms at mixing with his peers. This child exudes confidence and makes few demands on his mother. He is absolutely no trouble. I doubt whether any of us has met this child, but he seems to exist in the ether, and it is easy to feel inadequate as mothers when our own children fail to be like him.

As soon as a mother acknowledges that her child has his own unique feelings, she is dealing with a person. If she compares him to the ethereal child, his behaviour might not tick many boxes. But he is genuine, which means he can be unco-operative and intractable, just as she can.

> I take B to a music group once a week. I feel a bit annoyed because he never joins the circle or holds an instrument and takes part. He wanders around outside the circle. Perhaps I should stop taking him. After all, I'm paying for it. [B, 15 months]

But if her child doesn't enjoy going to the music group, does it mean that his mother needs to be 'all things' to stimulate her child? Surely she is a person too, with her individual limitations.

> I took G to a playgroup. I never feel at ease in groups, and I'm sure G picked up on it. I wasn't being myself, and it upset me that G wasn't being her usual self either, so no one could see how lovely she was. I felt terrible afterwards. I felt I'd ruined everything for G. But then I thought, *No!* That's what I'm like. I'm not into groups. G will just have to find some way of being different from me. She's such a sociable child. She loves being with other people. [G, 9 months]

It can be a challenge for a mother to trust herself, rather than strive to conform to what other mothers seem to be doing. One popular view today is that babies need to learn to be independent, and that close relationships with their mother might delay this.

> There's all this talk of separation. So if you are still carrying your child in a sling at fifteen months [*which she was*], you can feel a failure as a mother. You have failed to separate. There's all that

thinking that says the mother is holding her child back. What that theory fails to take into account is that a mother who is carrying her child will find that her child will make it perfectly obvious to her if she is holding her child back. [*She gestured a child making restless movements in her sling.*] So why don't mothers trust their own judgment? But, even though I think that, I have that niggling voice that says I could be holding G back. [G, 15 months]

All kinds of social situations today indicate to mothers that they are expected to separate from their babies, and that they will hold back their babies' development if they insist on staying connected.

It's taken for granted that you will want to put your baby into a crèche. There was a painting class I could take G to. I asked if I could bring B. I knew I could easily hold him while helping G to paint. But the answer I got was: 'You don't have to do that. There will be a crèche.' The problem I have with *that* is, not only whether you would put your child in the hands of a person you have never met, but your child hasn't met them either. It's as if your child wasn't human, but like a parcel, to be handed from one adult to the next, as if they were all the same. [G, 3 years; B, 9 months]

Children aren't parcels. Each is an individual person who is developing in his own way. It isn't necessary to rush him. A mother can count on her child wanting to be independent. But he needs to be ready for each new stage. Unfortunately, the sheer quantity of social opportunities seems to pressure mothers into sending their children into social situations before they are independent enough to enjoy them. There is a great deal of social encouragement to send children to nurseries and playgroups, no matter whether they feel confident without their mothers. A British journalist wrote: 'The government has encouraged a huge expansion in group daycare over the past ten years. Ministers insist that starting children in nursery as early as possible improves their communication and social skills and gives them a better chance of doing well in later years.'[89]

Some children are ready and get a great deal of pleasure from nurseries and playgroups. But do they all?

> I started 1B at playgroup last week. He *hates* it. He wakes up in the morning crying: 'Please don't leave me!' At the playgroup, he clings to my knees and he won't join the other children. And I'm thinking, *Where* did I go wrong? Should we have started earlier? Is he too dependent on me? Am I holding him back? Will he be a child of ten still clinging on to me? I don't know what the answer is. I feel *lost,* really lost. [1B, 3 years; 2B, 14 months]

> Of course I could make G go to a nursery five days a week so that I could work full-time. [*She was working three days a week, when F took care of G.*] She might be happy. But there'd be a price to pay. People confuse a child being able to manage things with what is good for them. If you go to a nursery, you'll learn skills, but they are more like: 'I can take care of myself. I can speak up for myself.' There would be an *outer* confidence. But I want G to know that we'll be there for her until she really *can* take care of herself. That way, I hope she'll be confident *inside*. Not to pass judgment on any other mother who has made a different choice. [G, 17 months]

Some people would argue that it is good for children to be plunged into nursery. They state that children don't need mothers to fuss and make everything easier for them. Children have to learn to fend for themselves. Are they right? Obviously, children vary. I have found that this whole area can bring up painful memories for some adults who feel that they were compelled to cope with situations as small children in which they did not feel safe.

One woman came as a student to the first class of a course that I was teaching. She started speaking about her childhood, and out poured memories of her upbringing. She didn't come back for the rest of the course. I suspect she felt guilty for having been so honest. This is part of what she said:

> Everyone said how wonderful I was as a child because I was so independent. I could do things no one would *dream* of letting a child do at such a young age. At the age of three, I could cross over a busy city road to go to my nursery by myself. And it *was* good. I don't want to blame my parents. Only, deep down, I . . . I . . . wish someone had been there to protect me. I wish someone had said: 'That's dangerous. She's too young. Don't let her do that.'

This brings up an important question. How can a parent know if a degree of independence is too much for the child? When this woman was a three-year-old, she must have appeared proud of her independence. It would have seemed disloyal to her parents for her to think otherwise. The most she could imagine, from a 'deep-down' reaction that she only allowed herself to feel as an adult, was that *someone else* might have argued the case for more protection to her parents.

There is some significant research by neuroscientists, trying to demonstrate when small children experience too much stress. But most mothers aren't neuroscientists. They haven't (at the time of writing) got the means of measuring their children's cortisol (stress hormone) levels. Is there any simple way a mother could check, not whether she is holding her child back, but whether she is propelling him forward, too suddenly?

A very helpful part of mothering is to enable children to identify their own feelings in words. Not all mothers do this. However, those who do seem to start casually, before the child can speak.

> I don't think parenting is the same as mothering. There's all that *emotional* mothering that I give. I know B needs it. And when he smiles at me – I'm glad he's such an expressive little boy.
> [B, 9 months]

If I'm feeling upset or I'm angry, and B looks at me, then I say: 'Mummy's upset' or whatever I'm feeling. [B, 14 months]

1B used to get hysterical about things. Like one day I left his library card at home and he couldn't have the book he wanted. It seemed awful. There was nothing we could do. But now he is nearly three. His language has come on, and he is quite calm, so we can discuss options. [1B, 2 years; 2B, 12 months]

It is often a revelation for a child to discover that a dreadful feeling he had when he got lost in a supermarket was 'fear', or that sometimes he has two feelings together, such as anger and sadness mixed. No one but the child can actually know what he is feeling. But his mother may be the best person to help him identify the appropriate words. A child who can use a word to explain his feelings will be able to communicate them verbally, rather than need to demonstrate them in actions.

G is very happy at nursery. Just once or twice, she's come home and told me: 'I wanted you. I wanted my mummy.' [G, 3 years; B, 8 months]

This is accurate language for a three-year-old. It communicates to her mother exactly how she felt. Once the mother understands how her child is feeling, it provides a bridge to span the distance between them. The woman who had been such a capable three-year-old that she could cross busy roads by herself (see p.131) didn't seem to have that kind of bridge to her parents.

Mothers can do much to enhance the understanding of their children. It seems terrible that many are haunted by the fear of holding their children back. Children don't learn only through 'educational' activities. Ordinary life is full of education. A child who is toddling after his mother around their home while she makes beds and tidies clutter off the floor can learn not just what his mother does, but a kind of rhythm of how she does it. He might well want to copy her. The whole rhythm and repetition of everyday actions is important for children.

So is it possible for a mother to hold her child back? Yes, but not in the way she might think. Because her child is sensitive to her, likes to please her and spends time with her, her approval can enhance him. In the same way, her disapproval can stop him in his tracks. Children are experimental. It's amazing to see the risky, repetitive, expensive, time-consuming or messy projects they think up.

> I keep telling 1G that milk is a food, but she likes to paint with it. The other day, I said, 'Let's clear up all this milk,' and started wiping it. But she cried, 'That's my *tree*!' [*1G had created a 'painting' of a tree out of milk.*] I try to be patient, but I'm sleep deprived. I hear my voice say all those things that I told myself I'd never say to her. I'm not being the kind of mother I wanted to be. [1G, 2 years; 2G, 5 months]

It is easy for a mother's patience to run out at a moment like this. Children have ideas that stretch way beyond adult horizons.

> I can have a much more interesting conversation with B than with most adults. If I go down to the pub, there'll be a conversation about some politicians. It's all opinions. I'll have heard it all before. When B talks it will be something new and original. [B, 23 months]

Children see possibilities where we do not. They are being scientific, rather than trying to annoy us. Yet, however confident they sound, they are easily hurt by our impatience. They can stretch our adult understanding beyond our limits. For all the wisdom and experience we have gained, we seem to lose the inventiveness that our children still have.

There are moments when our children feel too much for us to cope with. It's easy to hold children back when we are tired, it's long past their bedtime and we feel sure that their ideas simply are not viable. Because we love them, we can only hope that if they really want to do something, they will persist, in spite of us.

CHAPTER NINE

Learning to take turns

The traditional idea of motherhood was that a mother would gracefully sacrifice her own needs to satisfy those of her children. She would always put her children before herself. Her reward would come when she grew old. Then her children would repay her for all the care they had received.

The idea of grateful children caring for their aged mother might sound attractive. But it certainly did not always work out in practice. Besides, feminist writers have exposed the basic inequality: a traditional mother was expected to renounce her own youthful potential and to sacrifice the best years of her life to facilitating the development of all the other members of her family.

'The time is come', wrote Florence Nightingale in 1852, in her passionate essay, *Cassandra*, 'when women must do something more than the "domestic hearth", which means nursing the infants, keeping a pretty house, having a good dinner and an entertaining party.'[90] We are the daughters of her dream.

Today, at least in the West, the pendulum has truly swung. Housekeeping and childcare are rarely taught at school. They used to convey not only practical skills, but a whole set of values that went with them. Looking back at women's history, we can see the reasons for such a strong reaction in our day. But it has given new mothers an unforeseen difficulty.

Most girls growing up in the 1970s and 1980s were encouraged by their parents and teachers to prioritise their own needs. They were to recognise their potential as women, and to challenge male hegemony in every field. This generation of young women has made giant strides. They have pushed through barriers to women's career opportunities. In one generation, women have worked to open choices that had seemed entirely reserved for men.

However, once they become mothers themselves, they say they feel deskilled. Prioritising one's own needs simply does not 'work' for a new mother. That single-minded energy and determination that opened career doors does not help women to care for their babies. The journalist Mary Kenny, writing under the interesting heading, 'The party's always over when motherhood begins', comments: 'Being a mother is a hard task: it may be natural but it also goes against the grain of modern freedoms, and the endless emphasis on "personal choice" that is today's mantra. A mother has no "personal choices" in the absolute sense of the word.'[91]

Overnight, the nurturing values they may have been taught to despise suddenly become relevant. New mothers are often shocked to discover that they themselves have to shelve their own immediate needs. Just as their grandmothers did, they have to prioritise their newborns. But, unlike their grandmothers, many weren't expecting to.

M: I was an only child, and I didn't have many children around me when I grew up. I've always been very independent and done exactly what I wanted. But suddenly, now B's born, I realise I've got to put the brakes on. Suddenly it's got to be about *him*. I'm learning how to do it.

Me: But doesn't it have to be about you too? Don't you need to factor yourself in?

M: Maybe. But I haven't got to that stage yet. I'm still trying to get used to putting B first. [B, 6 weeks]

Women today have been encouraged to recognise that they do not have to dedicate their lives to the interests of their families to achieve their desires. As mothers (or daughters, sisters and aunts), girls and women know they have a right to satisfaction too. But a new mother often feels as though her right has been suspended because there never seems to be time for herself.

It's so obvious that being a mother means sharing your time with your baby so you have very little time to yourself. That's what being a mother means, doesn't it? And yet it came as a total surprise to me, and at first I found it very hard. [G, 2 months]

Situations arise which the mother simply had not envisaged. It can be a rude shock.

One morning, B was asleep and I thought it would be the ideal moment to grab a bath. So I ran the bath and I was just sinking into the hot water and had got my hair wet when I heard . . . [*imitation of a baby crying*]. So I had to get out and breastfeed him on the bathroom floor. And I can remember thinking, Your needs are *huge*. I have needs too. My needs are to get warm and dry, and to dry my hair. But my needs are as *nothing* beside yours. [B, 3 months]

How do mothers learn to respond to their babies without having to shiver while they breastfeed on the bathroom floor? Mothers gradually learn to expect their plans to be interrupted at any moment. With some thought, they can plan for exactly these contingencies. Then, when her baby cries for her unexpectedly, a mother can interrupt herself with minimal discomfort.

This means that she can no longer put her needs first in her usual way. But neither is she undertaking that huge kind of personal self-sacrifice that she had been taught to avoid. Mothers today feel entitled to satisfaction, not sacrifice. However, it need not be a battle between her baby's needs or her own. The two of them can be together on one team. So perhaps without spelling it out like this, mothers learn to prioritise the needs that benefit the team.

> I start to do something I need to do, and I'm hoping I can finish it while G plays. Then she wants my attention, so I stop what I'm doing and be with her for a while. Then she seems as if she'll be all right by herself, so I go back to what I was doing. [G, 9 months]

> G wants me near her all the time, so I can't just go and load the dishwasher, for example. But if she's happily playing on the kitchen floor, that's a bonus because I can use the dishwasher. And if she's playing in the bathroom, I get a chance to clean the toilet. [G, 10 months]

These aren't solutions for every mother-and-baby team, but they do show how these mothers found ways to do tasks without a head-on confrontation with an unwilling child. Mothers also discover that, by making small adjustments, they can still fit in their own needs, though usually several hours later. In the beginning, they may find it takes a lot of thinking to make this work. It gets easier as mother and baby get to know one another. But at first it can feel strange.

> You sit there with the baby, and it all looks peaceful and calm, especially if the baby's just been breastfeeding. But inside yourself you're thinking, I haven't made it to the loo yet. And there's a drink of water I should have had . . . [*She was cut short by loud laughter of recognition from listening mothers.*] [G, 5 weeks]

Between equals, 'taking turns' is usually by mutual agreement. With a baby it's different. When mother and baby both need something at the same moment, it has to be the mother who decides which of them will hold back for the good of their team (usually herself, but not always) while the other one takes their 'turn'. Then the second person waits (or is distracted, or falls asleep if he is a baby) while the first person has her turn. This new way means that the mother's turn is justified on behalf of the team. The emphasis has changed.

I like to have a shower every morning. I've just discovered that B is happy for me to have one, as long as I leave his nappy off. So I leave him on the bathroom floor on a towel, and he kicks while I shower. [B, 7 weeks]

Sometimes, B's playing under his baby gym, and he can be there for twenty minutes to half an hour while I do a few things. Then our eyes meet across the room, and he seems all right, so I carry on. [B, 4 months]

I spent a long time one morning [*breast*]feeding G and then holding her while she slept. When she woke, I got up to get myself some lunch, and G started complaining. I said: '*You've* got a nerve, after all I've done for *you*. If I don't eat, how will I have the energy to make your milk and look after you?' Of course, she couldn't under-stand a word I was saying, but I needed to explain it to her. [G, 7 months]

These mothers were all 'negotiating' with their babies. This enabled them to feel responsible for what they decided. Their assumption of responsibility gave them a strength, which made it much easier for them to act in love. It's revealing to see how mothers feel when they don't negotiate, but devote themselves to their babies in the traditional way.

With G, I used to think that my love should have no limits and that I should give her *everything*. That's what I took for granted, so I didn't look at her for signs of her own limits. I used to get very tired. But with B it's different. He gives me time. He shows me that he is ready to sleep at around seven in the evenings, and then I have seven hours. I take them and am very thankful to him. [G, 3 years; B, 5 months]

It might feel hard at first. At night, many mothers wonder whether they are sacrificing too much. Most newborns, especially if they are breastfeeding, cannot sleep through a whole night without being awakened by hunger. Of these, many continue to wake at night during their first year, sometimes frequently. This gives mothers a choice between leaving their babies to cry with hunger, or waking up whenever their babies do, to feed them. One night of broken sleep is manageable, but months of them are exhausting. Mothers make different choices.

First mother: B still wakes up several times most nights. My feeling is that he needs to be lying beside me. F says B is just 'playing me up'. But I don't think B understands where I am if he's not beside me at night. [B, 10 months]

Second mother: You could let him cry. I did that to G. It sounds awful, but I felt she needed to get over a hump to reach her sleep. She's fine at night now. [G, 7 months]

First mother: If I let B cry, he gets louder. I don't know. He's happy as long as I am there, so I feel that's where I ought to be.

If a mother is impatient for her baby to fall asleep, so that she can have her turn to fulfil some of her own needs, her tension can communicate. Then her baby responds by being too tense to fall asleep. If she can relax, he does too.

I've noticed that B goes to sleep much quicker if I'm carrying him around [*in a sling*], getting on with things, than if I'm actually trying to get him to sleep. I look down at his little face, and suddenly his eyes are closed. He likes to feel part of the family. [G, 3 years; B, 5 months]

I used to think that the mother's impatient longing for her turn when her baby fell asleep was a recent Western problem, and that traditional mothers were calmer and more patient. But, one day, looking through an anthology of ancient texts by James Pritchard, I found his translation of a lullaby from ancient Sumer – the earliest known civilisation of the ancient Near East, sometimes called 'the cradle of civilisation'. It was situated in what is now Iraq during the fourth and third millennia BC. This is one verse from a longer poem:

> Come Sleep, come Sleep,
> Come to my son,
> *Hurry* Sleep to my son,
> Put to sleep his restless eyes,
> Put your hand on his (kohl)-painted eyes,
> And (as for) his babbling tongue,
> Let not the babbling hold back (his) sleep.[92]

Professor Pritchard comments that the son in this lullaby seems to be ill. Perhaps this explains why his mother is desperate. No doubt she has been looking after him all day. She needs a respite, and calls on Sleep as her only resource. I have read this poem aloud to several groups of mothers, and all of them recognise the urgency of the Sumerian mother's feelings, all those millennia ago.

Mothers who care for their babies at night may appear to be making enormous self-sacrifices in terms of their own sleep. True, but, from what they say, it sounds a different kind of bargain. They are 'trading' quantity of sleep for a better quality. When they have finally helped their babies to fall asleep, they feel satisfied with themselves, even though there is less time for their own sleep. Their own turn for sleep can then feel more peaceful.

A sense that it won't always be like this can help mothers to keep going.

Everything that's convenient for us seems to be bad for babies. Convenience foods, convenient nappies, convenient sleep times. Babies *aren't* convenient. But when you think about it, what do they need? Just three years of you never getting proper sleep. It's only *three* years of nights. And then you've got a really happy child. At least, that's what I'm hoping. [G, 13 months]

Some people seem to think that babies must need their turns entirely for feeding or being soothed to sleep. However, even the youngest babies are social. They enjoy certain pleasures so much that they want to share their turns with their mothers. Sometimes this can give mothers great pleasure. But not always.

G likes to make eye contact the whole time. I couldn't read a book while she's awake. It wouldn't seem right. But there's part of me wishing for more intellectual stimulation again. [G, 3 months]

I used to get bored when B was younger. He'd love to lie on his changing mat and kick. It was his favourite thing. He could have done that for an hour. I had to be there because he could have rolled off and hurt himself. But, to be honest, I'd had enough after ten minutes. [B, 4 months]

Finding ways to keep interested rather than feeling bored and resentful was important to many mothers. They realised that it was good for their babies to share what they (the babies) enjoyed. Psychoanalyst and paediatrician Donald Winnicott put it simply: 'If you [*the mother*] are there enjoying it all, it is like the sun coming out, for the baby.'[93]

I've spent hours with B watching diggers at a site, building a round-about. You learn a lot, doing that. And I've found it fascinating for me too. The movements of the diggers are balletic, if you really watch them. [B, 3 years]

I've done this kind of thing myself. Through the mother's words, I can remember the cold wind blowing; I can feel the icy feet, the longing to be back home with a hot cup of tea. It would be easy to say: 'That's *it*. I've had enough. We're *going*.' And yet . . . There is something serious and dignified about the child's watching that can make it a privilege to share it, even for a long stretch, however cold it has become.

Gradually, as the baby develops, he can wait for longer, and his mother's team thinking adjusts. Instead of continuing to put her needs 'on hold', she finds she can fit in more turns for herself sooner.

Me: Why is 2B crying?

M: Because he wants me to support him to stand up. But he'll have to wait because I *must* find my glasses [*hunting in her bag*]. [1B, 4 years; 2B, 7 months]

G wanted more and more attention. There seemed no end to it. So finally, I told her I needed some 'Mummy time'. After that, it would be her time and we could do something that she liked together. At first, she protested, but she understands now. We've done it for about a week, and it's much easier. [G, 18 months]

As mothers learn to work out who most needs a turn, they initiate their children into the process too. We are definitely not born with this wisdom. Our original understanding is that our needs are desperately urgent and must be met immediately. Yet taking turns is a vital part of social life. How could we communicate if we did not take turns at being speaker and listener? How could two toddlers enjoy the same toy if an adult did not help them to discover that they could simply divide the time, rather than pull for total possession of the toy? Today, the flow of traffic on roads is controlled by dividing roads into lanes, and having traffic lights, and a set of rules over which lane takes priority at every road junction or roundabout. Traffic jams can be an irritant, but the organised system of turns means that we can be confident that the jam will resolve in time.

We can manage the complexities of adult social life provided we can trust one another to exchange a turn. It isn't always easy to agree on what is a fair exchange, but at least we can negotiate within a concept of fairness. Social life works incredibly well when we apply this fundamental human discovery.

What happens to children who have never learned how to take turns? It is so basic to most of human communication that children are at a great disadvantage without this understanding. A child who doesn't receive the experience of doing this from a young age seems to end up very puzzled as to why snatching and grabbing at what he wants never seems to get him very far. He is speaking a different social language from the language of turn-taking. Our education system has remedial schemes to help children in this predicament. But these are far inferior to the spontaneous education that a mother can provide. Most mothers never sit down to teach their children formally. Like so much that mothers do, it is conveyed through everyday life.

The mother is always in charge of how the two of them spend their time. But she can decide to give her child a turn to choose.

I told B we'd go to the park, and we left the house. B started walking the other way. I decided that, instead of insisting, I'd let him take the lead, and we ended up having a wonderful time. He toddled up the main road, and then he indicated that he wanted us to cross over, so we did. He went into the railway station, and then he climbed down the steps to the platform. Then a train came in, and

B was so excited. I thought, Oh, *no*, what have I done? We'll be here all day. But, after the third train, B had had enough, and we went back up. When we got home, B was very tired, but I felt really *satisfied* that I'd been able to go with him the whole time. Nearly always, it's me who says where we go. [B, 14 months]

I do what she wants, and then she does what I want. She likes going to the playground and sitting on the step [*running board*] of the roundabout. She can sit there for a long time. And I feel more relaxed doing what *she* wants than doing what *I* want. [G, 15 months]

If you think how often you say, 'No, you can't have that,' 'Don't touch that!' 'Come on, we're going out now.' I'm always giving orders. So I wanted to let B make some of his own decisions. I like him to know I have listened to him. [B, 3 years; G, 4 months]

Unfortunately, babies are too young to reward their mothers with deliberate turns. It can be upsetting when a mother has been generous in giving her baby a good 'turn', but the baby does not 'co-operate' and, for example, fails to have a nap at the expected time. The baby is too young for a two-sided bargain. That becomes possible much later. It's not the baby's fault that the mother lost her turn because he never shook hands on the deal in the first place. So with whom can the frustrated mother get angry?

I've dropped practically everything I do except my yoga class. I really enjoy that. Only, last Wednesday, B kept crying because he was tired, and just refused to fall asleep. I tried everything. So I had to take him out [*of the class*] for the first time ever. I didn't realise how much I minded until after. I just thought, Well, I'll flow with it. But I felt really angry with him. And that's dreadful because I love him *so* much. [B, 6 months]

One afternoon, I just wanted to be on my own. Just for a few minutes to get my energies back. But B kept following me wherever I went. My moment of greatest *shame*, yeah, I may as well tell all of you, was dragging B to his bed and throwing him onto it and yelling: 'What do you WANT?' And do you know, even then, he wouldn't let me alone. He followed me out of the room, singing, manic, kicking toys. [B, 3 years]

Mothers and babies seem to build up private systems of turn-taking, in which babies learn what to expect. However, family members may have different ideas and ask for a turn at holding the baby. But how is the baby to know that this is only for a limited time, and that he will soon have his mother back again?

We went to my family for Christmas. My mother and my mother-in-law were both longing to hold B. So I decided to have a shower and let them look after him. I showered for nearly twenty minutes, which was great. When I came back, my mother-in-law said: 'I feel it was very important for your development as a mother that you were able to do that.' But it was nothing to do with my development as a mother. I took B upstairs for a breastfeed, which I always do after my shower, and he was *furious* with me. He refused to breast-feed and just cried. I felt he was saying, 'What did you have to do *that* for? I was just getting used to being in this strange house, and you go and . . . ' [B, 8 months]

All kinds of third-party questions about turn-taking arise which require complex ethical thinking from the mother.

I keep questioning whose needs come first. Would I ever put the needs of someone else's child before the needs of my own child? I suppose, in an emergency, I would. [B, 10 years]

Slowly, children themselves discover how to take turns. It seems to start as a light-hearted game, much sooner than we might think.

I like the intimacy at night. We talk to each other. I say 'Hello!' and she laughs and says things back to me. [G, 7 weeks]

When B wakes up, he looks at me and we play games together. Like I stick my tongue out at him, and he sticks his out at me, and he roars with laughter. And then I do something different, and I can see him wondering what face muscles to use so he can do it too. [B, 9 weeks]

When F talks to G, I can hear them having this nonsense conversation, and both of them pausing to listen to the other one. [G, 2 months]

I won't bore you by telling you all the lovely things B does. Probably I'd be the only person in the room to think they are lovely. Well, every time he touches my nose, I open my mouth and say, 'Bah!' He thinks it's hilarious. [B, 12 months]

The mother is usually much more competent at her turn than her baby.

B was playing with a rattle and a box, and he indicated that he wanted me to play the game with him. So I took the rattle, and I shook it louder and longer than he did. And I noticed when I gave it back to him that he threw it across the floor and wouldn't play with it any more. Now I'm learning how to play with him – but being less good than he is. [B, 8 months]

It is amazing how generous young children can be when they start to give their mothers a re-turn.

G likes feeding *me* now. It's really sweet. She takes a spoon and pushes it into my mouth and she's so delighted when I take it. [G, 8 months]

I see G often trying to be helpful. [*I asked for an example.*] Oh, well, I don't like getting up in the morning. I can see G sit up, all bright and awake. Then she can see I'm still sleepy, but she doesn't complain. She snuggles back, has a breastfeed, and I can see her trying her best to go back to sleep. [G, 9 months]

When F's mother was ill, G heard us talking about her and suddenly she said, 'That's quite sad.' And F has bad acne. He brushes his back with a special brush. The other day, G picked up the brush and said, 'G will brush Daddy's poor skin.' [G, 23 months; B, 7 weeks]

With older children, the exchange is more obvious:

First mother: I'm hoping to get a lot of work done this half-term week. [G, 9 years; G, 7 years]

Second mother: How will you do that with two children? [B, 8 months]

Third mother: I was wondering that. [G, 7 months]

First mother: We *know* each other. We respect each other. I know they'll respect my need to work.

When a child has learned to share with his parents and other adults, he will eventually be able to take turns with other children. But transferring this experience can take longer than one might think. Children need time before they really feel safe with their peers. From years of observation, I think children are expected to take turns with other children long before they have learned the basic questions, ethical and practical, about turn-taking, and long before they feel confident about managing them.

It can be difficult to decide the fairest criteria for how to prioritise turns, especially if there are several siblings or visiting children. Decisions may be age-related ('After all, you are older and G is only a baby') or obey social codes ('We'll give B the first turn because he is our visitor'). It must take children a long time to get the measure of our complex systems of balancing of needs and rights.

First mother: 1B's lower lip wobbles when he wants something and he has to share it. His toys are important to him, and he hates sharing them, though he can be generous with them too. He says, 'It's *mine!*' and there's such a lot of emotion in it. And that's where I'm stuck. I don't know what to say to him. I'm afraid of saying the wrong thing and then he'll have a lifelong memory: 'She made me share that toy.' [1B, 2 years; 2B, 5 months]

Second mother: You don't *have* to socialise. Children go through stages when it's difficult. It can be very embarrassing with other people there. If it's just you and the children, B doesn't have to share. [G, 2 years; B, 7 months]

First mother: That's a new idea to me. I always think I *have* to be social. But your idea feels like a . . . a *weight* lifted off me.

B doesn't like to share. Like if he's playing a boat game, he likes to be the captain himself. There was another child in the playground one day who wanted to join in B's game, and I could see how upset B was. When other children come along, B gets anxious. He doesn't like children grabbing his things. [B, 3 years]

Do children have to be made to share their intimate toys and games? Or could they be excused from the process of sharing until they are mature enough to enjoy it? At what age is this likely to happen? These are fascinating questions about our development as social people. Mothers who have experienced these situations are in a good position to comment on their observations. But it must be a considerable time before children really understand about waiting for their own turn.

It's not good for children to have their own way all the time, is it? But it's hard to know when they are old enough to wait for you, and for how long they can manage. I find that quite difficult. [G, 7 months]

149

I have to remind myself that G doesn't understand everything. For example: 'Wait a minute!' I think it's hard for her to grasp what that means. [G, 3 years; B, 4 months]

Older children get an introduction to learning to wait for their turn when a sibling is born. The older child discovers that the baby usually comes first, and waiting may feel long, unaccustomed and frustrating.

I've lost my temper with B so many times. So I thought I'd better take them both out, and I decided I'd do absolutely everything B wanted me to do. At home, he's always got to wait while I look after G. So off we went. B wanted to go to a playground – and we had a *wonderful* time. I was able to have a coffee and sit down with G. I said I'd watch him, and he was happy for me to do that. And I noticed that he didn't want anything unreasonable. Everything he asked for, I could do. It was a really *happy* time for *both* of us. Then we went home, and I noticed that the nearer we got to our door the slower B walked. I said, 'Come *on!*' and I was getting irritated. Then, just when I could see our door, B threw himself down on the pavement and wouldn't get up. That's when I exploded. There I was, shouting insults at my son. I felt we'd so nearly done it and now we'd failed. But, when I thought about it, and it took many hours of thinking, I realised that the day *hadn't* failed. B lay down in the street *because* it had been so nice. I suppose he couldn't bear going back home and having to wait for me all the time while I looked after G. [B, 3 years; G, 6 weeks]

Surely it makes a great deal of difference if the mother understands how difficult it can be for the older child. This is discussed in more detail in Chapter Twelve.

When siblings are older, they work out how to take turns between themselves, especially if they spend a lot of time together. Often, they do it through play, and can be very inventive. When my two sons were small, I had to leave them in a place without a single toy, but they were soon laughing away. They had invented a game in which one had to blink, or pat his head, or shake his hair, and the other one had to try not to laugh. As soon as one of them laughed, they reversed roles.

Marbles, skittles, hopscotch, cards – all the traditional family games are based on children knowing how to take turns. Conflicts arise between older children about whose turn it is, and what is fair. This can lead to quarrelling. However, even a 'civilised' quarrel depends on taking turns. Since quarrels have been shown to be a regular part of family life, the ability to take turns can be useful in providing a familiar structure in which a dispute can be discussed and resolved. Participants seem to resort to violence only when their confidence in turn-taking breaks down.

As children grow older, they also take turns at behaviours that their mothers never meant them to copy.

Since G was born, I've been much crosser with B. And now he does it back. I used to say, 'B, if you hit G one more time, you're not going to be allowed to . . . ' And I make him miss a treat, or not play with a favourite toy. And now he does it right back. He'll say, 'I'm feeling *very* sad, Mummy, and if you can't make me feel better in *one* minute, I won't eat my food.' What you say comes back to you. [B, 3 years; G, 7 months]

I thought B was taking a rude tone of voice to me, so I told him: 'B, your tone sounds really disrespectful. If I'm honest, I'm thinking you sound as though you think I am bad and useless.' Then he said, 'You know what, Mum? When I was about thirteen, you used to speak to *me* like that, and I used to think *I* was bad and useless too.' At first, I wanted to defend myself. But it was a gift, and I tried to accept it like that. [B, 16 years; G, 6 months]

As far as we can tell, we are all born with enough sensitivity to learn to take turns. Yet this very sensitivity can work against us. We learn from unhappy experiences as well as good ones. If our mother doesn't offer us fair turns, we may be influenced by this early experience.

How could there be an unfair system of turn-taking? The existential psychotherapist R. D. Laing found a stark example in a published case study which described a mother with her six-month-old baby. The mother would smile at her baby, and he would smile back. However, if ever the baby gave his mother a smile, she never seemed to return it.[94]

We can imagine what a baby might learn from such an early and often-repeated experience. As an older person, he would probably feel secure at responding to contact, provided the other person started it. He might have much less confidence in making a friendly overture himself for fear that the other person would blank him. Laing thought this might have a profound effect. 'But emptiness and futility can arise . . .', he observed about this infant and mother, 'if [a person] feels he is not able to make any difference to anyone.'[95]

Equally, this scenario could cause problems if the two roles were reversed. An unhappy mother might only smile when her baby smiled, but never initiate smiling herself. This could easily leave her baby with the impression that every exchange was up to him. Without him, the baby might conclude, his mother (and therefore other adults) might rarely smile. This baby might end up with the opposite experience to the one Laing described, with the sense that his input was crucial. The importance of his own initiatives might then become a heavy burden.

Learning to exchange *equal* turns can seem so obvious when it works well. Yet it is exactly here that relationships easily go wrong. Some adults say they enjoy living alone. However, when they explain why, they usually say that they don't like sharing their private space, and feel more relaxed on their own. In every case, they express a fear that another person could be overpowering and that they might succumb to that person's demands.

Richard Byrd, an explorer, wrote: 'I should be able to live exactly as I chose, obedient to no necessities but those imposed by wind and night and cold, and to no man's laws but my own.'[96] American journalist Anneli Rufus complained that she found socialising as exhausting as giving blood. 'After three hours, I'm drained, even if I love the person I'm with.'[97] Equally frank was the novelist Kate Atkinson: 'Living with someone is like taking on another life. I can see where I have gone wrong with relationships in the past and for me it's true. I am only truly myself when I am with me . . . I always find when I'm with other people I'm thinking, Hmm, I have to make an effort.'[98]

The conviction that a person cannot be herself with other people is very common. It's one of the reasons why so many adult relationships start off well and then founder. The first relationship is the one we are born into, usually with our mothers. As babies, we are the less experienced party. This first relationship makes a strong impression on us. If our mother doesn't give us fair turns, then we may do two things in response. First, we might make every effort to appease her, because this is a good way of getting what we need from her. Second, we would take care *never* to get ourselves into this overpowering kind of relationship again.

Our vigilance might also lead us to misinterpret the behaviour of our partner. In vain, he or she protests that he/she does not want to dominate or control us. If we have known these kinds of relationships from a young age, it is difficult to believe there could really be a more equal one.

Moreover, dread of being overwhelmed and having to subjugate their needs to the needs of another person seems to be a key reason why so many women say they do not want to become mothers. They don't see the role as a strong one. They perceive it as having to be in thrall to their babies. Many mothers have said that they feel trapped. It can be difficult to recognise that they really can be in charge of the relationship.

> At first, I felt as if I was two people. One was my usual self, who wasn't a mother. The other was a person called 'mother' who wasn't myself. At first, I did everything that seemed right for the 'mother' figure to do. It felt like duty. Then, one week, I decided to relax. And I discovered that I was doing the things that the mother figure would do, only it was because I really wanted to. For example, I was holding G, and it wasn't duty. When I relaxed, I found that I *wanted* to hold her. [G, 21 months]

A different kind of turn-taking arises when parents work out how to share their parenting equally. This subject is discussed in Chapter Eleven. One advantage when another person takes the mother's turn is that it enables the mother to see how much she is enjoying her turn herself. Without a break, it is difficult to realise this.

> Now, on Tuesdays, F looks after G, and I take a train to a regular appointment. So last Tuesday, I get to the station and I buy a paper, and then a coffee. And then I think, Well, this is my morning off. So I buy a croissant. Then I get on the train with my paper, my coffee and croissant and I find a seat, and at first I really enjoy myself. And, do you know, after about *ten* minutes I'm bored with the paper and I think, Is this *all* I was mourning for? Is this *all* I gave up G for? Because I know that if I had been spending the morning with G, it would have been *quite* different and we would have been enjoying ourselves. [G, 9 months]

There is also a very generous kind of turn-taking where a giver does not expect any return from the taker. Instead, the giver trusts that he is part of a much larger system of turn-taking. In this larger scale of taking turns, a mother uses her turn as mother to be generous to her children, which she hopes will help her children to grow into generous adults, and also parents, in their turn. There is no guarantee that this will happen, and a mother takes a risk that her best efforts may not succeed. But it must be very satisfying if she lives to see that it does.

> I had a *real* mother. She did things for us, and I'd like to reproduce the mothering I was given. It gives me a lot to build on. The only changes I'd like to make for G are tiny things. [*I asked for an example.*] My mother taught us ice-skating. But she didn't teach us to ski. So now I'm terrified on a ski slope, whereas if I'd learned it earlier I know I'd be enjoying it. But that's not really important, and I'll probably leave out something myself. [G, 5 months]

However, this generous turn at being a mother does not always happen today. It seems to be part of a recent social change. David Elkind published a book in 1981 with the significant title, *The Hurried Child: Growing Up Too Fast Too Soon.* He observed:

> The concept of childhood, so vital to the traditional American way of life, is threatened with extinction in the society we have created . . . If child-rearing necessarily entails stress, then by hurrying children to grow up, or by treating them as adults, we hope to remove a portion of our burden of worry and anxiety and to enlist our children's aid in carrying life's load.[99]

There is a strong case for arguing that many children today don't get a proper turn at being children. A great deal of pressure is put on them, from a young age, to be self-sufficient, self-comforting, understanding and forgiving of adult foibles. But surely childhood, at least here in the West, is a time to be protected by experienced parents who enable their children to grow up slowly, and to learn by degrees the enormous complexity of modern adult life.[100]

> Our society seems really disrespectful to children. There are so many things that B mustn't do. Everywhere we go, there are things

B mustn't touch and mustn't explore. There is almost nowhere we can go where B can be himself. It's so difficult. I just want to respect B for being who he is, *a child*, so he will feel respected and give respect to other people. [B, 21 months]

If a child is not given time to behave as a child, we are losing our chance to develop as mothers. This deprives us too. 'We, and our kids, lose if we can't surrender to mother love,' wrote Brenda Hunter in her book, *The Power of Mother Love*.[101] But what kind of loss is it? What kind of turn do mothers get?

One mother, who had hired a nanny so that she could take on some freelance work, observed:

You can leave your job, and it doesn't make nearly as much difference as you might think. Somebody else can do it, even if they do it less well than you. But if you have to leave your baby, your baby will notice the difference immediately, and for your baby only you will do. [G, 4 months]

This can create a pressure that not all women enjoy.

What is *wrong* with us? Mothers are *necessary*. Is it so very difficult to be necessary? Is it so very hard to *be* there if your child needs you? Something is wrong with us that we find it so difficult. Being there is *major*. If we are not there, our children feel abandoned. I *like* to be there for my children. I *know* I'm not perfect. But I'm their mother. [G, 3 years; G, 15 months]

Any position of responsibility makes us visible and so shows our imperfections. But it is also a chance to develop much more of our potential. Especially, taking a turn as a mother can show us that we can negotiate how we love.

Mothers learn that love doesn't have to mean a grand sweeping gesture of devotion that denies their own vital needs. The small daily exchange of turns is a good way of loving. Then mothers don't need to build up a sense of resentment at the inequality of their relationship. Even with small exchanges, a mother may feel depleted because she seems to have given too much of her energies to her baby. But her discontent can alert her to the need to review what she is doing and adjust her system where necessary.

This more equal way of loving allows mothers and babies to feel safe when they share their lives intimately. A mother needs to feel safe enough in order to create an intimate relationship with her baby.

CHAPTER TEN

'I can't do intimacy'

Does love have to mean being intimate? Not everyone enjoys the closeness of an intimate relationship.

Yet, intimate relationships give us something special. We develop, as individuals, right through our lives. But we don't do this in isolation. Other people inspire us and hold keys to our potential.[102] Whoever we are, wherever we live, we need other people to bring out different aspects of ourselves. We can't do this on our own. We have to be close enough to someone else for it to happen. An intimate relationship isn't all we need. But living *without* one can leave us feeling that life is pointless. It is surely significant that many people who describe their sense of futility also seem to have no intimate friend to talk to.[103]

On the whole, we choose carefully whom we trust for an intimate relationship. This seems sensible of us, because the right person at the right moment can transform our lives. However, the very prospect of being transformed can feel unnerving. Quicker than thought, one adult will push another away. Intimacy depends on both parties being willing.

Once we have started on one of these reciprocal intimacies, it doesn't seem wholly reversible. Difficulties may arise, and some relationships founder. Even so, although we may quarrel and break off further relations with an 'impossible' person, we have opened something of ourselves to him or her, and cannot completely close up again. Their influence remains an important part of our story.

Most of us start along this road by learning intimacy, however imperfectly, from our mothers. A newborn has a special solitary look. He hasn't experienced a close relationship yet. Even newborn multiples don't seem to relate to one another as they do to their mother.[104] A mother is usually the person who initiates her child into intimacy.

Intimacy is, at its best, an opportunity to receive and give love. At worst, a mother can intentionally use or exploit her closeness to cause pain. No mother is perfect, and it's easy to cause accidental pain. However, if a mother creates overall a generous first experience of intimacy with her child, her child will have a chance to discover what an intimate relationship can offer.

Intimacy is not a luxury. As adults, we *need* it. I can see this, as I sit in the large basement of a city café at the end of a working day. The place is abuzz with conversations. 'Have you noticed that we have a real problem with Martin?' 'Frankly, I felt em*barr*assed for him.' 'I knew at once what she was driving at.' At last, the chance to drop one's guard, to be honest, and to confide in one another after the tense constraints of the day. From what I can hear, it's mostly about the effects of one person on others. Probably none of these is a major intimacy. People enjoy easy, intimate conversation to recover themselves at the end of a working day.

I sit back and try to imagine each adult as a small pre-verbal baby. Each *must* have been one. The idea makes me blink in disbelief. Every one of these lively people sounds so lucid. Yet, long ago, not one of them knew how to talk, let alone articulate intimate thoughts. Most of them owe their first steps towards expressiveness to their mothers.

How do mothers know how to be intimate with their babies?

Are there guidelines to follow? It seems not, because although mothers have existed for millennia, they haven't created a mothers' rulebook. Have they been negligent? Or does their long silence suggest that there are no rules for this, and that each mother is capable of finding her own way?

> Over my career, I'm very organised. I like to decide on my goals and plan my future backwards from them. But relationships are different. I don't have goals for F and me. So with B I just go by ear. And it's all been easy so far. [B, 3 months]

However, some mothers feel a good deal less confident.

> I don't know how to be intimate. I can do meals and baths and . . . But I can't do intimacy. [*Rush of tears.*] I suppose no one did that for me. [G, 18 months]

It must have been hard for this mother to try to relate closely to her daughter if she herself had missed this experience. Yet I could see that her little daughter kept running up to her mother and obviously *did* feel close to her. Perhaps doing meals and baths with a child *are* ways of being intimate. Intimacy can happen unexpectedly without either person trying. It certainly isn't necessary for a mother to limit herself to set ideas of how intimacy 'should' be.

Also, for this particular mother, it must have been difficult even to manage a meal or a bath. She was ill, and employed a nanny to help her. One day I asked the nanny how she was getting on. She replied: 'G really trusts me now. We have great times together. But sometimes G just needs her mum.' Surely those times are indications of the mother-and-daughter intimacy.

Mothers don't realise how much they know. They make sensitive observers, because they can get much closer to their babies than any onlooker or researcher. By piecing together some of their observations, we can start to create a broad idea of how intimacy starts.

The pregnancy months seem, as we saw (pages 55–6), to be a kind of prelude to intimacy. The moment of birth is intimate in itself because the mother's body opens up and the baby emerges from inside her. Birth doesn't just open her body physically. It seems to prepare her to open her essential self in readiness for her baby.

It is difficult to describe the moment of birth without giving the impression that one person's experience is the way it *ought* to be. Some mothers have frightening birth experiences. For others, it is an exciting discovery. 'The flower opens. Thick petals part,' wrote Sheila Kitzinger in her poem, 'A Celebration of Birth'.[105] Another mother said: 'Giving birth is such a spiritual act. I wish I could have given birth in a church.' A third mother was more prosaic: 'Giving birth was the only thing that has ever stopped me talking. Normally, I *always* talk. When I gave birth, it was a shock. I couldn't utter a *single word!*' All three are trying to describe something momentous, and each woman conveys it entirely in her own way.

A mother's first impression of her baby is usually the cry, the sight and feel. Yet I remember how smell was an important part of it too. People don't talk about smells much. It would be helpful to collect precise details of the impact of smell during the early moments of relating to our babies.

The newborn may know his mother better than she knows him. As a foetus, he knew his mother from within. He got to know the different ways she responded to events, and the changing rhythm and tension of her movements. He could hear his parents' voices. It is not the same as being able to see them, though it surely prepares him. It is hard for us to imagine. We would need to 'rewind' our own immense database of relationships and try to remember how it was in the womb. Like breathing, seeing our mother is something we start at birth, and learn to do so quickly that it's hard to recall how.

Many mothers mention the immediacy of eye contact. Sheila Kitzinger, who has five daughters, describes a sequence when a newborn has had time to relax after her birth: 'Then she opens her eyes and looks straight at you. It brings a shock of delighted surprise. This is not just "the baby"; here is a *person* . . . It is the first encounter.'[106] Frederick Leboyer, who wrote *Birth Without Violence*, and who had been present at many births, describes the newborn's expression: 'The first look is unforgettable. Immense, deep, grave, intense, these eyes enquire: "Where am I? What has happened to me?" . . . We discover that, beyond any doubt, a *person* is there . . . '[107]

It is revealing to study newborn behaviour through photographs. Lynne Murray is co-author of the photographic book, *The Social Baby*. Here is the evidence for newborn actions that mothers must have witnessed for millennia. Some people claim that newborn babies are only interested in their food. The photos in *The Social Baby* tell a different story. A series of photos demonstrates how a midwife put a newborn called Ethan 'to the breast, but in fact he's not interested in feeding; he wants only to look at [*his mother's*] face. Ethan watches his mother intently again. As [*his mother*] talks to him, Ethan's face becomes more mobile and expressive.' We can see from the times printed on the photos that Ethan's birth had been only *ten minutes* earlier.[108]

With her newborn in her arms, a mother can look down at him, while he can look up at her.

> When G wakes up, she seems to come from a long way off. She seems animalistic. She doesn't make eye contact. I think, Where has G gone? Then she looks at me, and it's as if she's back. She gazes right into my eyes, like soul gazing at soul. [G, 2 months]

> At first, B would just look up at me with this staring face. His eyes

looked blank, without moving. An adult will usually respond to you. I think I used to feel a bit afraid of him. [B, 3 months]

M: When B was younger, I'd be breastfeeding him and I'd see him gazing up into my face. Just . . . looking at me without blinking. It made me feel very responsible.

Me: In what way?

M: Well, I'm the face B looks at. [B, 4 months]

It can feel awkward to allow our faces to be scrutinised, day after day. We might wish we could touch up our appearance like a celebrity photograph, so that we would look smiling and impassive. Instead, we don't have much privacy. We have to show our real faces, in our 'up' moments and our 'down' ones. Our eyes especially express every nuance of emotion for our babies to see.[109] Babies seem to learn to 'read' facial expressions, by studying the subtle changes on their mothers' familiar faces. This process seems to prepare them to understand non-verbal cues, before the verbal ones. (See Chapter Four.)

However, there is no recipe for intimacy. Mutual gazing is not essential. Blind mothers, blind babies and others still find ways to contact one another.

B *never* made eye contact with me. He still doesn't. Other mothers used to say: 'We gaze into each other's eyes and it's so lovely.' I used to think, What am I doing wrong? I thought I had to get B to make eye contact. But it's all fine now. I suddenly realised that we have lots of communication between us. [B, 3 months]

In other words, by all kinds of combinations of looking at, touching, hearing, smelling one another and also tasting, if the baby is breastfeeding, mother and newborn start to respond to one another. As quickly as that, a whole new intimate relationship is under way.

So what is a 'person'? How does a newborn communicate to his mother that he is not just a baby, but a person? One mother tried to explain, though her child was no longer newborn.

M: G is a real *person*.

Me: In what way?

M: Well, she . . . I don't know. It's an odd thing to say but she's independent. I mean, she depends on me for all kinds of things, but she's . . . like she *waves* to things. That's all her idea. If she likes something, she waves to it. Sometimes I see her wave, and I don't know what it's to. It's obviously a wave, not a random movement. It shows that she's got her own world. Of course, she doesn't know all of my world, and I realise that I don't know, and will *never* know, all of hers. [G, 10 months]

A person, then, is someone with his own ideas who makes autonomous choices and decisions. Alessandra Piontelli was thinking of 'a person' in the same way when she was making pioneering ultra-sound observations of babies in the womb.

I could no longer regard the foetuses I was watching as non-persons, as each of them seemed already to be an individual with its own personality, preferences and reactions.[110]

After birth, mothers frequently observe how thoughtful their newborns look, as if they are processing many impressions. Even when they are asleep, their eyes move below their closed eyelids, suggesting that they have dreams. While physically so dependent, they seem to have ideas of their own.

Mothers could have challenged a widespread philosophical theory of '*tabula rasa*', a blank slate. This idea was as old as Aristotle. In this tradition, the seventeenth-century philosopher John Locke claimed that babies were born without any ideas: ' . . . a foetus in the mother's womb differs not much from the state of a vegetable, but passes the greatest amount of its time without perception or thought, doing very little . . . '[111] Locke believed that babies acquired ideas after birth, through gaining experience. It was brilliant of Locke to ask himself when we start to have ideas. His clear answer influenced thinking for centuries. Yet it didn't occur to him to question mothers. Surely mothers could have enlightened him.

Some people, even today, talk about babies, not exactly like blank slates, but not like persons either. They admire the soft skin, the gurgling sounds, the way a baby can look 'delicious' or 'yummy' and 'good enough to eat'. In this kind of conversation, the fact that a baby might have thoughts and feelings of his own tends to be disregarded.[112]

Another way of overlooking the person of a baby is to relate to him as if he were the mother's exclusive possession. He certainly is her own child – but he is more than that too.[113]

This means that we don't all start from similar experiences. Some of us are treated as persons all along, while others get a more mixed experience. However, it is not possible for a mother to start a truly loving and intimate relationship with her child unless she is aware of him as a person.

But if a mother recognises her baby as a person, does he recognise her as one? This question is hard to answer, though people have speculated. It's difficult for us to guess what babies experience. Nevertheless, it is interesting to listen to what mothers say. After only a few weeks, a mother may remark: 'G really knows me now,' or, 'B and I have long conversations.' Clearly, they already feel as though their understanding is reciprocated.

The psychoanalyst René Spitz saw that mothers did something vital to establish communication with their babies. But what was it? He had the humility to concede that he did not know.

What occurs within the dyad [*of mother and baby*] remains obscure. How, for example, can we explain the near-clairvoyant manner in which a good mother seems to divine the needs of her baby, to understand what his crying means and what his babbling? We speak of maternal intuition, of the mother's intelligence; but essentially we know little of what goes on in her in this respect.[114]

Are we getting any closer to understanding? Which words would describe how a mother relates to her child? We usually select the best words from a spectrum of possibilities: intimate/remote, open/closed, warm/cold, soft/hard, light/heavy and so on. You might imagine that a sensible mother would choose a 'midway point' between all these extremes. She could choose middle-distance, halfway open, tepid, medium-hard, and so on. She could then claim to be relating to her child from a balanced or neutral position.

But this isn't what most mothers do. Typically, a mother will hold her baby right in, in contact with her warm body. Her touch tends to be strong enough to be protective, yet sensitive enough to adapt to her baby's movements. Her voice sounds soft and gentle. Her eyes widen with tenderness. A baby's breath is often sweet-smelling, and I wonder whether a mother's breath might smell sweet to her baby. Usually, mothers start at the extremely warm, soft and gentle end of the spectrum.

The very origin of the word 'intimacy' is also at the same end of the spectrum. '*Intimus*' is the Latin superlative of the preposition, '*inter*', which means 'between'. So the meaning of an *intimate* relationship seems to be one that is most intensely *between* two people. 'Intimacy' is not a neutral, middle-of-the-road word.

That may be exactly how it feels to a newborn. If his mother is breastfeeding him, she probably needs to hold her baby warm and close to her. Many formula-feeding mothers instinctively do this too. In order to survive, babies need to be fed frequently, day and night. This means that many babies start their lives by being held close to their mothers every time they feed. In this way, the maximum sensations can be exchanged *between* the two of them. These babies are surely getting a very good start to intimacy.

The mother/baby relationship differs from a peer relationship. A newborn is at the beginning. He won't always want to stay close to his mother. Their relationship will change. Yet the first stage can feel trying for some mothers. They may feel trapped by such closeness. After all, it means that their babies are getting to know them. Adults usually expect that a person who knows them will judge them. It can take time to see that babies have no point of comparison to make such judgments.

However, both parties need to be honest with one another. Lies and deception are the enemies of intimacy. That is not a problem for the baby because he is too young to be able to tell lies. But it's different for his mother. Her thinking is sophisticated, and she might find it painful to be honest, even to herself. However, babies see us, hear us, smell, taste and feel us. Using their senses, they really get to know us. They probably end up knowing our bodily reactions at least as well as we do. In this sense, the exchange *is* truthful.

> Someone told me you should always be honest to your baby. And it *works*. When 1B was small, he was crying, and I was smiling and trying to soothe him. I kept saying, 'It's all right. You'll be all right.' But it wasn't honest because that wasn't what I was feeling. Really, I felt *scared* because I didn't know what to do. In the end, I said, 'I'm sorry but I don't know what to do.' Because that was the truth. And guess what? Immediately he stopped crying. [1B, 4 years; 2B, 7 months]

Being truthful helps a mother to feel relaxed with her baby. For a mother who discovers this, it can be astonishing. She may never have been intimate with someone to this extent before.

Intimacy becomes more complex as children grow and can manage more subtle communications. Even experienced adults don't find intimacy easy. It depends on understanding one another's signals. Which of us has learned infallible understanding? Surely even our closest relationships are littered with mistakes and misunderstandings. Which of us has not had a moment of silence misread as coldness or disapproval? How often have we intended to communicate a simple message, but the person we were talking to decoded our message 'back to front'? Which of us has never regretted something we said, or regretted failing to say it?

People sometimes talk about intimacy as if it were an absolute, which has to be turned totally on and kept full on, like a light switch. If that is how people perceive intimacy, it is not surprising that some people say they don't like it. However, the more we examine intimate relationships, the more subtle and complex they appear. They seem to depend on our learning to use a metaphorical 'light dimmer' or 'volume control' to control the quantity of light or sound desired. Both parties discover the art of adjusting the amount of intimacy to levels which feel right for a particular moment.

For a mother, this 'volume control' means that she can have times of holding her baby while her thoughts are far away. Equally, she might be physically far away, but feel intensely connected to her baby. Many variations are possible.

Is it only the mother who can use the 'volume control'? Or do babies have any choices? At first glance, it can look as though a newborn has no choice at all. But closer study shows that even a newborn can increase or decrease the connection.

In *The Social Baby*, photographs and text show how newborns are able to reduce contact if it overwhelms them. Isabelle, for example, is one week old: 'As Liz [*an adult*] moves in, too close for Isabelle, her expression changes and Isabelle becomes more serious, she frowns and grimaces, and turns away, shutting her eyes. As Liz continues to try to engage with her, Isabelle steadfastly twists away, keeping her eyes shut.'[115]

Some mothers learn to notice and to be sensitive to signals from their babies. They back off when their babies look uncomfortable. If a mother learns to do this, it is such a subtle adaptation that neither she nor the adults around her may notice her achievement. Yet she has taken a crucial step towards helping her baby enjoy their relationship, rather than finding it overwhelming.[116]

If mother and baby get used to noticing one another's signals, they learn to understand and predict one another. They create many implicit agreements on the kind of assumption that 'I'll do this while you do that'. This makes it possible for them to live together as a synchronised 'we'. 'We do everything together,' mothers say. It doesn't mean they have both submerged their individuality. Both are very individual. But, like skilful runners in a three-legged race, they have managed to combine sufficiently to co-run in harmony. They have become a working team.

> I'm convinced that babies understand you. Once, in the early days, I was so tired, I didn't know what to do. G was crying and I said to her, 'G, I'm so tired, I can't go on any more.' And the next thing I knew was that we were both waking up because we had both together fallen asleep. [G, 2 months]

> He lets me know when things are getting too much for him and he needs my help. He turns round towards me. [B, 6 months]

> I can really read B's signals now, like one night he woke up holding his ear and I knew it meant he had toothache and needed comfort. I patted him and then he was all right. [B, 9 months]

When mother and baby start to understand one another, little moments of everyday life become a pleasure for both.

> I was expecting to love my baby. But I didn't expect that I would like her. I've just discovered that I *like* her. I like being with her.

She's fun to be with. She's already made me laugh five or six times, this morning. [G, 9 months]

We like hanging out together. This morning we took the train. G loves going by train. Then we walked in the park and went to the playground and we had such an enjoyable time. G and I 'get' each other. I 'get' her, and she obviously 'gets' me too. When we are going out, she finds my shoes and bag. She makes me laugh – and I make her laugh too. [G, 19 months]

An intimate relationship might suggest a cosy couple who are always 'at one' with one another. Yet this does not seem to be the case. Fortunately, there can be harmonious moments. But more often, even two people who know one another well have misunderstandings. Sometimes the mother simply cannot get her baby to understand what she is doing:

There's just been a few times when I've been in a hurry to get somewhere and G doesn't understand that. She wants to do her thing. So we are pulling different ways. Then we *really* fall apart. [G, 7 months]

Sometimes it takes time for a mother to work out what her teammate is complaining about.

B definitely has a boredom threshold. I used to put him in his little chair in the morning, and hurry round, getting my breakfast. But now, every time I sit down to eat it, I can see he's had enough. So now I sit him on my lap while I eat. Come to think of it, maybe that's what he *wants:* to see what I'm doing. He likes watching me eating. He seems very interested. [B, 3 months]

M: B always whines at me like this when he's tired.

Me: Do you feel told off?

M: I do, yes. I feel he's whining because he thinks I'm a crap mother for not helping him get to sleep. I feel he's angry with me. [*She was*

170

holding him to her chest to try to soothe him and bouncing him rhythmically, while he writhed against her.] But, actually, I don't think he *is* angry. Now that I think about it, I think that's what I *hear*. I hear it as anger. But maybe he's feeling something quite different. I'm sure of it, actually. [*B relaxed and nestled against her neck. M in surprise:*] He's *never* done that! [B, 7 months]

Intimacy is complex and subtle. To an onlooker, it can seem as though mother and child are having an easy time. Like a grassy field, it seems green and smooth from a distance. Only someone walking across the field can really feel the constant hollows and bumps. Usually there isn't much level ground.

At first, continuity is crucial. Mother and baby need plenty of time to be together so that their relationship can develop. If a mother is contracted to return to work early, it can make this process slower and more difficult. The fact that employers offer short-leave contracts indicates how *little* this relationship is understood and valued.

The 'team' element needs to be respected. Mother and baby are learning to trust and communicate with one another. They have begun to discover what to expect from each other. It's easy for other people to make suggestions which ignore how many intimate signals have already been 'agreed on' between the two. Typically, a well-meaning person turns up to 'give you a break from your baby', without stopping to check whether the mother actually wants this. Not all mothers do.

My mother-in-law took B for a walk for two hours yesterday. B has never spent that time away from me in his whole life. But she insisted. She said, 'He'll be all right with me,' and took him. It felt a total *wrench*. I could feel it in my whole body. And I think B felt it too. She told me that B cried for half an hour. I said, 'Why didn't you bring him *back*?' She said he fell into a sound sleep after. I was very upset. I thought it was probably the sleep of despair. [B, 3 months]

Sometimes a mother miscalculates:

You don't realise how close they are to you until something happens. B was asleep, and I was wondering if I'd have time to pop out to the shop. I knew I shouldn't – but B never wakes up. So I told F and G, and then I went. F phoned me when I was five minutes away from getting back. I could hear B crying through his mobile. B has *never* cried like that, never in his entire life. I got home and B was in a terrible state. Neither F nor G could calm him. It was me he wanted. [G, 3 years; B, 6 months]

But aren't mothers grateful to have time away from their babies? Don't they feel trapped by constant babycare? Some mothers certainly describe feeling trapped. But we shouldn't assume that this is true of everyone.

I felt I needed a break, and I decided I could ask F to look after G at the weekend, and I could go maybe for a run in the park. After I'd imagined it, I decided I didn't really want to do it. I just wanted the *possibility*. That was all I wanted. [G, 3 months]

At one meeting, I brought an article by Geraldine Bell in the Observer,[117] which I thought might encourage mothers to voice their negative feelings. I read out a passage which included the words: ' . . . being with children all the time can be very boring, draining and frustrating'.

First mother: Being a mother can be boring and . . . all those things she says. But many people think that's *all* it is. That's all they see. The real story may be invisible to everyone else. Just you and your husband see it. There's all that warmth and joy that comes from having two of the loveliest children on this earth. [G, 2 years; B, 8 months]

Second mother: Yes, the biggest shock of motherhood to me was how much I loved G. If anyone had told me I would, I wouldn't have believed them. I'd have laughed and thought they were in some *fairy*land. I'm so happy with G I don't want to spend a moment without her. [G, 8 months]

First mother: Even if someone offers you babysitting, you say: 'No thanks. I thought I wanted it, but I don't *really* want an evening away from my children. Maybe in three or four years . . . '

There are many ways of loving, and this intense connection does not suit everyone. But it's more common than people seem to think. If the relationship is intimate, both mother and child may feel relaxed together and anxious apart.

I have been thinking that B has separation anxieties that he doesn't *need* to have. I'm always there. But, the other day, I was talking to someone in the park, and I looked up and I couldn't see B. He wasn't anywhere. Immediately, I felt the panic rising [*indicating her stomach*]. Where could he be? It was only for a few seconds and then I saw him. He was behind something – I think it was a tree. But it made me think, Is this how *B* feels when he can't see *me*? [B, 16 months]

A baby gets into a terrible state *because* he has an intimate relationship with his mother. At a certain stage of their relationship, he feels lost without her. But why? Why will no one else do just as well? What have mother and baby created together?

If a mother relates to her child as a person, the child feels relaxed and safe with her. Then special moments of intimacy happen between the two of them. These are unexpected times when a single moment seems to open up like a flower and spread wide. The usual everyday hurry of life seems to slow down. For me, these moments seem like wide seas of stillness, though another mother might have a similar experience in excitement and activity. Intimacy doesn't have to be any particular way.

These unexpected moments happen when mother and child are

sharing something simple. Yet it feels full of wonder. Babies and young children tend to be much more open than older people. Opportunities for particularly intimate moments seem to happen more easily with them than between two adults. Some of these moments are brief but intense. Others are a less intense side-by-side togetherness that can last for some time.

After the birth, they took B away to be cleaned, though I didn't want them to take him away, but they did it anyway. Then I could hear a baby crying. I looked at F and said, 'That's our *baby*.' I'd had a C-section, and I had a moment of doubt, just then, about whether I really wanted a baby. They brought him back and first they gave him to F. Then they put him into my arms. B was still crying. The midwife was saying it was good for C-section babies to cry. But I *couldn't* listen to him crying. I kissed the top of his head, and talked to him, and kissed him many times. He stopped crying. That's *got* to be one of my best moments. [B, 4 months]

G laughed the other day. I was sitting on a blue birth ball, with G in my arms, bouncing up and down. Then I did one very high bounce. I could hear her give a real laugh and feel her chest expand. I was all rainbows. I tried the same thing next day, but it didn't work. [G, 7 weeks]

The first time B smiled, I cried. It was months ago and one of the best days of my life. It started with his eyes first, all bright, and then travelled to his mouth and cheeks and *all* of him smiled. It was such a beautiful smile, I was thankful I was there. [B, 9 months]

On my way to our house, I waved to G because I could see her standing at a window and she waved back. Afterwards, I could see her looking very thoughtful. I asked her what she was thinking about, and she said: 'I *love* you, Mummy.' It was incredibly moving. I thought it was because she had seen me through a window from a distance. [G, 2 years; B, 5 months]

Mothers often find these moments too intimate to describe:

> But the words you use about how you feel about your children sound *mawkish*. Even when you are talking to other mothers. It's beyond words, how you really feel. [G, 21 months; B, 13 days]

Perhaps for this reason, there aren't many descriptions in print. An exception is *The Philosophical Baby.* Here, the book's author, Alison Gopnik, has tried to encapsulate motherly love. She is a developmental psychologist, and most of her book is a summary of recent research on babies' mental development. However, she is also a mother herself. Every so often, she seems to burst out of her 'researcher's voice' with impatience, because as a mother she completely understands questions that researchers find problematic.

So in her section on love, she suddenly exclaims: 'We love our children just for the particular characteristics that we couldn't possibly have anticipated – my oldest son's intensity, talent and straight-backed confidence; my middle son's brown curls, wit and intelligence; my youngest's luminous smile, warm blue eyes and sensitivity.'[118]

Then she must have read this through and felt unhappy about it. 'In fact, these lists don't capture it either – I just love *them*, not even because they are my children, but just because they are Alexei, Nicholas and Andres.' We can hear how warm this is, and from the heart. What she loves – what many mothers love – is the irreducible wonder of each child.

Why are these moments of love so important? Do they flatter our vanity? Do they give us an inflated view of the goodness of our children, and therefore, by extension, of ourselves? Or could it be that something truthful is exchanged? When we marvel at our children, are we seeing something true about each new person that is easy to lose sight of, as we struggle through the worries of daily life? When our children marvel at us, do they remind us that we, too, are unique and wonderful? How often do we think, when we read an obituary or attend a funeral: I'd no idea that person was so interesting? Our children provide these timely reminders that living people are wonderful too.

We can have wonderful moments listening to music, watching a sunrise or going for a run. But there's a mysterious energy generated by a two-person exchange, such as between parent and child. For a moment, they can really see the goodness of one another. The mother finds she can relax from looking over her shoulder to see if she is keeping pace with other mothers. Nor is she on a treadmill to improve herself and her child. She can see how the two of them are all right, now, exactly as they are. They are all that they need to be.

A mother can see that she is helping her child to develop. But he is helping her too. Each child has the potential to awaken in her something previously unknown.

I used to be a party girl. Last Saturday night, I went to a party again, the first one since G was born. I breastfed G to sleep first, and it took far longer than usual. Then I got up – and to be honest I felt like catching up on sleep, on the sofa. But I made myself go. And I had fun. But it was like looking at myself from the wrong end of a telescope. I talked about work and I drank three glasses of white wine. That's a tiny bit like I used to be. Only I'm in a new phase of my life now. I feel different, not *completely* different, but I've changed. I was *so* glad to get back to G again and my other self. [G, 3 months]

Being a mother is like shifting into another gear. My work is cerebral, and I think I live a lot in my head. But having G was like needing to use *all* my senses. When I'm with G, it's like I'm using the whole of myself. [G, 21 months]

M: I'm a singer. *Was.* I stopped when I realised that B really needed my undivided attention. It took me a while to get used to it. It was strange, getting used to having no affirmation at the end of a concert – all that applause. You have to learn to do without it.

Me: How did you manage?

M [*Sudden smile*]: You realise you don't need it. [B, 4 years; G, 4 months]

The relationship is in continual flux. Intimacy with a baby is closest at the beginning. The baby, after all, began life *inside* his mother's body. Slowly the two grow more apart.

For the first three or four months, mothers instinctively tend to hold their babies to face themselves. After that time, they often turn their babies to face outwards so that the babies can study other people. Later, babies learn to crawl, and can move away from their mothers at will. Mothers discover a less physical, but still intimate, connection which continues between them.

G used to want me to hold her and cuddle her to sleep. Now I pat her chest, and she loves it. Her little hands clasp my hand. Eventually I hope my presence will be enough to reassure her for sleep, and then just the *thought* of me. [G, 9 months]

B is very independent now. He says: 'Mummy, I want to play with [*the boy next door*]. I will go down our steps and through their gate and up their steps and ring the bell. I don't want you to come with me. You are *not* to say you will come in for a cup of tea.' [B, 4 years; G, 3 months]

When children are ready to enjoy being with their peers, mothers can see a new development.

First mother: When another child cries at G's nursery, G is always the first to put her arm round the child and say, 'It's all right. Don't cry. G is here. You'll be all right.' [G, 2 years; B, 2 months]

Second mother: G is exactly the same: 'Don't cry. I'll help you. You'll be all right.' [G, 4 years]

As they grow older, children can extend the intimacy that they have known at home to their friends at school. And children who have known intimacy at home choose their friends carefully. They are not intimate with everyone. Often, this makes life a lot harder. These are the children who care deeply about their friends, stand up for them, demand fairness and justice, and refuse to compromise. A mother might compare her furious child to another easygoing one and think she has brought her child up 'wrong'. However, most children grow strong from learning to stand their ground and insisting on being heard. They are learning how to be loyal friends.

Children develop in physical growth spurts. Mothers report similar 'spurts' of growth in independence too.

G and I are very in tune. We weren't, a few weeks ago. She kept crying and nothing I was doing seemed to help. It seems to go in cycles because now we are in harmony again. But what I want to know is: is she able to communicate more clearly what she wants? Or have *we* got better at understanding her? I have to answer: both. It just takes time. I'll have to hang on to that knowledge so I can use it for next time. [G, 14 months]

Older children seem to value time when they can be close to their mothers again. This might sound obvious. However, I used to be puzzled to hear how often mothers would tell me that they couldn't get their small children to sleep in the evenings. So I started asking mothers what their children were doing.

First mother: If B doesn't want to go to sleep, he *won't*. He keeps on talking to me and using all his new words. [B, 12 months]

178

Second mother: G loves talking too. She doesn't like going to bed. She doesn't like being by herself, so I lie beside her, and sometimes I fall asleep before she does. One evening, I could hear her talking away, and then I could feel her wrapping a cover over me and tucking me in! [G, 4 years]

When I put G to bed, she has her story, and then a song, and then she loves talking. Lately, she's been asking about the meaning of words of a song, which I can't usually answer. I've never *thought* about the words. I've been thinking about these conversations, and I think they are the only time in the whole day when G has my undivided attention. During the day, I've noticed how patient she is. It helps to see this time as important to her – otherwise I might just dismiss it as procrastinating. [G, 3 years; B, 7 months]

One mother grumbled that she could never have a private bath any more because her daughters, both of primary-school age, would immediately walk into the bathroom and start talking to her. Her words evoked memories from several mothers at that meeting:

I used to *love* talking to my mum in the bath.

I would always come in and talk to *my* mum when she was having a bath.

It's intimate then; she's naked, and it seems such a special time.

It sounds as though having intimate time to talk to his mother is very precious for a child.

Once a mother and baby have become intimate, is their relationship established for a lifetime? Or can it be turned on and off at will, by either of them? This is a complex question. I think that true intimacy must be lifelong, and is not reversible, though most children want to grow up and establish a distance which feels comfortable. It might seem strange, then, that the mother of an older child often finds it hard to remember the baby he once was. One mother reflected:

> I think that forgetting how your children were as babies could be nature's way of separation. I mean, especially with boys, you are *so* intimate. You don't want to be thinking, I used to wash your genitals; I used to wash your bum. They need to be separate from all that. [G, 2 years; B, 6 months]

Yet the earlier intimacy seems to be renewable when mother and child need it. The understanding between them is usually important to both, and typically resurfaces very strongly in a crisis.

It is possible for a mother to betray the intimacy. To describe this, I find it helpful to use two terms coined by Martin Buber, the existential philosopher. He distinguished 'I–you relationships' from 'I–it' ones. We all, he said, use both ways of relating to one another. However, he believed that a newborn connects to his mother from the start as an intimate 'you'.[119]

The 'I–it' relationship is when one person relates to another for their usefulness, rather than as an equal person. Buber had to invent these terms, and I think they can be helpful to identify how mothers relate.

For example, a mother may relate intimately to her small child. Then a friend telephones and she adopts an intimate tone to her friend. As she talks, she tells a funny anecdote about her child, in which she and her friend are united as sensible people, while her child becomes an irrational 'he' who does comical things in the manner of an 'it'. This can relieve tension, and it can be a tonic to share a laugh. But even a small child can sense changes in his mother's tone of voice. If his mother changes tone in this way frequently, he might find the change disturbing.

A second common example of this kind of switch is when a

mother is finding it hard to reconcile the love she feels for her child with her outrage when he does something that she thinks is wrong. She may usually relate to her baby as a lovable 'you'. But when she is angry, though she addresses him as 'you', her tone of voice suggests that he is an 'it', an alien creature for whom she has lost sympathy. Again, her child may be startled by this somewhat inconsistent 'you'.

Perhaps the odd occasion helps the mother more than it upsets her baby. However, impressionable babies grow up. If they have become used to this change in relating, they will eventually be in a position to use it themselves.

A more extreme situation is the sexual seduction of children. However, the 'I–it' distinction gives us a helpful way of clarifying it briefly. Intimacy is often associated with sex. However, that would be between two consenting adults. It's different if a parent invites a child to have a sexual relationship. Even if the child seems willing, the invitation is primarily for the parent's pleasure. The child is, in other words, for the parent's use. The child has therefore become a tool, an 'it', instead of a 'you'. This cannot be true intimacy.

The situation may have been set up in a way to confuse the child. An adult might seduce a child into a sexual relationship with the semblance of an 'I–you' dialogue. The child might feel as if he were being treated as a special 'you'. But in no way can this be called true reciprocal-love intimacy.

Some relationships run into difficulties. The two most obvious ways are for mothers to relate either too remotely or too intrusively to their children. Of course, it is only too easy for *all* of us to do both. However, babies usually signal their reactions when we do. There is then an opportunity to adjust. In any case, some imperfections on the mother's side don't seem to result in disaster. There must be a wide 'error margin'. The relationship goes awry when a mother *continually* overrides the signals from her baby.

A mother at the 'distant' extreme keeps herself apart from her baby, even when they are together, usually by being very busy. It can leave the baby with a sense of infinite longing for more connection, and also feeling unimportant and burdensome.

> My mother was *not* maternal. She used to say she wished she'd never had children. [B, 6 weeks]

> My mum was at school when I came along. She had me as an act of defiance. After I was born, I was taken away from her. I don't know who brought me up for my first six months. It's never talked about. At six months, she took me back. But the bond never really happened between us. And I'm thinking, *Six months!* That's six months of conversation she's missed, six months of getting to know me. I've learned so much about G. I know who she is. My mum never had that. [G, 4 months]

> Mum was always deep in a book. There were five of us, and we always used to say that you'd have to put a *bomb* under her to get any attention. [G, 7 months]

At the other extreme are mothers who are afraid of seeming too remote. Often, they set themselves the task of being completely available for their children. This can turn into a rigid ideal. They don't observe signals from their babies that would tell them when their babies have had enough. Probably their babies soon stop trying to give them. Instead, mothers exhaust themselves, and typical statements are: 'By the end of the day, I've nothing to give any more,' 'I'm drained dry,' 'I need a break.' A mother in this position may be wracked with guilt that she is not doing enough. In reality, she and her child would both prefer less interaction, but her 'idea' is that this would mean she had failed to be a good mother. One mother burst out:

> *M*: I hate it, hate it, hate it. I hate it from the moment I wake up

in the morning to the moment I go to sleep at night. I used to have a *life*. I had so many interests before I had G. I love going to the theatre. I'm a theatre junkie, an addict. I used to love looking at my watch at four in the afternoon and deciding which play I'd go to that evening. I'd ring up, book it and go. I'd love it. I haven't been to anything for nineteen months.

Me: What is the 'it' that you hate?

M: Motherhood. It's blasphemy to say that, isn't it? But there's no mind-space for oneself. I've got to entertain G and think of things to do *all* day. It's so boring. I look at my watch and think, Three more hours till it's time for bed.

Me: I notice you say you hate 'it', but you don't say you hate G.

M: I don't. I love G. But it can be hard to keep them separate. [G, 19 months]

In a theatre, we can sit back and watch the dramas of other people. It sounded to me as though this mother felt she had to be too intensely face to face with her child, and longed for more distance, like a member of an audience in a theatre. I was impressed at her commitment to persevere, even though she said she hated it. But I also wondered whether she was giving herself and her daughter an uncomfortably close relationship.

Some mothers seek a tight closeness in a kind of denial that their children have separate identities. Virginia Woolf gave a very perceptive example of her mother's relationship to her step-sister, Stella: 'They were like sun and moon to each other; my mother the positive and definite; Stella the reflecting and satellite.'[120] She went on to give precise details. I have not read anywhere else such a sensitive description of a terrifying kind of closeness.

The two most frequent fears that adults voice about forming

intimate adult relationships are either that they will be abandoned or that they will be overwhelmed. This seems to correspond to the two ways in which mothers can relate insensitively to their babies, either by seeming withdrawn and remote when they are together, or else by being too close and overpowering. When adults say how much they fear to start a new intimacy, they often sound as if they are describing experiences they have already had.

Babies who have had unhappy relationships with their mothers usually hunger to find love and to form loving relationships as adults. But once someone has been hurt in this tender spot, it can be difficult not to expect to be hurt again.

Is there, then, a recipe for a good relationship that will avoid these two extremes? This might sound a reasonable question, but there doesn't seem to be a universal recipe which has the answers. As we can see, it's not that 'anything goes'. Some relationships are definitely abusive. It's more that good relationships are individual. I have heard mothers torment themselves with 'wishing I could get it right', or sobbing, 'I know I've done it all wrong'. But usually, so it seems to me, these mothers have created good relationships, which have simply reached a difficult phase.

If a mother hasn't established a close relationship at the start, is there anything she can do years later, if she wants to make up for it? There must be all kinds of possibilities. My discussion groups are for mothers of younger children, so I haven't got information on this. It would be interesting to hear what mothers have done.

How do children develop intimacy if their mothers died young? These children often seem acutely aware of how much they have missed. One woman, writing in the *Guardian*, described how she had tried to find out who her parents were, but no research unearthed any record. All she knew was that her mother had left her to be brought up by the elderly midwife who had delivered her. The midwife led an isolated life and the little girl 'grew up in an almost silent house – no voices, no laughter'. In her late seventies, she explained how the lack of a mother had affected her and 'added to the uneasy sense I sometimes feel of only brushing past this earth.'[121]

' . . . only brushing past this earth.' This is how she felt to have grown up without knowing her mother, or even having an intimate relationship with the elderly midwife who looked after her. It is easy to overlook how important *having* an intimate relationship is, in itself, even if it wasn't ideal. That early intimate closeness seems to be crucial. It teaches us that we matter, that our mother has some stake in us, and therefore we feel grounded or rooted in life, and are not 'brushing past'.

Usually, there are more adults available for a child. Even if the mother is not present, the longing for the special kind of intimacy that mothers give is so strong that a child will seek out at least one other person, perhaps a grandmother, aunt, neighbour or schoolteacher, to get some experience of it. Some fathers find they can relate with mother-like tenderness when the mother is not available. Perhaps children don't always find as much as they want, but it must be virtually impossible to experience none at all.

Even so, not everyone enjoys intimate relationships. They can seem too *intimate*. No one has described the 'problem' of mother–baby intimacy better than Aldous Huxley. *Brave New World* was published in 1932, and has turned out to have been brilliantly prophetic. Huxley himself lived long enough to discover just how much of his futuristic world vision had actually been realised. One catchphrase in Huxley's future world was: 'Everyone belongs to everyone else.' Family intimacy had become obsolete. Babies were conceived in test tubes and brought up in nurseries with their peers.

But there was a Controller, one of the ten World Controllers, who knew the history of the 'bad' old days when children were brought up by mothers. This Controller recounted some long-ago 'world history' to a group of students:

> What suffocating intimacies, what dangerous, insane, obscene rela-
> tionships between the members of the family group! Maniacally,
> the mother brooded over her children (*her* children) . . . 'My baby,
> and oh, oh, at my breast, the little hands, the hunger, and that
> unspeakable agonising pleasure! Till at last my baby sleeps, my baby
> sleeps with a bubble of white milk at the corner of his mouth. My
> little baby sleeps.' 'Yes,' said [*the Controller to his horrified students*],
> 'you may well shudder.'[122]

Huxley rightly saw that, in order to create impersonal relation-ships in which 'everyone belongs to everyone else', one would have to start with babies. Mothers, he saw, provided the intimacy of love, which helped their children to form personal relationships later on. Impersonal care prepares a child for less intimate, less demanding, more work-orientated relationships.

Today, Huxley would surely recognise, not just the increase in peer-group childcare available today for young babies and small children, but the increasing ideology that has developed with it. Professional care is sometimes described as superior to maternal care. ' . . . daycare . . . can teach your infant or toddler lessons about co-operation, independence, self-sufficiency, and even friendship he wouldn't learn were he at home with you.'[123]

What happens to a child who is cared for by several people, but doesn't develop a close relationship with any of them? From what I have seen, these children often seem to grow into sociable and easy-going adults. They can negotiate awkward social situations without fuss. They don't complain easily. They often look for pleasure in material things, because material pleasures seem so much more dependable than people. They are competent and seem good at having fun and enjoying themselves.

As children, they don't seem to have the social problems of

fitting in and submerging their individuality, as more mothered children so often do. They are able to share and to compromise. They seem happy and well adjusted. Seen like this, their upbringing has been successful. In contrast, it looks as though children who *have* received intimate mothering are at a disadvantage, because they are less good at fitting in.

But are they? What happens when a minimally mothered adult wants to form an intimate relationship? Only here do the problems really show up. A person who has spent his childhood learning how to adapt to other people and to avoid being a trouble might not know how to manage closeness to another person. Closeness is not synonymous with fitting in. To be close, and yet different, to connect together and yet respect one another's individuality, is a special art that mothers teach by doing. It must be terrifying to feel deeply attracted to another person, but to have very little experience of that whole dimension of relating.

Research surveys reveal how widespread this must be. About half the households in Britain today comprise people who live alone. Many of them claim that this is a positive choice. It's only by listening to, or reading, what they say that one learns that the positive reason often has a negative side to it. Frequently, the solitary person has wanted and tried to live with a partner. But then the two found that each confirmed the other's worst fears of a bad relationship. They felt safer breaking up than staying together. They describe this as being liberated from the disappointment of relationships and, in that sense, they feel positive about living alone.

Because so many now choose to live alone, it suggests that there might be a widespread shortage of mothers who have enabled their children to relate intimately. Many mothers are returning to work early (though not always by choice), which makes intimate relationships much more difficult to sustain. Fortunately, mothers who have started relating intimately to their children usually manage to continue, despite the exhaustion of combining employment with mothering.

Perhaps though, the real reason for the larger national trend is simple. Many mothers may be returning to work early *because* they do not see an important role for themselves at home. They are not literally failing at intimate relationships. Rather, too many of them never thought that relationships were an integral part of their motherly work.

CHAPTER ELEVEN

Turning into parents

What happens to the couple relationship when a new mother starts to get to know her baby intimately? Up till then, most couple relationships are based on intimacy between two. Now they are three. Can the intimacy of the couple survive the change?

Many couples say they go through some bumpy times as they adjust to their babies. A baby needs a lot of attention and it's often the mother who gives most of it. At first the intimate couple twosome can seem eclipsed.[124] Some relationships founder soon after the birth, and the couple decide to split up. Some mothers become single parents. Others find second partners, and form blended families. Some mothers are in lesbian relationships.

However, in this chapter, I want to focus on heterosexual couples who stay together. It is important to understand how a couple of two turns into a family of three. The couple intimacy, which might have felt very close and tender when they were two, changes its shape after a baby is born. Mothers describe some stormy challenges and problems. Yet, below the surface of their difficulties, their love for their partners continues to develop and mature. Some couples have children from earlier relationships. However, questions that arise from complex families would require much more space.

When a couple learn that they have conceived, there is a change which can feel like a separation of ways. The couple are 'expecting a baby', but they expect it differently. A woman has usually imagined having a baby, from her girlhood on. The great changes of conception and growth happen within her body. The father's role, at this stage, is peripheral. Before the birth, the coming baby can seem very much 'about her'. There might also be crucial decisions about the birth itself which require the mother's legal consent, in consultation with her delivery doctor.

A father's involvement during pregnancy is voluntary. He doesn't even need to be present at the delivery of his child. When mothers were routinely anaesthetised for the second stage of labour, birth would turn into a medical procedure from which fathers were excluded. Since the spread of the natural childbirth movement, many mothers are conscious and active during the whole birth. It has become an event at which fathers have discovered that they can have an important role.

If a father is present, it can become an intimate experience for both partners. Though part of the birth must seem unimaginable to his man's body, he can draw emotionally close to his partner. Suddenly, they can both see the momentous consequence of their lovemaking. A private act of theirs has resulted in a completely new life. When the baby is the result of artificial insemination, they can experience the birth as the moment of realisation of both their hopes. For every father, birth has the potential to be an incredible, special moment.[125]

After the birth, the newborn is usually placed in his mother's arms. Most people recognise that a mother has a passionate need to hold her baby. But, if the birth was intimate, don't a father's arms ache for his baby too? After all, this is his very first opportunity to enjoy direct contact. Often, however, if birth was in hospital, practical pressures can intrude on the early hours of the new family. Hospitals are short of space, and usually only mothers are given beds.

> After the birth, F held the baby while I was cleaned up. Then the baby was put into my arms. At some stage, F was told to go home [*from the hospital for the night*]. He told me that as soon as he got home he started having doubts and thinking, Oh dear; I don't think I love B enough. But when he got back to us next morning and he could *hold* B again and see him, he said that feeling went. [B, 4 months]

It sounds as though having an opportunity for physical contact with his newborn is important for a father. Because of his biology, he is a step behind the mother at this stage, in getting to know their baby. Obviously, men don't all feel the same. But it sounds as though many couples need time to stay together to cherish their baby, especially after the intense intimacy of childbirth.

Back home, life has changed for both of them. If the mother is breastfeeding, she may sit for hours with their baby at her breast. The father may feel a warm, glowing pleasure at the sight of them.

> F likes to watch me breastfeeding G. I think he finds it beautiful. [G, 8 weeks]

The father can feel included in the early intimacy of his partner and baby, and strongly protective of them. He may be glad to give practical support, which is remembered gratefully, years after.

> When F came home, I'd tell him: 'I'm *starving*.' I'd have been breastfeeding G it seemed like all day. He'd be right at my side, holding a sandwich to my mouth. [G, 22 months]

However, not all fathers feel so positive. Mothers, whether they are breastfeeding or formula-feeding, usually do most of the babycare. So some fathers feel there is a mother–baby dyad from which they are excluded. There seem to be endless broken nights, with mothers absorbed by their babies. At first, especially at night, these fathers say they feel they have lost a wife more than gained a child.

Before the baby's birth, most men receive some mothering from their partners. But once women become mothers, this mothering is withdrawn from the adult partners and focused on the needy babies. So men have to adapt to much less emotional mothering.

Some fathers seem to feel in competition with their babies for attention from their partners. Listening to mothers, it sounds as though the birth can bring back hurtful boyhood experiences. Some had been abruptly displaced from closeness to their mothers by the birth of a younger sibling. A new baby can seem like a repetition of that difficult time. Some men protest, sounding more like older brothers than fathers: 'I never seem to get a turn,' or, 'The baby seems permanently plugged in,' or, 'Why can't I be your little man too?' Other men withdraw, feeling unwanted and depressed.

The whole couple relationship is now in flux. A new mother may be exhausted, and still recovering from birth, so not yet confident about making love again. But she might long for her partner to be tender to her and to affirm her in her new role as a mother. If a father is feeling tired, unsure of himself or hurt and rejected, he may overlook just how defenceless his wife feels.

This morning, I asked F if he could make me a cup of tea before he left. He said, 'If I do that, I'll be late for work.' I couldn't help it, I just burst into tears. [B, 2 weeks]

I had no idea that parenting couldn't be shared. I was so lost, looking after G at home. I kept saying to her, 'What do you *want*, G? What do you *want*?' When F went back to work, I felt like crying, '*Take me with you!*' [G, 2 months]

F can't get a visa to come here. He's in a different country. It's not his practical help I miss. I can manage all the practical things on my own. But I miss not having a second opinion. If G comes out in red spots, it's good to be able to ask, 'What do *you* think?' [G, 2 months]

A mother's long hours of babycare can increase a sense of separation between the couple. If mothers are doing twenty-four-hour babycare, they will be quicker to learn what their babies are like. They will then have an advantage, which they can use to help, or hinder, the sensitive period when the couple relationship opens out to become a family of three.

A mother can use her new understanding of their baby to bridge the gap between herself and her partner. ('Look! The baby keeps turning to face you as you walk around the room.') Or she can use her advantage to be the 'expert' on their baby and close the father out. She can transfer the intimate twosome relationship which she used to have with him on to herself and the baby. ('You're very late home. The baby's much too tired to play with you. You start your dinner, and let me get him to sleep.') This turns the father into an alien outsider. Adrienne Burgess, Head of Research at the Fatherhood Institute, comments that if couples keep repeating these roles, then 'relationships tend to get very sticky'.[126]

In traditional families, the parents had differentiated and distinct male/female roles. But today these distinctions are changing, both at work and at home. Couples may have discussed the kind of parents they hope to become. However, trivial daily situations arise that they didn't anticipate. Perhaps the mother asks her partner for some simple help, but he has no idea where the clean baby vests are – or whatever she asked him for. He thought this was 'her domain'. This infuriates her. It sounds to her as if he has placed her and the baby in a realm that has nothing to do with him.

> F works abroad during the week. He texted me to say that he kept looking at the beautiful photos of G that I'd sent him. By then, I was clearing G's poo and sick. He and I are on different . . . We are in traditional parent roles. [G, 4 months]

> F *dips* into being a father. He doesn't feel it like I do [*about being a mother*]. [B, 6 months]

At this stage, the baby may offer his mother something that her partner cannot. The baby is totally accepting of her. He knows her intimately, *literally* inside and out. He needs a lot from her, but his wishes are usually obvious and possible for her to provide. So when she gives him what he needs, as, for example, her breast milk, he pats her breast and laughs in delight (when he is old enough), and she feels he is really pleased with her. Few of us have ever experienced such an accepting love before in our lives. It can be a wonderful experience. A mother may feel close to her baby, and contrast his grateful love with the grumbles of her adult partner.

Why do new fathers often grumble? Turning into a father sounds difficult. If he is sole breadwinner, a new father may work hard for his family. He returns to his home with the expectation that now he can relax. However, many mothers lean heavily on their partners for practical and emotional support that, in traditional societies, is usually given by the mother's mother, female relatives or female neighbours. No mother was expected to care for her baby alone. Today, most female relatives, friends and neighbours are at work and, therefore, unavailable. A new father may be surprised at how much of his 'free time' is redefined by his partner as 'family time'.

> *First mother*: It's the *expectations* that are so bad. I look forward to the weekends. And then one comes, and it's just more hard work. There's no break. F doesn't do snacks and he doesn't do nappies. He doesn't even wash up. By the end, I'm really disappointed. It would be better to have more realistic expectations. [B, 2 years; B, 7 months]

> *Second mother*: But you couldn't manage without expectation, could you? You need that 'beacon light' of the weekend . . . Friday night . . . [*Groans of agreement from the rest of the circle.*] [G, 7 months]

> B brings out the best in us and the worst in us. He makes us into parents, but I never dreamed we'd argue so much, not me with F. But we're getting to the stage when we can finish arguments quicker. They're mostly because I think F isn't doing enough for B. He's *our* baby. [B, 11 months]

Listening to what mothers say, I can see that misunderstandings often arise because an employed father regards his work as structured, whereas time with his family seems an opportunity to relax. However, a mother will usually have a much more structured view of the long day with the baby. Perhaps she asks her husband to change the baby's nappy while she has a quick shower. She prepares everything that he will need, and grabs her towel. In her mind, she has made it easy for him and it's fun changing their baby's nappy. She has set up a generous deal. But the father hears her differently. He is aware that he never has enough time to enjoy his baby, and his understanding is that this is a precious chance to play while his wife showers. Yes, he knows she asked him to change a nappy, but that isn't the important thing. The post-shower conversation between them is better left unwritten.

Sometimes, it makes sense for the mother to resume work while the father becomes the chief child-carer. This is a recent development. In that case, many of the observations about parents' attitudes to leisure time and work time will be reversed.

Men in traditional roles, who may be working overtime away from home to support their families, often complain that they would like more physical affection from their partners when they return. But many mothers have been looking forward to their partners' return as a time to recover from the intensity of babycare. One good solution to what appear to be opposite needs is that the father cuddles his baby while the mother has a few moments to herself.

> My partner works very hard, and he says, 'I'm doing it for G.' But my dad used to work very hard and he never interacted with us. I want G to have a proper father. And I want F to hold her and to *enjoy* it. I want him to have more of what I'm having. [G, 4 months]

Once a father finds ways of enjoying being with his baby, the three-way family relationship starts to develop.

> G can now go to sleep when F is holding her. He *loves* it. I think it's one of the best things for a bloke. He doesn't want to let go of her and put her down. He holds on to her and says, 'I don't think she is *quite* asleep yet.' [G, 9 months]

> We have B in bed with us. F didn't like it at first. But now he's developed his own relationship with B, and he loves it. I had my knees up in bed, one night. Suddenly I could feel F giving my knees this *wonderful*, soft stroke, and he whispered to me: 'M, I think B is sitting up, under the bedclothes.' [B, 10 months]

Not all fathers enjoy this. However, one group of mothers thought that, although the fathers said they wanted more sex, they might be underestimating their (fathers') own need to cuddle their babies.

First mother: F keeps saying he wants time for just the two of us. Whereas I think it would be nice, but I don't feel I need it like he does. [B, 4 years; G, 10 months]

Second mother: F would like more time with me. He says he really misses it. So I'm trying to fit it in. [B, 13 months]

Third mother: G comes first on my list, then B, and then F. F definitely comes last. I wonder why that is. F would like sex but, as far as I'm concerned [*laughing ruefully*], sex is just one more thing to do before I can crash out in sleep. [B, 3 years; G, 11 months]

Fourth mother: Do you think we get more *cuddling* than men do? I'm always cuddling G. I get my cuddling needs met. Then, when F comes home, I want to get away and be alone, whereas *he* wants to be close and cuddly. [G, 11 months]

[*The other mothers said they found this a helpful observation.*]

This is interesting. If new fathers feel excluded from the mother/baby duo, and if they also have too little opportunity to cuddle either of them, this might explain why some new fathers tell their partners that the early months feel lonely and bleak.

However, some men seem to feel guilty for *wanting* to cuddle their babies.

First mother: F doesn't want me to keep picking G up when she cries. He wants her to learn independence. But I've seen *him* picking up G and rocking her when she cries. I think he has a conflict about it. [B, 3 years; G, 4 weeks]

Second mother: F is the same. He keeps saying we should leave B to cry it out, so that he'll learn to sleep through the night. But the other day, B cried and F picked him up right away. He said: 'I'm being a real softie.' [B, 9 months]

It would be interesting to learn from men whether many of them feel awkward about holding and cuddling their babies. Does this make it harder for them to feel that they belong to the family?

Employed work is paid, so has obvious value. Parenting is unpaid, and can seem to have less value. It's easy for tired parents to undervalue one another's parenting. Some mothers report that their partners protest that maternity leave goes on for too long, and that mothers should resume earning sooner. Mothers, in turn, complain that fathers don't give practical help unless it is demanded of them.

There has been some research to show how appreciative new mothers are when their partners wash and clean for them.[127] So it's interesting to hear that practical help isn't all that mothers want. This is not to say the washing up doesn't matter. However, the contribution that mothers really value may sound like nothing at all. Yet mothers feel very moved when partners give it:

> You lose all your sense of perspective as a mother. There's nowhere to step back to. When things were hard with B, and I couldn't understand him, I just wanted to *die*. But F comes home in the evening and he says, 'You've been having a bad day.' For me, it was just going on for ever. [B, 3 months]

> My mum stayed with me for two weeks. After she left, I just fell apart. I was so depressed. I was phoning my husband at work and saying, 'You've *got* to come home. I can't *cope*.' I thought he'd come rushing back. I was surprised that he said, 'Come on, M. You can get through this. I know you can.' He was really supportive to me. [B, 3 months]

> In *our* house, mothers are important. Everyone knows that F is earning the money, but *I've* got the important job. F says he wouldn't

be able to concentrate at work for a *moment* if he didn't feel confident about me. [B, 4 years; G, 12 months]

It may sound like nothing, but it surely isn't. Mothers say it makes all the difference to know that their partners truly believe in them.

Mothers often long to give support in return. Almost certainly, this was part of their role in the earlier couple relationship. But, once a baby is born, he needs a great deal of his mother's energy.

F's father had a heart attack – at least, we *think* it was – we all *rushed* to the hospital. And he seemed fine. He was sitting up in bed. Thankfully the prognosis is good. But I've just realised . . . [*Her hands rushed up to cover her face, and she burst into sobs.*] I'm sorry. I didn't realise I felt so strongly. I'm feeling so *sorry* for F. There's never time to talk. F looks after B, or I do. I've asked F how he is, but I don't *know* how he is. I'm sure he feels it. [B, 6 months]

When F comes home in the evening, I get ratty. If I'm honest, it's because I'm trying to listen to what he is telling me, but G needs my full attention at the same time. [G, 20 months]

These are genuine concerns. They show that mothers may want to give their partners much more loving attention than they can manage with their small babies. Also, a moment's thought tells them that their partners aren't having a much easier time, even though they do less babycare.

I'm envious when F goes off to work. But work's not Nirvana when you get there. It's only when you *can't* work that you think it is. And F often feels he's missing out on seeing enough of the kids. [*All the mothers listening to her agreed that their husbands felt they were missing their babies and children by going out to work.*] [G, 4 years; B, 2 years; G, 3 months]

There's a popular idea that women should nurture the couple relationship.[128] So many mothers feel duty-bound to organise special couple time.

Everyone said I should make time to go out with my husband. So I did. And it was nice. But I wasn't relaxed. I noticed my shoulders were tense and I was holding my breath. Quite honestly, I don't think it was worth the effort. We've got a small balcony that looks over the park. We could put our candles and glasses of wine on it. I could relax then [*because G would be near*]. [G, 3 months]

By the end of the day, I'm *so* tired. But F says he misses me and I feel sad about that. So sometimes we watch a DVD together. But *all* the time I'm watching it, I'm calculating inside myself how much less sleep I'm going to have. [G, 4 months]

I hate to say it, but it was easier when F *wasn't* there. Now I can't go to bed in the evening when I'm tired because I feel I should talk to my husband. [G, 10 months]

Don't mothers have any romantic feelings left? Listening to them, it sounds as if small, spontaneous reminders of their romantic warmth work much better than dutiful efforts.

The other day, we were all shopping and I saw a couple in a café, looking as if they had all the time in the world. They had time to enjoy their tea. No sense of rush. I pointed them out to F: 'See them? Do you remember? *We* used to be like that.' [B, 2 years; B, 3 months]

I *don't* think, when you've got children, you need to go out without them. I know there're many people who embrace the opposite school of thought. But I don't agree. F and I went out with just 3B in a backpack, and we went into town, and it was, '*Hey!*' We felt just as romantic as when we only had our first child. [1B, 6 years; 2B, 4 years; 3B, 4 months]

F and I went out together while my sister looked after B. It was just round the corner to get a curry, but we *held hands* all the way there. It was the first time I'd been out without B for fourteen months. And we talked about B the whole time. B – and F's work. [B, 14 months]

Some people regard parental conflict as inevitable. Surely, they say, the present situation is unfair. Isn't the solution to divide childcare, so that fathers do more? Wouldn't it help if babycare were equally shared, divided fifty–fifty down the middle, between both parents? This idea was taken up by Amy and Marc Vachon in Boston who run an organisation called Equally Shared Parenting.[129] British mothers may not have heard of it, but they are aware of the idea. They may like the idea of equal sharing. So it is very interesting to hear that, when mothers praise parental equality, they usually add that, on reflection, they would feel insulted to be treated as equals with their partners.

I think men are taught now that they should come home from work and do fifty per cent of the childcare. My partner really wants to. But he can't just rush home and slot in. He's got to *ask* me. Oh, I dunno. Maybe I'm not being fair. But I've been with B all day, and I really know what he wants. [B, 3 months]

My husband says he's got to be allowed to make his own mistakes. He says: 'I want to be your *partner*, not your helper.' But I don't want G to get upset from his mistakes, and I know what she needs by now. I don't want to hurt his feelings – but I'd definitely prefer him to be just a helper. [G, 3 months]

I don't want to put F to shame. But sometimes I want to tell him not to hold B as he does. So I say it. Then F says, 'You're always telling me what to do. Then, just when I'm using my own initiative, you criticise me for it.' He's right. Maybe I'm being unreasonable – but I'd like to have some *respect*. After all, I'm the one who looks after B most, and I know what B likes. [G, 2 years; B, 3 months]

These comments are significant. Mothers certainly start by feeling lost and helpless. But slowly, even though they continue to say how hard it is, they do start to make discoveries about their babies. This must be confusing for fathers. They may be expecting a more equal division of babycare. If a mother doesn't make clear that, despite her disclaimers, she doesn't feel like a total beginner any more, her partner might not realise how much she has learned. Perhaps fathers are not expecting to see how capable their partners have quietly become.

First mother: My partner is always saying that I make too much fuss. It *enrages* me. It really gets to me. Like when *he* looks after G, he says it's all pretty normal and straightforward. [G, 4 months]

Second mother: My partner says that too. He keeps saying that looking after G is perfectly simple when he does it. But what he doesn't seem to understand is that that's because I've organised it so *well*. There's all that work that he calls 'fussing' which has gone into it beforehand. [G, 6 months]

I've got it all worked out so that everything around me is in its right place. There's a folded muslin towel by the changing table, and a dummy just at the right angle. It's my whole system. I don't know how to explain. But when F has been looking after B for a few hours, everything is scattered, and I think, *Oh*! It's not that F is doing anything deliberately wrong. It's just that he doesn't realise. But if I explained it to him he'd think it was all so petty. [B, 6 months]

But how petty is it? One mother used a revealing image to explain:

M: My husband looked after the older ones when 3B was born.

202

Me: Was that nice?

M: Well . . . it was a bit annoying as well.

Me: Did he do things differently from you?

M: He didn't know my system. Like a temp changing everything on your desk. [1B, 6 years; 2B, 4 years; 3B, 6 weeks]

The office desk is now a respected image in people's thinking. If a temporary worker sat at someone else's desk in their office, they would be expected to tidy everything and leave the desk as they'd found it. The desk arrangement would be treated with respect. Why should a mother's system be any different?

Something new seems to have arisen. I have noticed that mothers do not apologise so frequently for being 'only a mother' as they did when I started Mothers Talking in the early 1990s. It seems that women now expect to become competent at work. So this gives them a certain standard when they become mothers. They take pride in learning to become good at being mothers too.

If I ask for help and I'm too apologetic, F will say, 'Sorry, I haven't got time.' So now I say, 'I'm going to have a shower. Here's B. Have fun.' And he's fine about it. [G, 2 years; B, 6 months]

I've gradually turned F into part of the family. For example, I don't keep saying 'Thank you' when he does something for G. And if he tells me he's done something as if it's a favour, I say: 'Well you're only G's *father*.' Luckily we both share the same sense of humour. So now we work well together as a team. But I had to *work* for it. [G, 8 months]

I think women today are prepared to stand up to men. My mum didn't. If my dad asked her to do something, she'd do it. I don't think men today realise what's hit them. If B and I are awake at night, and F says he can't sleep, it's not *B and I* who have to get out of bed. I just tell F to sleep in a different room. [B, 18 months]

But perhaps not everything has changed.

First mother: As soon as F gets home, I start apologising: 'Oh, I'm so *sorry*, I haven't had time to do this and that.' And he says, 'Stop putting words into my mouth! That's you. *I* haven't said anything.' [G, 3 years; B, 3 months]

Second mother: I say it too. 'I'm so *sorry* . . . ' [G, 6 months]

Third mother: I'm exactly the same: 'Oh, I'm *so* sorry . . . ' [B, 22 months; G, 4 months]

Despite all the talk about parenting being fifty–fifty, mothers may have created very sensitive relationships with their babies. This is a real achievement. A mother can easily feel hurt if her partner overlooks all the work she has done. At the same time, there has also been a change in the role of fathers. Traditional fathers used to leave their small children in the care of mothers or nurses. Children learned their first lessons 'with their mother's milk' and 'at their mother's knee'. Traditional fathers became involved as their children grew. But today, fathers are starting to share *babycare*. There is obvious potential here for confusion over how much a father should do.

Problems often arise when the couple make assumptions about what the other one 'really wants'. Typically, the mother feels she is nobly protecting her partner by doing all the main babycare herself. In a reciprocal way, the father feels he is being generous by standing back and letting her take all the parenting decisions. But neither has asked the other's agreement to these self-allocated roles. So instead of each being grateful to the other for being so thoughtful, each feels irritated because they can't understand the logic of one another's actions.

It can be tough. F and I feel ourselves disconnect, and then it's easy to think F is just doing things to annoy me. What helps is for us to talk. We have a rule that if one of us says, 'I don't like it when you . . .' and adds whatever the annoying thing is, then the other one is *not* allowed to say, 'Well, *I* get annoyed with *you* sometimes.' That may be important too. But it's a separate point. First we give enough time to the first person's point. [G, 9 months]

When both parents feel tired and uncertain, instead of supporting one another, both sometimes try to feel better by demoralising the other one, in a kind of competition to be the better parent. Having a baby can feel such a responsibility that as soon as something goes wrong (as it's bound to), both parents feel at fault. Rather than admit it though, each tries to find a way to blame the other one.

First mother: If G falls and hurts herself when I'm looking after her, I feel especially upset that it happened on my watch. F and I are a bit competitive about our parenting. He'll say, 'Why did you let it happen?' [G, 8 months]

Second mother: In that case, just wait until your daughter has a fall when you are both there. F and I were both with G visiting a friend, and she was on the garden step. We were joking that she could fall off it, when suddenly she did. I was quicker and stopped her from hitting her head on the ground. Then F and I looked at one another, and realisation dawned: 'I can't blame *you* . . .' [G, 13 months]

An unpleasant extension of this kind of blaming is when one parent tries to turn the family into two 'teams' of competing sides. This kind of conflict can go on for generations.

First mother: My husband is always in competition with me. He wants to be the better *mother*! [G, 5 months]

Second mother: Your husband sounds a bit like my dad. He was in

205

that kind of relationship with my mum. He still *is*, though he's old now and ill. I wish he wouldn't. If only he'd stop. [B, 5 months]

Me: Has it worked? Has it made you love him more than your mother?

Second mother: No, definitely not.

I was my father's favourite. I didn't like it. I felt 'wrong'. It was too heavy for me. Much too heavy. [G, 3 years; B, 5 months]

It sounds as though competing to be the favourite parent is a very unfair way to involve a child. Babies especially seem generous in their love for both parents.

In the world of work, the separate roles of women and men have become interchangeable. Why shouldn't it be the same with parenting? One broad answer is that most mothers bear their own babies, and some go on to breastfeed them. This seems to give mothers the possibility of a more tactile and tender intimacy with their babies than the more vigorous style that many fathers create.

I can see G start to fidget in her chair and I can tell that she's beginning to have had enough of sitting there. She'd prefer to be lifted up and in someone's arms. But F thinks I'm making too much fuss. G would have to up her distress levels before he would pay her attention. [G, 3 months]

The other day, G was in her high chair, F was feeding her soup and talking to his brother-in-law. He turned to face him and I could see him getting interested in the conversation, just when G had her mouth open for more soup. And I thought, Can't you wait ten minutes and talk to him after? *Please* give G her soup! I think he thinks she can wait for as long as he can. [G, 21 months; B, 13 days]

However, it's easy to judge fathers by maternal benchmarks. Many parents were themselves brought up by their mothers, while their fathers gave little practical help. It can take time for both of them to recognise that fathers can discover their personal *fatherly* ways to relate to their babies.

When G was a baby, I used to feel I had to do everything for her myself. I treated F as second class. I never said anything, but of course he knew my feelings. But then I hit the wall of my limits, and I couldn't give any more. F said, 'Let me take her. She'll be all right with me.' He's a film-maker, and one day he said to me: 'I want you to see that G can be happy when I'm looking after her.' So he filmed her, crawling from room to room, very happy and smiling at the camera. He had taken her to an art exhibition, and I could see that she was *really* happy with him. I was *very* glad he'd made that film. [G, 3 years; B, 3 months]

When B wakes in the night, I try not to feed him if I know he's not hungry. But it's no good. He just *abseils* down to my breasts. Last week, I had a fever, and one night F said, 'Let me take him.' So I handed B over and F took him upstairs. He closed the door, and I could hear B crying. I was upset, so I texted F: 'Bring him down?' And he texted back: 'No.' After half an hour, B fell asleep. Next night, F took him and B fell asleep in one minute. Now F and B have really bonded, and it's lovely. [B, 7 months]

I feed B to sleep in the evenings, and F has G. Sometimes I can hear her crying, 'I want to see my mummy. I need my mummy.' By the time I've got B to sleep, I'm *dying* to cuddle her. But I can hear F with her, and he's settling her very well. If I go in, I'll disturb them. Besides, it's *his* cuddle. He's done all the work to deserve it. [G, 2 years; B, 5 months]

Men themselves seem surprised to find how much they welcome fatherly involvement. They may be tired, but they do not seem to want their partners to protect them, as if they were small boys. What men seem to value is to be regarded as essential fathers.

I was so tired, I said to F, 'Can you take G?' So he did, and I went straight to bed and slept as much as I needed to. F was nervous at first, but he enjoyed it. He told me after, 'You can really do things with G now. She's interested in everything.' [G, 7 months]

I was having a terrible time with F. B was waking every two hours at night, and F wanted me to sleep-train him. Then he read a book written by a father which listed twenty-three points that a father could be doing for his child. F won't usually read a book, but reading a *list* appealed to something male in him. He was like, 'Do I only do *two* of these twenty-three things? I need to up my score.' So now he gets up at night when B cries, and pats him to sleep. Now *he's* very tired, but he tells me he feels much better in himself. He feels he's really contributing as a father. It has made a *huge* difference to me. It isn't just the sleep, though that's wonderful. It's also the responsibility. Previously it was *me* that had failed because B kept waking up. Now we do nights together, so the responsibility for B is shared. [B, 9 months]

I'm in the 'in' department and F's the 'out' department. I give food and breast milk. F does the nappies. [B, 3 years; G, 3 months]

One fatherly trait seems to be to relate to their children in fun, and not to mind doing things which might seem thoroughly silly:

G makes me laugh. She makes us both laugh. She keeps insisting on F wearing a sort of tin mixing bowl on his head. [G, 14 months]

Even so, fathers who do a great deal for their children may not realise just how important they are to them.

I took G to stay with my mother. G was a bit out of sorts, and we put it down to teething. Then, on the weekend, F joined us, and I took G to the station to meet him. G smiled as soon as she saw him – and she didn't stop smiling for several hours afterwards. She'd obviously been *missing* him. [G, 6 months]

'Very few fathers', observed Adrienne Burgess, Head of Research at the Fatherhood Institute, 'have a clear idea of their importance to their children.'[130] Fathers seem to value confirmation that they truly matter. This can be especially exciting when it is expressed by their child.

> I heard F say: 'Daddy loves B. Does B love Daddy?' And I thought: 'What a *stupid* question! He shouldn't be prompting B like that.' But then I heard this little voice answer: '*Yes.*' It was incredibly moving. [B, 21 months]

> G cried all the car journey, for *hours*. It was dreadful. She cried, 'Mummee, Mummee!' I kept thinking that the minute we got home I'd look after her. F was driving as fast as he could down the motorway. But then she cried, '*Daddee!*' And I noticed he stopped at the next roadside restaurant, and got her out, and grabbed everything in the shop that he thought she'd want. [G, 22 months; B, 2 months]

One mother explained to her husband that his contribution needed to be not occasional, but frequent:

> I told F there were three of us in this family. We really need more of him at home. I said it was like the central heating. No matter how warm you are when the heating is on, you start to feel cold when it's off. It's like that when it's B and me all the time, and he's not there. [B, 21 months]

As fathers discover their own ways of relating to their children, mothers begin to trust their individual fatherly styles.

> F is a professional speaker. In the mornings, I can hear him talking to G. They talk for five minutes. It's lovely. [G, 8 weeks]

> In the morning, F takes G, and I can hear him losing his temper in the kitchen. I used to tell him not to talk like that in front of G.

But I know *I* get cross. And he gets over it quickly, and I can hear him singing again. I've learned to let him be cross. [G, 2 years; B, 2 months]

I've learned to appreciate F for what he does. This morning, he didn't put many clothes on B. I was going to tell him off. But then I saw the weather forecast. They predicted a warm day. And I'm glad I held back because I saw B looked really nice in the jacket F had put on him. [B, 3 years; G, 3 weeks]

Textbooks and popular wisdom often advise parents to agree on how they both want to parent, so that the child will receive the same response and learn 'consistency' from both of them. So some mothers try to ensure that both parents are consistent.

I won't let G bite me. I had to stop her. It's the one thing I feel really strongly about. Her teeth are sharp. I've seen some children hit their mothers. G is not allowed to hurt me. F doesn't mind so much, but I had to talk to him about it so we would be consistent. [G, 9 months]

However, parents *are* different. Some people assert that children need consistency because they will be confused by their differences. Not all mothers confirm this. Some notice that their small babies study their parents minutely, and learn to distinguish between them.

G has a different laugh for F from the one she uses with me. He plays more boisterous games with her and for him it's . . .[*she demonstrated a laugh with a wide-open mouth*], but for me it's . . . [*she demonstrated a half-open mouth*]. [G, 4 months]

G is not allowed to pull my glasses off. I feel strongly about that. It gets very irritating, especially when I'm breastfeeding. F doesn't mind, so G pulls *his* glasses off. But usually she remembers not to pull mine. [G, 13 months]

Just as F is Greek and speaks in Greek to B, but I talk to B in English, so B appears to be 'bilingual' in responding to our different ways of looking after him. [B, 22 months]

The advantage of a father having his own style is that he can take over when the mother is feeling tired and exasperated.

I had been trying to get G to sleep for an hour and a half in a *hot* room, with the window closed because of the noise outside. And she was crying and not going to sleep. So I phoned F – he had just gone out to play hockey – and I said, 'You've *got* to come back!' So he did. He came back and he took G and fifteen minutes later she was asleep and he went back to hockey. We talked about it afterwards, and F said, 'You know what? I wasn't *against* her.' That's what it was. I was in that 'I've-got-to-*win*' state. I expect G was picking that up. [B, 3 years; G, 9 months]

When G won't do what I ask, I say to F, 'Oh, *you* deal with it!' And he does. He's got this jokey way and he takes time to make it into a game with G. So G does what he asks. But she won't do it for me. [G, 20 months]

Unfortunately, if a father is slow or reluctant to take an active part in parenting, the mother has to look for support elsewhere.

My mum and I make a great team looking after B. B loves her and she is wonderful with him. I go to my mum's every day. I don't like coming home. F is working very hard, and I do support him. But when he takes B, it's as if he's doing me a *favour*, not as if he wants to. He never offers. The other night, I was so tired ... [*tears*]. Here I go! I asked F if he could possibly manage to take B for one hour on Saturday mornings so I could get a bit more sleep. And he said: 'I can't commit to it.' [B, 6 months]

Not all men become fathers willingly. This might sound surprising. It used to be women who complained that they were trapped into motherhood because their husbands demanded children. Yet today, this situation can be reversed. It seems that a proportion of men feel trapped as fathers. They didn't want children, but consented because their wives were insistent.

Sometimes, a mother is ill after the birth, or feels too distressed to care for the baby. Then it falls to the father to take care of their child. Many fathers rise magnificently to a crisis. But what happens when it's the father who becomes depressed?

> My partner wishes it was still us two. He is depressed. He says he doesn't feel the same to me any more. He doesn't desire me. [B, 5 weeks]

> *First mother*: My husband is out of work at the moment. He lies in bed and cries. It's just like postnatal depression, only *he's* got it. He says, 'Oh, I should be so happy with a lovely baby.' [B, 5 months]

> *Second mother*: F works from home, and it's very nice having him, but I think he often gets depressed. [B, 13 months]

> *Third mother*: F gets depressed too. I'm *sure* he does. And *he* works from home too. [B, 3 years; G, 11 months]

Fathers who lie in bed in tears during the day don't seem to get much sympathy from their partners. It can seem self-indulgent to a mother who is working so hard and would welcome support. 'It's like having *two* babies,' is the usual wry comment.

When parents feel distant from one another, it can seem a personal problem between the two of them. But they have become a family. Even young babies seem sensitive to tensions between the parents.

> When F and I argue, G stops playing and goes quiet and she doesn't smile. Her eyes go from one of us to the other, and it's as if she's thinking, I'm really confused now. So afterwards I sit her on my

lap and I explain what it was all about. I say, 'It started when Daddy said X and then Mummy said Y.' And I bring her back. I know she can't understand my actual words, but it's still working because her *smile* comes back, and in the end she's ready to play again. [G, 4 months]

F and I used to quarrel in front of G. G would go pale, withdraw, and play silently in a corner of the room. A marriage guidance counsellor pointed it out to us. We were both shocked. Since that day, we've agreed to save our quarrels for later. [G, 20 months]

My friends are all advising me to leave F. It's hard. I could so easily give all my love to the children and leave F out. He's being a brute. But G senses the tension between us and she says, 'Daddy, kiss Mummy!' [G, 3 years; B, 2 months]

Tension increases when a couple don't talk to one another. Sometimes it's from lack of time. Sometimes one of them doesn't enjoy talking. Each feels ill used and nurses a store of complaints. Each has withdrawn from the other. Their original intimacy feels at risk. Couples find it can take courage to reach out to one another across the no-man's-land of hurt pride.

I didn't like the amount of drinking that was going on in our home. I mean, I've been a party girl myself. But F would get through a bottle of wine per evening. It didn't seem right. Then he couldn't be there for G. So I wrote him a letter. I said I'd seen him being a wonderful father to G. I said I wanted him to be like that again. I said I wanted him back. I missed him. 'When you're drunk,' I wrote, 'you're not *you*.' So now, when G goes to sleep in the evening, we have a bit of time together. It feels much better. I know it's not solved for ever. [G, 3 months]

We've banned arguments about which of us is the more tired. We're parents. We both *are* tired. [G, 5 months]

I got angry with F because I came downstairs from getting B to sleep and he was watching television and not giving me any attention. So then we had one of those silly arguments. And the upshot of it was that we decided that every time I wanted his attention I was to give him a hug. That's really working for us. [B, 6 months]

Some couples resume sex soon after the birth. But many mothers need longer to recover from the birth, physically and emotionally. Luckily, couples discuss sex much more frankly with one another than earlier generations did.

There *must* be sex after childbirth. G is the living proof. But not much, even now. On holiday this summer, F was drinking a lot of red wine, while I was eating sweets and chocolate. I pointed it out to F, and he said, 'I'm glad you said it, because I was going to bring it up.' We both miss sex, but F would like some, whereas I am far too tired. [B, 4 years; G, 12 months]

When we started [*making love*], I felt swollen up. F said, 'What's happening?' I said, 'I don't know. I feel swollen.' No one tells you that could happen. It was fine after we'd realised. [G, 15 months]

Mothers have developed sexually as a result of having a baby. Despite being tired, and despite protesting that they look 'a mess', they look glowing, tender and feminine. They hold their babies with growing confidence, looking shy, yet graceful. It adds a new element to a couple's relationship when a father discovers that his partner has developed from a young woman into a beautiful mother. Unfortunately, because of the current idealisation of pre-maternal beauty, mothers are led to believe they ought to recover their *previous* looks. There is expensive cosmetic surgery available now with special operations for 'the mummy tuck' to restore their previous looks. But don't mothers realise how lovely they have become? The psycho-analyst Daniel Stern and his wife, Nadia Bruschweiler-Stern, struggle to put the change into words: '[*Her*] face is rather private, quiet and poised at a central still-point, full of love without any external sign. This face has an unearthly beauty.'[131]

Their description is only one way of wording it. If fathers perceive their partners' new sexual beauty, perhaps they could put it into words or photograph some more individual portraits, so that the rest of us can better recognise what we see. My husband organised a seminar[132] attended by thirty adults of whom sixteen were mothers with their babies. He was moved by them, and commented after: 'I shall *never* forget the beautiful sight of the sixteen mothers gently rocking, singing to, or talking to their babies. It would have needed a great painter to do it justice.'

A mother's beauty costs nothing, any mother can achieve it – and perhaps these are exactly the two reasons why it is not valued.

There are no fashions marketed specifically for mothers, so they often say they don't know what to wear. People talk scornfully about a 'mumsy' look. I'm puzzled that no one has designed clothes that distinguish mothers from other women, creating a distinct style that maximises maternal beauty. At the moment, 'beauty' is equated with the springtime of a woman's sexual development. But when a woman becomes a mother, she reaches the summer of her femininity.

Very little has been said about the look of a new father. Becoming a father doesn't seem to make such an immense change to his sexual and social identity as becoming a mother usually does. But it's certainly there. A father now knows the outcome of sex. He may feel profoundly awed at the reality of his baby. The joy and pride in his voice are audible when he says, 'This is my *son*' or 'I am her *father*'. He too looks different. His eyes brighten noticeably; his face flushes and his shoulders assume a more ponderous, responsible look.

I can remember when I was about three saying to my parents, 'I know you are my mummy and daddy, but what are your real names?'

So they told me, and after that I couldn't call my father 'Daddy' any more. He was very annoyed. He said, 'People won't realise that I am your *father*.' [B, 8 months]

What happens to the couple intimacy as each sees the other one developing as a unique parent?

It's amazing seeing F turn into a father. If we didn't have a baby, I'd never have seen that side of him. [B, 6 months]

I've been thinking quite deeply about things in the last few weeks. I find I like myself more, now I've become a mother. I like G, and that makes me like *myself* more. But it's also had the same effect on F. His self-esteem has grown and grown during this year. It's really lovely to see. [G, 13 months]

B was crying and F said, 'I think he's crying from a chest pain, *not* a tummy pain.' And my reaction was, 'Oooh! That's my *man!* He's really tuned into being a father now. He's *got* there!' [B, 23 months]

The couple intimacy is no longer exclusive. It has become more elastic. The two of them have more space between them than they used to. At first, both may fear the unfamiliar space. What people dread are repetitions of earlier painful relationships. If a person was hurt as a vulnerable child, it is only too easy, as a tired and stretched parent, to expect to be blamed, or belittled, or ignored, or whatever the hurtful behaviour once was, by the partner. Because the couple relationship is so intimate, it can easily re-open ancient wounds. Most people seem to have raw places from childhood. Either may attack the other to pre-empt getting hurt again. When a couple hurt one another so deeply that they carry the pain all day, it's obviously more than the surface event that has provoked it. It is easy to darken the present relationship with shadows from the past.

Often, when couples feel estranged from one another, this is based on layers of misunderstandings. If they can calm down enough to talk, these can be unravelled. For example, person A did indeed hear the special request of person B. But person A thought it essential to 'show some initiative' or 'show that I can't be pushed around'. However, this left person B feeling the special request had been unheard. As the sequence of reactions and counter-reactions becomes clearer, it's hard to know whether to laugh or cry.

Couple intimacy originally develops when two people realise that part of their attraction to one another is that they share certain values. They may have also been influenced by recent ideas of fairness and equality, to create a harmonious relationship based on connection. But having children reveals their differences too. The couple see themselves separate into mother and father. However, just because they are different, it does not mean that their differences need to threaten or undermine the other one. Couples learn first to tolerate and then to trust and, gradually, rely on these differences. They can then recover a sense of 'we', that is, a couple with a definite identity as a pair of parents.[133]

A loving relationship has much to offer. It is a great pity to see a single *one* of them founder through early misunderstandings. Even a mature couple relationship is never perfect or finished. To outsiders, a mature couple relationship probably looks much more secure than it feels from the inside. But the feeling of unsteadiness is because the relationship is alive and still growing. As outsiders, we might imagine that the mature couple were always so calm and comfortable together. But we can be virtually certain that the two had to work for all the maturity that they have achieved.

Whenever a couple relationship survives, deepens and matures, this must surely be one of the most wonderful creative achievements in life. Their intimacy seems to generate and spread out a great deal of peace and warmth that reaches all of us.

CHAPTER TWELVE

Intimacy with two

New questions arise when a mother has more than one child.

Me: What's it like, having two children?

M: Do you mean being a mother for the second time? Or having two children to mother? For me, they are different questions. [G, 3 years; B, 4 weeks]

That sounds to me a good distinction. So I'll start with the first question of what it's like to be a mother for the second time, and then move on to the question of having two children to mother.

It might sound unnecessary to remind ourselves that it is only possible to have one first child – or first children if they are multiples. Yet never again will we be so inexperienced. Also, when a second baby is born, the older child may seem to his mother almost like a young companion. The mother may feel less alone with her new baby.

It's easier with two children. When B cries, I say to G: 'It's all right. B's just crying because he wants . . .' And then I say 'food' or 'sleep' or whatever he wants. Naming the problem out loud to G calms me down. If I was by myself with *one* crying baby, I know I'd be in a state. [G, 2 years; B, 8 weeks]

Before the second birth, mothers often seem to expect the second baby to be the overwhelming experience that it was the first time. For some mothers, though not all, part of having a second baby is the surprise at how much more relaxed they have become.

I am much calmer as a mother this time. I hardly worry about B at all. [G, 3 years; B, 4 weeks]

It's different with the second one. Not to say B doesn't take up a lot of my attention. But it's not at all a . . . a *blur*, like it was with G. When I had G, I could hardly cope with anything else. Like if I went to Soho with G, it was as if I had gone to Mars. Everything looked so completely strange and unfamiliar. Whereas now, I've been back to Piccadilly, and I noticed that everything looked exactly the same as it always did. [G, 2 years; B, 8 weeks]

With a first baby, the mother usually has much more time than when she has a new baby and an older child to look after.

It's going too quickly. G's my third [*hugging her*]. She may be my last. I love her as a baby so much, and the early part is almost gone. [B, 7 years; B, 5 years; G, 3 months]

Sometimes, if a mother has had difficulties with her first child, she can see the second child as 'easy' by comparison.

B didn't sleep through the night until he was three. Then he suddenly did, almost on his third birthday. For eighteen months, he found nights difficult. To him, they were too quiet and dark, and the idea of sleeping for ten hours didn't appeal. I found that very hard. I knew I had to stay there with him. People said I should leave him to cry it out. But I *couldn't*. It seemed a double-whammy: can't sleep plus being abandoned by his mummy. G is completely different. She doesn't wake up nearly as often as he did. [B, 4 years; G, 3 months]

This means that a firstborn is likely to have a different experience of his mother from his younger siblings. This different experience surely continues as an ongoing story which extends right through life. You could, for example, ask an octogenarian pair of siblings: 'Which one of you is the older one?' You could be certain that, if both had retained their normal powers of memory, neither of them would reply: 'Goodness, absolutely no idea! Just give us a moment while we go and check our birth certificates.' No, the difference is meaningful. Being older or younger gives each a different family history, and may suggest certain character traits for both. For example, 'I've always been the responsible one,' or, 'I'm *still* treated like the baby of the family.' Even in a family of many siblings, the birth order always seems to carry a great deal of meaning for each of them.[134]

Rebecca Abrams, in her book with the evocative title, *Three Shoes, One Sock and No Hairbrush, Everything you need to know about having your second child*, points out how much parents underrate the difference it will make to their families when they have a second child: 'From conception, the second child makes a difference, but it's not the same difference that a first child makes . . . The pervasive model of mothering is of mothering *one*. From the moment we conceive our second child, this model of mothering becomes inappropriate, yet it continues to inform our expectations about what mothering two will be like, or ought to be like.'[135] Ms Abrams points out that our expectations get in our way, making it harder to recognise and to confront the new difficulties that arise.

During the second pregnancy, the coming child may still feel 'unreal'. The mother is more concerned about the child she can see. Frequently, a mother who has built up an intimate relationship with her first child starts to have serious concerns about how the two of them will relate when there is a newborn to care for.

> Now I know there'll be another baby, I realise that my time alone with B will be limited. It feels so *precious*. I love him more than *ever*. He's talking now. Our times together are really wonderful. [B, 2 years; 4 months pregnant]

Parents are now advised to prepare their child for the coming baby, and there are many children's books about the birth of a sibling. But one mother pointed out how important it was to check their contents first. Books can suggest problems which the older child might not have thought about yet.

> I edit what I read to G. There are lots of stories telling you how the older child behaves very badly after the birth of a sibling, and after a while the behaviour gets better. But that hasn't been our experience. Why should I read G the story of a child being unhappy after the birth of a sibling, when *her* experience has been quite different? [G, 3 years; B, 2 months]

The developmental psychologist Judy Dunn, who made an extensive study of sibling relationships, makes the interesting point: 'In families where the mother discussed caring for the baby as a matter of joint responsibility and talked about the baby as a person from the early days, the siblings were particularly friendly over the next year.'[136] The significant phrase is 'talked about the baby as a *person*'. It might seem easier to talk about 'the baby' in the abstract. But preparing the older child to meet another person, someone who is as much a 'person' as himself, sounds a realistic way for mother and child to prepare.

Some mothers are able to conceive within a few months of giving birth. This means that some first children may be too young for preparation. Instead, the mother needs to prepare herself for mothering two children so close in age. The novelist Rachel Cusk discovered that she was pregnant again when her first child was six months. She described her response to the news: 'Motherhood, for me, was a sort of compound fenced off from the rest of the world. I was forever plotting my escape from it, and when I found myself pregnant again when Albertine was six months I greeted my old cell with the cheerless acceptance of a convict intercepted at large.'[137] Although this way of thinking may sound negative to many women, it must have been daunting – especially because she was 'plotting her escape' from motherhood – to face the prospect of mothering two children who would be fifteen months apart.

When the next child is about to be born, a new question arises. Who will take care of the first one while the mother, often accompanied by her partner, is giving birth? Many mothers cannot relax unless they feel sure that the older child will be looked after by someone they can trust.

First mother: Last week, I looked after my sister's older child while she gave birth to her second baby. I wanted to protect my sister too. I'm the older, and I felt *very* protective. I could tell she felt very relieved that she could trust the person looking after her child. [G, 7 months]

Second mother: It makes a *huge* difference to the birth. I had a close friend that G loves. As soon as I knew that she could look after G, then I could relax and get ready to give birth. [G, 2 years; B, 2 months]

Third mother: I can remember my aunt looking after me when my younger brother was born. [*The whole circle of mothers was alert with interest. The third mother said it had been a good experience. She had been about eight years old and her aunt had been especially supportive of her.*]

Fourth mother: My friend had four children close together. We looked after her older three when her fourth was born. She said it made a tremendous difference to her feelings at the birth, knowing that her older three would be well looked after. She told me she'd had some earlier experiences that had been more difficult. [G, 9 years; G, 7 years]

It would surely help if we were all aware of the strength of a mother's concern for her older child during the birth of the next baby. It's the one occasion when she cannot give him proper attention. Family and friends of the birthing mother might be keen to care for her older children if they realised what a great difference this would make.

What happens to the mother's intimate relationship with her first child when a second child is born? During the pregnancy, many mothers worry whether they will be maternal enough to love two children. They frequently say they worry that they have given so much love to their first child that they might not have enough 'in reserve' for the next one. (There were a few examples of this on page 21.)

Nearly always, the birth of the second baby brings a surprising discovery. Mothers find that love is not finite. It does not need to be stored in reserve, divided up or taken away from the older one.

I was worried that my feelings might change for 1G. But they didn't. You just get more love. It's a wonderful thing. [1G, 2 years; 2G, 2 months]

I loved G so much, I didn't see how I could possibly love another one as much. But, when B was born, the love seemed to come from nowhere. I think we must have the capacity to love an infinite number of children. [G, 3 years; B, 6 months]

Rebecca Abrams points out that not all mothers love their second child easily or immediately. Such immediate second-time love hadn't been her own experience. She agrees that motherly love does 'come' for a second baby, but not always at birth. She adds:

'Loving more than one child at once does not always come easily; the real problem is our expectation that it should.'[138]

> 2G is very different from 1G. 1G seemed like the one I loved, and 2G looked alien. They *look* like little aliens when they're new. I felt no rush of love for 2G. I felt so *guilty* that I was failing to bond with her. But I didn't know her then. She's got a completely different personality from 1G. [1G, 2 years; 2G, 2 weeks]

If the mother falls in love with her second baby, immediately or gradually, what happens to her feelings for her first child, with whom she had previously been in love? Is she wholly in love with the second one now, or does she have two different kinds of love, as a mother kangaroo can produce two different kinds of milk?

A common pattern is to love the first child unreservedly, up to the moment of the new birth. However, as soon as the mother sees how tiny her newborn is, she starts to see her previous 'baby' as enormous and very mature, and expects him to manage almost as well as she can.

> I was an older child. Before 2G was born, I felt very worried that I wouldn't have enough love for both of them. All my sympathies were with 1G, and how she would cope with another baby. But as soon as 2G was born, I found myself changing. I was surprised that my sympathies were with the baby more than the toddler. I felt 2G really needed me, whereas 1G could cope *really*. But she's only two and a half. [1G, 2 years; 2G, 5 weeks]

> 1G is so *big*. I get angry with her for not being mature. [1G, 6 years; 2G, 2 months]

Jane Patricia Barrett wrote her PhD thesis on 'Mother–Sibling Triads'. She confirms this pattern from her own research, and suggests that it can continue for some time.[139]

I myself can remember being startled at losing that sense of protectiveness towards the older child because the new baby needed it more. This changes the quality of the intimate relationship. Protectiveness is not the same as love. But it might feel like it to the older one.

So how does the older child respond to the sudden change to his intimate relationship with his mother?

> The first days were awful. 1B wouldn't come near me. He turned his back on me. He acted as if I had been unfaithful to him – like a husband bringing home another woman – and I felt as if I *had*. [1B, 2 years; 2B, 6 weeks]

Is motherly love fickle? Do mothers switch their love to the newer arrival? It seems not. Many mothers care intensely about their older child, even while their immediate attention is on the needy newborn.

> Most of my thoughts are with G. I don't want her to feel left out. And she's been absolutely brilliant. I'm very proud of her. She's very helpful. Though it's usually a help I could well do without. She brings me a drink and a snack when I'm breastfeeding. She knows breastfeeding makes you thirsty. Afterwards we go back, wiping up all the spilt milk* off the floor. And she likes helping to change B's nappy. He likes to be changed quickly, and she takes twice as long as I do. But I want her to feel included, and it's good for her relationship with B. [G, 3 years; B, 4 weeks]

> [*M explained later that G believed a mother needed to drink milk to produce milk. M tried to explain, but G kept asking her how a mother's food could possibly turn into breast milk.]

> I admire B so much. He really understands now when I'm trying to rock G to sleep. One time, he said, 'Can I hold her? Shall I sing to her?' And he sang her everything from 'Baa Baa Black Sheep' to 'Early One Morning'. And in the end, G was asleep. Another time,

he fetched him and me a drink of water each. He thought of it and did it all himself. I really *admire* him. [B, 3 years; G, 5 months]

But it isn't easy at first. Most mothers have a difficult time trying to combine giving the attention that their newborn needs with the different kind of attention that the older one wants of her. The hardest part is at the beginning, when the whole situation is new, everyone is tired, and the siblings haven't discovered their own relationship yet.

The hard thing is the difference in timing. B is a baby, and when I slow down for him it gets really nice, doing things at his pace. But for G everything needs to be very quick because she's three, and it's hard to do things at the speed that she likes. [G, 3 years; B, 3 months]

It might sound like a good solution to have one parent for each child. Many fathers are overjoyed to get closer to their children.

G says to F and me, 'You are *my* parents. I want B to go to *his* parents.' I find that very hard. Then, the other day, G said to me, 'It's all right. You *can* be B's Mummy. I don't mind any more. I'm going to have *Daddy*.' [G, 3 years; B, 5 months]

But for a mother who has developed an intimate relationship with the older child, it can feel an intense loss.

I feel as if I just look after the baby. G asks for her daddy now. I miss her so much. But, at the moment, F is away and we're staying with my mum. My mum looks after the baby now, so I can take G to the park or for a hot chocolate – things we *used* to do. [G, 3 years; G, 10 weeks]

B and I seem far apart now. It started in [*my second*] pregnancy when . . . [*tears*]. I couldn't lift him up when he wanted. Now I'm

226

always with G, feeding her or changing her nappy. He asks for his daddy now. We split everything between us. F does everything for B and I breastfeed G. I feel I've failed B as a mother. [B, 20 months; G, 4 months]

One mother described how happy she felt when, instead of getting her husband to care for the older child, she asked him to look after the baby.

F took B for a walk recently, so G and I could have time together. It was really lovely. G was completely happy. We did baking. [G, 3 years; B, 6 weeks]

So although many mothers describe getting irritated with the older child, their pre-sibling relationship remains strong.

M: I find B very annoying. It sounds terrible, but I do. He keeps wanting me to talk to him about monkeys. It's his 'thing'. All day.

Me: How do you keep your temper? If you do.

M: Oh, I do, I do. He *expects* it of me. He thinks of me as his good-tempered mummy. I don't want to let him down. [B, 3 years; G, 4 months]

I hadn't appreciated, until writing this section, how deeply mothers care about sustaining the intimate relationships with their older children. There is often a special animated tone of voice in which mothers describe their firstborns.

I was asking myself if I loved G *more* than B. And, in a way, I *do*. Your love grows with your child. At first, their needs are so simple and you are just grateful that they are all right. Now G has grown, and there's much more of her to love. But I'm sure B will *grow* into that amount of love, as he gets older. [G, 3 years; B, 5 months]

[*I was curious about this. As B grew in months, I noticed that he did*

*indeed 'grow' a more individual kind of love in his mother, exactly as
she had predicted.*]

What, then, happens to the new baby? What kind of love does
the younger child get? Many mothers describe how their behaviour
is more casual with subsequent babies than it had been with their
first.

First mother: I don't think I can leave B to cry. [B, 9 months]

Second mother: I was the same with G. I couldn't let her cry. But,
this morning, I was changing G's nappy and B started crying. And
I just *knew* he'd be all right. I knew I'd have time to finish changing
G's nappy. I could tell from the crying. First children and second
children get such a different experience. [G, 21 months; B, 13 days]

M: I do let B cry if I'm not quite ready to go to him. I didn't
with G.

Me: But isn't that because you can hear that it's . . . ?

M: Just grumbling, yes.

Me: Would you react differently if he suddenly gave a high-pitched
cry?

M: Yes, of *course*. [G, 3 years; B, 6 weeks]

It might sound as though second babies were getting a more
casual kind of love. But this seems unlikely. Second-time mothers
have gained experience, and can make finer judgments to identify
which cries are urgent. Second children seem to get a more assured
response.

When a mother has a second child, her first child becomes the
older of two children. She has to learn how to balance the interests
of two children, not one, with her own. At the same time, she
needs to help her first child to adjust to being the older of two.

228

There are other questions which might trouble her. Does she have much less time for the younger children? Or does her experience enable her to grow in warmth and love to each child, so that her youngest has the best of her? Does a mother who was a second-born herself have a special affinity with her own second-born child? Does she relate more comfortably to female children, because they are more familiar? These questions are intriguing, but beyond the scope of this book.

So a second child may give his mother plenty to think over. He is not just an add-on to the family. He changes it. Everyone in a family is sensitive to all the others. Judy Dunn tries to outline the complexity: 'The way in which a mother behaves toward one child in her family is intimately related to the way in which the other children behave toward her and toward each other. And the more closely one examines the connections between family relationships the more complex the patterns appear to be.'[140]

The mother can suddenly see her older child in a new way:

By accident, 2B put his arm on 1B's back. 1B said: 'Look, Mummy, 2B is looking after me!' I was very moved. [1B, 2 years; 2B, 3 months]

Having a second child is a very rich experience. I've seen G change from my daughter to B's big sister. It's a whole new side of her. Not that she's always very nice to him. [G, 3 years; B, 5 months]

A family of four or more people is much noisier and busier than a family of two adults and a baby. The second child is born into a good deal of loud interaction. There is usually something interesting going on.

I feel furious with G at least once a day. She's so loud and wild, I often wish she wasn't here. But one afternoon F took her out, and I suddenly realised what an important part of the family she is. Because without her it was very quiet, B got bored, and I had to entertain him. I didn't get any of the work done that I'd been meaning to. Normally, B's entertained the whole time, just watching G. [G, 2 years; B, 5 months]

With a single child, the mother has to be the main entertainer. With two or more children, she suddenly notices how much the siblings enjoy one another. Sooner than one might expect, the older sibling starts to relate to the baby.

B loves having baths with G. And the other day, he brought her all the wrong toys for her to play with. It's the first time I've ever heard G give a real belly chuckle. She thought B was hilarious. [B, 3 years; G, 4 months]

It's lovely to hear their laughter. 2B thinks that 1B is the funniest person on earth, and 1B is very flattered. So he is always doing things to make 2B laugh, like jumping up and down and waving his arms. [1B, 22 months; 2B, 5 months]

1G and B play beautifully together. They fight as well, but an adult could *never* play with a child the way another child can. I couldn't, anyway. Children need children to play with. [1G, 3 years; B, 2 years; 2G, 2 weeks]

Sibling relationships aren't only playful. Older siblings sometimes express negative feelings towards the younger ones. Despite this, older siblings often sound very protective of them too.

I'm afraid to leave G alone with B in case she hurts him. But if G thinks that B needs me, she will say, 'Mummy, B is cold, he needs his socks. Mummy, come *now*, B *needs* you.' [G, 3 years; B, 5 months]

First mother: B says to me, 'Drop her, Mummy. Go on, *drop* her!' [*A bit later, at the same meeting*:] G nearly fell off the bed today. It was B who saw and saved her. Then he said to me, 'Mummy, I think

G is too old for the bed. She should be in a cot. She should be in *my* old cot.' [B, 3 years; G, 8 months]

Second mother: So one moment he wanted you to drop her, and the next moment he actually saved her. [1B, 6 years; 2B, 4 years; 3B, 5 months]

Could these be examples of the innate sibling rivalry, which many people say is inevitable? Sigmund Freud, who himself was born into a large family, reflected on this rivalry which he saw as a crucial part of family life. He was a pioneer, determined to make sense of his own childhood, and the stories his friends and patients told him. 'Many people, therefore,' he wrote in *The Interpretation of Dreams*, 'who love their brothers and sisters and would feel bereaved if they were to die, harbour evil wishes against them in their unconscious, dating from earlier times; . . . a child's death-wishes against his brothers and sisters are explained by the childish egoism which makes him regard them as his rivals . . . '[141] Other psychotherapists have valued this theory, and the idea has now become a cliché.

There are several questions to consider: whether conflict between siblings is rivalrous; if it is, whether it is innate, or whether there are other explanations.

The assumption that siblings feel rivalrous towards one another might make sense of all the quarrels that go on between them. However, in this theory of sibling rivalry, Freud attributes the source of the child's angry wishes to 'childish egoism'. This means that the source is located in the immature nature of the child himself. If we accept this, there is then no need to look any further to understand a child's rivalrous feelings. But suppose we don't immediately accept this and look further. Might a child's feelings of rivalry have some foundation, for example, in family circumstances? Should we not, before accepting that rivalry is innate and inevitable, look to see whether children's rivalrous feelings were *about* something?

Freud's theory does not take into account what the parents are doing. There are many ways in which a parent can influence the relationship that their children have with one another. A parent may indicate that the children have to compete for love. It is only too easy, and perhaps tempting, for a parent, especially if he or she is distracted and finding it difficult to give time and energy, to offer a limited amount of love for the children to share. When love is restricted like this, or when it is conditional, siblings scrap bitterly with one another for the crumbs that are on offer. They are rivals, but not because of their innate nature. The parents have set up a situation in which the children have to contend with one another.

'But is it fair to suggest', demands one study, 'that parents are primarily responsible for the extent of jealousy and disturbance in the firstborn? Surely not.'[142] This kind of opinion is often stated. There is an abundant literature in which authors claim that parents are not responsible for their children's feelings. It is, they say, the children who are responsible.

It's true that children create their own feelings. But they may be provoked into jealousy. For example, a mother might stimulate rivalry between her children by constant competition ('Which of you can ask me more politely?') or by constant comparisons ('Can you do it as well as your brother?'). Children can be quickly hurt by being assessed only by comparison with someone else. It is then easy for the child who has lost the 'competition', or who has fared badly by comparison, to feel hurt and resentful.

It seems rare for adults *not* to compare siblings. The mother of two-month-old twins explained that she herself took care not to compare her two. But, she said, other people never stopped comparing them. Whoever visited to see the twins would first define the character of one twin and then compare it to the supposed character of the other one. She said she didn't know how to stop her visitors doing this.

'Sibling rivalry' may describe many sibling relationships. But

232

these might come about as a *result* of parental behaviour, rather than as feelings that are innate to children. There is some evidence to show that once parents avoid behaviours that stimulate sibling rivalry, this sibling behaviour invariably ameliorates and often disappears. Faber and Mazlish, two American parenting writers, introduce their book, *Siblings Without Rivalry*, with an acknowledge-ment of parental power. 'From all these sessions and all the work we had done in the years before comes this book, the affirmation of our belief that we, as parents, *can* make a difference. We can either intensify the competition or reduce it. We can drive hostile feelings underground or allow them to be vented safely. We can accelerate the fighting, or make co-operation possible.'[143]

Many books for parents include a special section on siblings. Authors advise parents on how to get their children to be nice to one another. The advice is often to manipulate the children into behaving better by rewards and punishments. However, this doesn't address the reason why the children aren't getting along in the first place. A mother might find that, on reflection, she could relate more evenly to the two of them. It's not necessary to manipulate children.

Competition and rivalry can be very exciting for a child, and fun. In competitive sports, for example, this is evident. But should a child have to compete for his mother's love? Surely a mother's love can be plentiful, and each child deserves a generous amount.

The question of sibling rivalry seems to have got tangled up with a related, but separate, problem. There are times when siblings quarrel bitterly, not out of rivalry, but because they are trying to sort out questions of fairness. After all, a pair of adult flatmates may quarrel for exactly these reasons. The two protagonists are therefore not in competition for the parents' love. This is different. They are working out what is fair. The actual issues may seem petty, and a parent may feel exasperated. However, the basic prin-ciples at stake are not petty, but serious.

The children may need their mother's help in articulating their viewpoints and restraining themselves from physical violence. This is essential work in the parenting of more than one child. After long periods, when the siblings seem to do nothing but bicker, a host of issues are resolved between them. Then they have learned to live, side by side, honouring their differences. This gives them valuable experience to use in solving differences with their peers.

It's not easy to look after one child and protect him from danger. It becomes harder with two.

> I'd love to be the sort of mother who lets her children do everything they like. But I'm not like that. The other day, I took them both to the park. 2B started to play in some mud, and he was really happy. Then I saw 1B running to climb a tree in the opposite direction. I needed to get to 1B, because it looked dangerous. I couldn't be there for both of them. And that's when I *snap*. [1B, 3 years; 2B, 16 months]

Mothers of one baby often wonder if they will be overwhelmed with exhaustion at the physical work of mothering two. But mothers of two seem to accept the inevitability of tiredness. So they don't complain of exhaustion – or at least not so often.

> It gets better. You'd think with two children you'd be even *more* tired. But it doesn't seem to work like that. With G, I was exhausted all the time. With B, I'm not fighting it. It's just how I am. It won't be for ever. [G, 2 years; B, 2 months]

> *First mother*: I feel really . . . tired. I can't . . . think of the right words. As you can probably hear. [G, 11 months]

> *Second mother*: I'm tired. I *am* tired. But I've got used to it. It's not at the forefront of my attention. [G, 3 years; B, 10 months]

> I go to bed early. I have to. The worst thing is fearing I'll be too

tired to cope with the next day. [B, 4 years; G, 12 months]

As with one child, the physical work may be tiring, but there is also the mental organisation, keeping everyone's needs in mind.

The most tiring thing is the planning. You have to work backwards through the whole day. I've got to collect B from his playgroup, and we'll need lunch, so I need to put lunch for B, G, and myself in the car. Then I'll need a pram for G so I can get somewhere else. It's *exhausting*! [B, 4 years; G, 12 months]

What happens to the mother's own personal life?

I feel I'm a 'doing' machine. I just get things done, all through the day, from moment to moment. I never have time to myself, or to do anything properly. I could be quite sad if I thought about that. [G, 4 years; B, 3 months]

First mother: 2G wants me to hold her all the time. I'm feeling frustrated because I so much want to finish writing a little book. Just half an hour's work on it makes everything in the week feel easier.

Me: How do you cope when there's no time to write?

First mother: I don't cope. I just *continue*. [1G, 4 years; B, 2 years; 2G, 2 months]

Second mother: So do I. I don't cope, just *continue*. [B, 4 years; twins, B and G, 7 months]

M: I look after G, I take care of B, I help my husband, I keep up with our flat, I try to keep up with the demands of my work. And this is all at the expense of one thing. It's 'me' time.

Me: What is 'me' time?

M: It's stillness, which is *so* hard to achieve at the moment. And eating chocolate. That's great! You can continue eating after being interrupted.

It's any time, any place. The only problem is if you get distracted and you don't have time to savour it. [B, 4 years; G, 12 months]

I was surprised to see from my notes how frequently mothers of two or more children feel desperate one moment, and calm again a few moments later. Mothers of one child don't often mention the abruptness of the change.

First mother: I can't understand how everything can be marvellous one moment, with two lovely children, and a minute later B is crying and G is having a strop. [G, 3 years; B, 3 months]

Second mother: Yes, or the other way round. Everything can be terrible, and you don't know how you'll get through it, and suddenly it's over. [B, 22 months; G, 4 months]

[*In tears.*] Since we've been back from holiday, it's been so hard. It's 2B. He is always very aggressive, very physical. He's starting to focus it on 3B. I don't understand how we can have a wonderful moment, like being at the top of a wave, and then very quickly, suddenly, *down* into a horrible moment, at the bottom of the wave. [1B, 6 years; 2B, 4 years; 3B, 5 months]

I've had a difficult week. First 1B was ill and then 2B was. On Friday, we had a terrible afternoon. 1B was lying on the floor because he felt too ill for anything, and 2B kept vomiting. 1B kept saying, 'Play trains'; I couldn't explain to him that 2B was ill, so I couldn't play trains with him. I kept watching the clock and wanting this moment to pass. And then 2B fell asleep, and then 1B was asleep, and suddenly it was easier. [1B, 2 years; 2B, 5 months]

M: We were in the park café, and there was a queue. G was screaming because she wanted a chocolate muffin *now*, and B was screaming because he was tired. I knew if I could get B from the buggy into his sling, he'd fall asleep, so I was trying to do that. Then G wailed, 'I want to *wee.*' I thought, Oh, *no*!

236

Me: So what did you do?

M [with a mysterious motherly smile]: I got B into his sling, and he fell asleep. Then I got G her muffin, and she was very happy. So then everything was all right. [G, 2 years; B, 9 months]

But sometimes two screaming children are simply too much.

One evening, they were both crying, and I shouted: 'Stop crying, both of you, because Mummy just can't cope!' [B, 4 years; G, 12 months]

Nearly every mother described how, especially if she had to give a lot of attention to the baby, her older child seemed very sensitive, emotional and liable to be furious with her.

Sometimes I give in to B when I *do* know better. When G was three days old, we decided to go for a walk in the park. B wanted to take a toy he had made out of Lego. I knew it would break and we'd lose the pieces, so I said no. He threw himself down on the kitchen floor, and I think all our neighbours must have heard his screams. It was a tantrum, and he doesn't often have those. So I said he could take it. He *ran* to pack it into my bag. Sometimes you have to go with their feelings and listen to them with respect. [B, 3 years; G, 4 weeks]

G is so emotional. She gets furious over tiny things. Like if she can't find a particular book, or if she can't get her doll's sock on to the doll's foot. I try not to belittle her if she's really upset, and I'm never sure how much to tell her it isn't really important. [G, 3 years; B, 6 weeks]

Two mothers noticed a similar kind of behaviour when their older children were with children of the same age:

First mother: When I'm around, G runs up to her friends and shouts, '*No!*' into their faces. I'm very embarrassed because I know their mothers. [G, 3 years; B, 7 months]

Second mother: That's interesting. 1B always pushes a little girl he knows. It's embarrassing because her mother is my friend. I think 1B is behaving badly. [*She and the first mother compared behaviours for a while.*] I've just thought of something. Could 1B be attacking this little girl because she doesn't have to share with a younger sibling? She will have to soon, but she and 1B don't know that yet. So she gets the full attention of her mother. I think that because there's another little girl who's got a baby brother – and 1B and she get on very well now. There's a real understanding between them. [1B, 2 years; 2B, 3 months]

I wonder if other mothers have noticed that their older children resent their child-friends if they are singletons.

There are moments when the older child seems to find fault with everything his mother does.

G loves her playgroup now. I say to her, 'Today we'll have a lovely day at home, with just you and me and B.' But she says, 'But I won't have any friends to play with.' So I say, 'All right, we'll go to the playground and perhaps you will make a friend to play with there.' But then she says to me: 'But that isn't a *proper* friend. I want one of my real friends to play with.' [G, 3 years; B, 3 months]

If you get *one* thing wrong when 1B is ill, everything is ruined. I'd turned on his favourite TV programme. I'd got him a tray of crisps and juice. But I'd forgotten to put the lid of the juice on the way he likes it. 1B was furious with me. [1B, 2 years; 2B, 6 months]

This kind of exchange can sound as though the older child is being tyrannical, and the mother is allowing herself to be treated like a doormat. However, it needs to be understood in context. It's characteristic of an intimate relationship. It doesn't usually happen if there is more distance between the two. The family is interconnected, and the tiny details matter to both.

I used to blame myself for getting upset about such petty little things. But now I can see that the children and I are a little ecosystem of our own. If one of us isn't happy, it affects all of us. [B, 4 years; B, 2 years]

This especially seems to be the case during long periods of adjustment when the older child, who used to be easy and good-tempered, now seems so easily ruffled and upset.

I find it helps to sing. I can't hear them so well then, and it helps to change my mood. One day, G was crying, and B started yelling to get my attention for himself. I started singing 'All things bright and beautiful . . . ' very loudly. I couldn't remember the words, so I went, 'ba-ba-ba'. As soon as I had finished, I heard B say: '*Again!*' [B, 23 months; G, 5 months]

I keep swinging one way and then the other. G wants something that B has, but I can't take it away from B to give it to her. B is still a baby. But if G has made a tower and B wants to touch it, I say, 'That is G's. We mustn't touch it.' I know B can't understand. But I say it for G. [G, 3 years; B, 7 months]

However, mothers aren't saints. It's not easy to have one's best efforts rubbished by an irritable child. Two mothers, both younger siblings themselves, and both with children of the same ages, had this conversation with one another:

First mother: I feel so tired, I haven't always got the energy to be nice. And then – I'm ashamed to admit this – I think I've got a cruel and mean streak to me. Sometimes I just want to *squash* B. Like he was a fly and I'm annoyed. I feel I really *want* to squash him. [B, 3 years; G, 5 months]

Second mother: I can really relate to what you just said. I wouldn't have had the courage to admit it. I've got a cruel and mean streak too. I'd like to squash B, even though I love him so much. The thing that annoys me most is when he hurts G. Then my love seems to disappear. And you know what? Maybe those feelings aren't bad. Maybe they're *normal*. [B, 3 years; G, 5 months]

Being able to share these moments with another mother is hugely helpful. It is honest, and being honest with oneself seems the most appropriate way to start solving difficulties. It can be less comfortable to own up to honest feelings alone with oneself. It is easier, and tempting, to blame one's children for 'making' one feel a certain way.

In time, mothers make a discovery. It often has to be 'discovered' many times, because it is such a surprise. It is that the mother doesn't have to solve everything herself. She can't, because she often comes in on a dispute too late to be able to make a fair judgment. She can help her children by giving them guidelines about how to decide what is fair. However, after some time, her children start to sort out issues for themselves.

G lets B have all her things. He takes this and then that, and she doesn't seem to mind a bit. But then her patience runs out. She's no pushover easy-going second child. She's got a will of *iron*. She hangs on to the one toy she really won't let him take. [B, 4 years; G, 11 months]

If mothers have to solve a dispute, they find that it doesn't mean treating both children alike. That doesn't usually work because even if two siblings get exactly the same product, such as two copies of a mass-produced toy, they themselves usually find some minute way of distinguishing the two identical products and of claiming that one of them is 'better'.

Instead, mothers learn, as their children develop, how different they are. Then their love can open out to each individual as an exciting and unique child.

Two children are much nicer than one. And I loved G very much.

I have a different love for each of them. [G, 23 months; B, 7 weeks]

At first, I was always comparing. But that wasn't helpful. G is so different from B. So slowly I learned to look at *her*, and to stop having comparisons in my mind. [B, 2 years; G, 7 months]

I was an only child. In fact, there was only me and my mum. I've always had a lot of time for myself – and now there just isn't *any*. But I *love* it. It's so rich and exciting. Of course, there's a lot of juggling, because F and I both work. But luckily, there's never been a problem with all three children at the same time. And it's fascinating to see each one grow and develop. Family interaction really interests me now. [B, 5 years; G, 3 years; G, 7 months]

Each of them is so different from the other three. They are *wonderful* kids. [15 years; 14 years; 13 years; 11 years]

We have three sons, at college and beyond. I keep three boxes in my closet. I put things in to give to each of them, but it's not about consumerism. It's my way of connecting with each. [3 adult sons]

These boxes sound a concrete way of doing what many mothers do metaphorically. They recognise each child as distinct from his siblings and collect together mental 'boxes' for each. This frees mothers from expecting their children to be similar, and from constantly comparing one with another. Once mothers describe loving each child individually, they find it easy for their love to flow to each. Each child, then, has his own unique and secure claim on his mother's love. There is no need for siblings to be rivalrous. There can be plenty of love for each child.

It sounds a lot of work to create an intimate relationship with each child, to treat each sibling as individual *and* to help each one to relate well to the others. Don't mothers have their own concerns to think about? However, bringing up two or more children is a major social responsibility. If mothers do their work well, it will help their children to relate to their peers, even those very different from themselves, to solve issues with them and to create long-lasting friendships. This is a wonderful contribution to our society.

You may have your doubts when you come across a family of squabbling children with their furious mother in a toyshop. But it's hard for outsiders to understand what is going on. You are not looking at the final result, but at the mother's work in progress.

CHAPTER THIRTEEN

Family relationships

When she is expecting her first baby, a mother will usually look round at the wider family to which her child will belong. Very likely, she will notice many cool or tense family relationships. Before now, they hardly mattered. But now she would like her child to be a part of a loving family.

Many grandparents want to support the new parents, and try to heal difficult relationships too, from their side. However, this chapter will view family relationships from the perspective of new mothers.

At meetings, mothers tend to focus on family problems.

> You don't want to land your child with all the disappointments you've experienced from your family. But you don't want them to be isolated from the family either. [G, 7 months]

This sort of remark might leave a negative impression of how problematic family relationships must be. But usually mothers are eager to use meetings to try to sort out problems. It's important to realise that many of their family relationships must be working too well to be discussed.

Families teach us so much. From being in a family, we begin to learn the immense complexity of human relationships. Perhaps, as children, we hear our parents recalling events in their childhoods. Then we discover that our grandparents' version of the same events puts our parents' accounts in a different light.

The philosopher Max Scheler believed that children first experience themselves as family members before they discover that they are also individuals:

> Only very slowly does [*the child*] raise his mental head, as it were, above this stream flooding over it, and find himself as a being who also, at times, has feelings, ideas and tendencies of his own.[144]

This is an interesting theory of how children develop. More often, psychologists assume that a child develops awareness of his own feelings first, and discovers his family's views later. I wonder whether any mothers have noticed which their own children developed first. Perhaps children with many siblings develop awareness of their families sooner than an only child.

Many families today are combinations of marriage, divorce, remarriage and blending. There aren't precise words to cover every relationship. Often, it's only at a family funeral that it becomes apparent how many people consider themselves 'one of the family'.

A couple may shyly announce to members of their families: 'We're expecting.' The couple may see this as an intimate revelation about themselves. However, their new baby will change the family 'geography' on both sides. The youngest member will soon forgo that special place, and the oldest members are affected too. 'You realise you are getting older when your grandchildren start having babies,' observed one octogenarian woman.

If this is the couple's first baby, they are now upgraded into parents. This may change how they see their own parents. Mothers often review the example of their own mothers with admiration.

There were six of us. Since becoming a mother myself, I appreciate my mother so much. I don't know how she did it. There was never money to spare – not like *we* have. But she always made us feel secure [*holding G tightly and rocking her, to demonstrate*] and safe. [B, 3 years; G, 3 weeks]

My mum is always talking to B and he *loves* it. I used to be annoyed with my mum for little things, but now when I see how good she is with B I can't admire her enough. My *nan* talks to babies. She's over ninety now, but she still does. It must run in the family. [B, 5 weeks]

I wasn't proud of my mother when I was young. She was very loving and always there for us four children, and I'm afraid I took her for granted. At school, the other kids were always saying, 'My mum's a this,' 'My mum's a that'. And I'd think, Why can't *my* mum be something? Why can't she have a job like the other kids' mums? But now I'm a mum myself, I keep thinking how *brilliant* she was. [G, 4 months]

If this is a first grandchild, the new grandmother is a beginner, like her daughter. She too has a great deal to learn.

I thought my mother would know what to do with G. I think of my mother as very experienced and competent. But I noticed that when she was with G she seemed very uncertain. That was a surprise to me. [G, 16 months]

'We *learn* to be grandmothers, just as we learned to be mothers,' observed Sheila Kitzinger.[145] What is there to learn about becoming a grandmother? Surely anyone who has been a mother knows about babies. The idea of a grandmother may suggest someone very calm and cosy. But she may not feel calm and cosy at first. Every new grandmother has to make the transition to her new role. She is now related to a baby whose primary connection is not to herself, but to her daughter or daughter-in-law.

Some new grandmothers are close to their daughters, and their styles are similar:

> My mum says exactly the same things to B as I do. I overheard her saying, while she was undoing B's nappy: 'Now I know you aren't going to like this.' That's exactly what *I* say, but my mum couldn't have known that. And there're other things, like that, that she says. [B, 2 months]

Other mothers find simple, practical ways of helping:

> I went round to my mum's. She took B and said, 'You are going to bed.' I said, 'I can never sleep in the day.' My mum said, '*Bed*! And take your jeans off.' So I went to bed and when I woke up it was two hours later. [B, 5 months]

> We went away for Christmas, and my mum came in and did all my ironing. She said, 'Well, I knew you wouldn't want to come back to a huge pile of ironing.' Only your *mum* would think of a thing like that. [G, 5 months]

Grandparents who live near enough may be able to give the support of a traditional extended family. If they move further away, the mother loses all the comfort and help they provided.

> My parents left our neighbourhood to move up north. We relied on them for help with the children. It felt like a *bereavement*. [B, 8 years; B, 6 years; G, 6 weeks]

At the same time, the new mother, once only a daughter, discovers that she also needs to be independent of her mother. This can feel unfamiliar and strange.

> I've no complaint about my mother. I think she was a very good mother to me. But going home undermined all my confidence. I suppose I *defer* to her. I always do. I listen to her and take her advice. But deferring to her with G seemed to undermine all I've learned. [G, 2 months]

I had an imaginary conversation in my head, as if I was on the phone to my mum just now. What I said was: 'Mum, you know a great deal about parenting and you've got a lot of experience. But some things about G I *do* know better than you.' [G, 6 months]

I always felt I needed to copy others. But being a mother has taught me that I can make decisions on my own. Even my own mother – I can't copy her any more. [B, 17 months]

It definitely helps the new mother if her *own* mother can feel proud of her. One mother brought her own mother along to a Mothers Talking meeting. The new grandmother started crying as she remembered:

My husband and I rushed to the hospital when B was born, and we saw him when he was only one hour old. And my husband . . . [*She tried hard not to cry, then she sobbed.*] . . . My husband, he *cried. I* cried. I didn't know I was going to cry again now. And what I thought then was, What a *wonderful* little mother [*i.e. her daughter*], what a *wonderful* mother! She was so good with B. Right from the start. [New grandmother, 3 adult children]

I was moved by this, and noticed how flushed the whole circle of mothers looked. The fact that her story moved all of us indicates, I believe, that grandmothers do not always express their enormous admiration and delight at seeing their daughters become mothers.

Sometimes the new mother wants to care for her child differently from the style of her own mother. The new grandmother can feel criticised and hurt because her own mothering, which she can't change now, is regarded as mistaken. But some new grandmothers are able to take a second look at their own mothering and decide in their daughters' favour.

When I was trying to breastfeed, my mum would say, 'There's nothing wrong with formula, you know, M.' My mum is a biologist, and I was saying, 'Mum, *you* should know. You know what animals do.' And she said, 'You are always so *stubborn*, M.' She was telling me how, when I was born, everyone said it was difficult to breast-feed. Not all women could do it and formula was proved scientifi-cally. But now I've learned to breastfeed, I think she's changed her mind. I think she'll end up the *biggest* fan of breastfeeding! [B, 2 months]

My mother keeps saying, 'Wouldn't it be nice if B came to spend the night with us?' She used to be dead against bed-sharing. But now, when I say, 'B always sleeps with us,' she says, 'Don't worry. B won't sleep on his own.' [B, 15 months]

The grandmother who had sobbed to remember her daughter becoming a mother (on page 247) then went on to recall her own mother, so that we got a picture of three generations of mothers:

My mother brought us up, Truby-King style.[146] She never cuddled us. She used to say, 'Pet, when you were babies, you slept through the night from the start.' She'll be ninety-two this week. It shouldn't matter what she did then. But, when it's you, you can't help thinking about it.

However, when the new grandmother had children herself, she found that her babies *didn't* sleep through the night, but woke and cried. She felt a failure:

My youngest was about eighteen months and he *still* wasn't sleeping through the night. I can remember sitting on the loo at night, listening to him crying. I'd be crying myself and thinking, I *shouldn't* have been a mum. I *shouldn't* have been a mum. And I'd think, Oh, *please* let him sleep through the night! Just once!

Her little grandson, aged about eight months, wasn't sleeping through the night either. His mother had told us she would comfort him when he woke up and cried. I think it must have helped her to understand her own occasional doubts about doing this when she heard the particular maternal history she had come from.

Some mothers remark that their own mothers talk as if their grandchildren are giving them a second opportunity to be mothers. The grandmothers get into a competition with their daughters over who knows best. This creates difficulties. Grandmothers are not the mothers of their grandchildren.

> My mother was always criticising me. She stayed in our holiday flat with us. Everything I did was always wrong, and she complained that I wouldn't do what she said. Finally, she complained to my brother about how I wasn't doing right for my daughter. And that was *it*. I told her what I thought – I was really angry, and she cried and left. I felt a bit bad about it. I mean, she *is* my own mother. [G, 6 months]

A particularly devious way for a grandmother to criticise her daughter is to address negative remarks, not directly to her, but to the baby. This creates two wrongs: the roping in of an innocent baby, and the bypassing of the mother.

> My mum makes little remarks to G. I don't think she knows she's doing it. She says, 'Oh dear, G. Your mum didn't put your socks on.' It makes me feel incompetent as a mother. [G, 4 months]

> When B's crying, my mum won't pick him up like I do. She tells him, 'Don't be silly. Stop making that silly noise.' She says picking him up will spoil him and stop him getting independent. [B, 5 months]

> F's mother and sister were asking me if I was still breastfeeding and if B was sleeping through the night yet. I felt criticised, so I ended up defending myself, which I didn't realise until I had talked it over with F afterwards. They were saying, 'You look tired.' And I was, 'No, no, I'm fine. I'm all right.' When I was out of the room, I could hear them saying to B, '*You* are making your mother ill.' [B, 7 months]

Some grandmothers assert themselves by constantly worrying about their daughters' ability to take care of themselves. They profess to be speaking 'for your own good'. To an outsider, they might sound concerned. But to a new mother, these comments express her own mother's lack of confidence in her.

> G wakes up at night a lot, but so far I've been okay about it. I'm like: if I can say when I wake up in the morning, 'Yes, I can face this day', then it's all right. But I went to see my mum and my mum was like: 'You've *got* to look after your*self*.' [G, 7 months]

> I phone my mum once a week, and I tell her things, but she's always trying to fix it, whereas I want her to *just listen*. I'm often in tears after the phone call. She seems to perceive me as quite fragile. She says, 'Can't you pull your socks up?' and 'Aren't you being a bit silly, darling?' [G, 8 months]

The most painful complaint that new mothers make about their own mothers is when the grandmothers don't seem particularly interested in their grandchildren. Instead of listening to their daughters, they seem entirely absorbed in their own concerns. Typical comments are:

> Everything I say is all about *her*.

> My mum never hears me. She can't listen. She immediately rebuffs what I say.

> My mum always says, 'Why are you being so *difficult*?'

> Whenever I complain, she says it's *my* fault.

> My mum always contradicts what I say. If I say, 'When I was eight, I was so unhappy,' my mum will say: 'Nonsense, you had a lovely time. Don't talk like that.'

Among new mothers the subject of their own mothers is *always* an emotive one. If the new mother's mother had died before her daughter became a mother, this is almost always a cause for tears. New grandmothers don't seem to realise how important they have become. Daughters usually long for them, however painful their earlier relationships have been. As an adult, a woman may be able to see her own mother in perspective. But once she has a baby, it is extraordinary how desperately she usually wants her own mother *as* a mother.

> My mum's mother died when she was a child. Rationally, I know my mum must have a lot of emotional problems. I can see that, when I don't need her. But, when I do need her, I lose that perspective. It's impossible to hold onto. I just want my mum as a mother. [B, 5 weeks]

> No matter how uncaring my mother is, I can't help hoping she'll turn into a good mother, *next* time, and that she'll just be an ordinary mother to me: a mother who *cares*. [B, 16 months]

> My mum was telling me that she never strove for perfection. She just wanted to be a good-enough mother. And I was going, 'Yeah, yeah,' in sympathy for her. But then I suddenly realised that her child was *me*, and I thought, Hey, *no*! What did you do for me that was only 'good enough' and not perfect? I want the *best* you can give me. [B, 17 months]

Some difficulties go back to the new mother's childhood. The mother's mother may not have helped her daughter to find the confidence to become a mother herself.

> Frankly, I've always been terrified of being a mother. Not just of the birth. Afterwards. Of not having enough to give. My mother always said to me, 'Whatever you do, *don't* have children! You haven't got the personality for it.' So I was terrified. And now I've done it. It's been hard, and I'm sure there'll be more hard bits to come. But

I can give more than I thought I could. And, when I can't, I just withdraw, and then I *can* again. [B, 4 months]

M: My mother was nineteen when she had me. It must have been hard for her. When I was thirteen months, she left me. My father brought me up. He was always very calm. He helped me and he understood me. When I was older, I saw my mother for regular visits. But my father was my real parent.

Me: So was it difficult for you to mother your own daughter after thirteen months?

M: No, the opposite. That's when it got easier. Before thirteen months, I kept thinking it might get too difficult for me and then I would want to leave. So I stayed with G all the time. I felt *terrible* if I ever left G with F, to go out to the shops. I kept wondering if this was the beginning of abandonment. [G, 3 years; B, 3 months]

Even women who have become very independent usually want a closer relationship with their own mothers, once they have babies.

One mother turned up to a meeting looking so different that everyone commented on it. She always looked beautiful, but that afternoon she glowed from inside herself. She said:

I think I understand my mother now. Instead of looking at all the things she *wasn't* doing for me, such as not offering to help me when I phoned her up saying that I was desperate and that I needed her, I suddenly saw where she was coming from. My mother is a very strong woman, and I couldn't understand why she hadn't been a better mother to me. So I asked her, and we had a good talk. Then I saw how she was with B, how gentle, and how much she loved him. And I thought, She can't have changed. She must have loved me too, and been playful and gentle with me. And I felt I could really *see* my mother properly, and I was ashamed it had taken me so long. [B, 20 months]

This seems to have been a turning point for her. Insights such as hers don't heal a troubled relationship just like that. But they make a difference. Despite a number of stormy encounters since then, I believe mother and daughter are basically reconciled.

It can be very moving to hear daughters reassess their own mothers.

First mother: One night, G's nose was blocked with mucus, so I sat on a chair, holding her upright, all night, so that she could sleep. [G, 14 months]

Me: Aren't mothers heroic? And yet all these details seem to get forgotten.

Second mother: I've been thinking about that and it makes me quite sad. I mean, I've been thinking about the things my mother did that were not good. But she must have done a lot of other things that *were* good. I don't know all the good things that she did. [G, 6 months]

Mothers think about their fathers too. Details about what their fathers did when they were young become treasured memories.

My dad is a natural pedagogue. He's great at answering a child's question with another question. He does sums with G, just for play. He used to do that with me. G *loves* it. [G, 3 years; B, 2 months]

My father used to read me books when I was little, and now I can hear his voice through mine, when I read aloud to G. I think I used to be hard to settle, and my mum would hand me over to my dad when he got home, and he used to walk up and down with me. [G, 14 months]

Grandfathers, especially, can sometimes use an old-style authority which parents rarely adopt today.

My dad is wonderful with my children, and they adore him. But he says: '*G!*' in a deep voice if G is doing something she shouldn't. G looks really frightened because she doesn't hear that kind of tone from us. [G, 3 years; B, 10 months]

However, other mothers recall their fathers with great pain. Both of the next two mothers said that their fathers would be shocked to hear what their daughters really felt about them.

First mother: My parents visited over the weekend, for 2B's birthday . . . When my father was a boy, he used to be beaten with the dog's lead. He's never done anything like that with us. But there's a *mental* way of bullying. I'm convinced it's just as bad. I've tried to tell him, but I can see he doesn't get it. He makes comments about me, but he never sees how much I really do. That leaves such a *hurt*. I can feel it deep within my chest. [1B, 2 years; 2B, 12 months]

Second mother: My father never seemed to be interested in me. I was the second child, another daughter, not the son that he wanted. At least, that's how I read it. He never abused me, but whatever I did didn't interest him . . . I said to my daughter: 'I'm always going to be *there* for you.' I was actually crying when I said it. [B, 22 months; G, 5 months]

Both mothers were determined to be better as parents. But both obviously loved their fathers and were deeply hurt that it didn't seem reciprocated.

New grandfathers may consider that this is the time to tell 'the truth' to their daughters. A daughter may have defied her parents when she was a teenager, and rudely hurt their feelings before leaving home. Now she is in the vulnerable position of becoming a parent herself. It's an easy moment to 'get even' with her. So daughter-blaming can be the order of the day:

My father arrived early at my place and he sat there, this *seething* mass of disapproval. G wouldn't go to him. She wanted me, which is only natural. But my father was like, 'Oh, you never come to see us. G doesn't know us.' But I stayed with them in the summer, and every day he would tell G that he felt sorry for her because I had made such a mess of my life. G doesn't need to hear all that. [G, 9 months]

However, becoming a mother can give a woman a new opportunity to become more assertive towards her parents. After all, most grandparents want to be connected to their grandchildren, so a new mother suddenly finds that she is in a position to set her own terms.

My mother's had five children, and she wants to help. But I find her very undermining. My family's ideas are quite dogmatic. They keep saying B's out to 'manipulate' me [*smiling down at him*]. But how *can* he be? So what I arranged was that I breastfed B, and my mother cleaned the whole house. She likes cleaning, and it's what she offered to do. [B, 4 weeks]

My mum makes little remarks about what I'm doing. So this time, before I visited her, I made a mental checklist of all the things she disapproved of. I asked myself about each thing I do, and I agreed with everything that I was doing as a mother. I said to myself, '*I am G's mum.*' So, when we got there, my mum's words didn't bother me at all. Like when she said to G, 'You'll have to come and spend the night with me.' But G can't, as she's breastfeeding. I didn't say anything and the visit was much calmer than usual. Then, when my mum was saying goodbye to G at the train station, I could see from her face how much she really *loved* G. [G, 5 months]

Today, a large number of grandparents are doing more than making the occasional visit. When new mothers are contracted to return

255

to work and look round for someone to take care of their babies, their partners seem to be the first choice, with their parents a close second. Not all grandparents live near enough. Even so, over half of all British grandparents today regularly look after their grand-children. Of these, 15 per cent do so for over forty hours a week.[147] The sudden increase in grandparent support is recent. Mothers often find themselves patching up relationships with their parents for this to work. Because they depend on the grandparents, they cannot afford to be too critical of them.

In some families, this might be an excellent arrangement. But on such a large national scale, it needs to be considered more carefully. Is there a good reason why so many mothers choose to ask their parents and in-laws to take care of their children? Or are these arrangements of convenience, because being at home them-selves or paying for childcare are not viable economic options? If so, we must be witnessing a triple unfairness. Many children are deprived of their mothers' daytime care. Many mothers forgo the experience of bringing up their own children. Many grandparents are bringing up two generations.

Often, the mother is returning to work exactly when her child is starting to explore new situations. Now he has to get used to a new intimate relationship as well. Visiting his grandmother is quite different from being dependent on her all day, without his mother. Mothers are aware of this and often return to work feeling uneasy. It would be interesting to hear from them whether they manage to sustain their intimate relationships with their small children.

It would also be interesting to hear from caretaking grandparents. Being a grandparent is different from being a parent, because she or he is legally *in loco parentis*. A grandparent doesn't have a free hand. Besides, a grandmother might feel she has done her turn at being a mother. She might aspire to be doing different work.

Similar issues arise when it is the father's parents who are doing the work-time childcare. I have grouped the 'in-law' discussions in this part of the chapter. From the mother's standpoint, the in-law relationship differs from the one she has with her own parents. She tends to be sensitive to her in-laws' comments, and anxious to measure up as a good mother in their eyes.

> My mother-in-law has eight children. I was a bit in awe of her when she came over. She came from the States, and I think she wanted to make sure we were all right. I kept wondering what she thought of me. After a day and a half, she said to me, 'You know, I think you're doing all *right*.' I felt moved and nearly cried. [G, 2 months]

> Normally, I'm a confident person. But my confidence went once I became a mother. In the hospital, when B was born, I had to change his nappy. F's parents were there, and his father said: 'Have you put the nappy on *properly*?' Normally, that would have meant nothing to me. I'm sure he didn't mean to criticise me. But it was all new and I remember feeling really judged. [B, 2 months]

The in-law relationship is usually a less intimate one. Often, the mother hasn't yet got to know her in-laws very well. So difficulties can arise because the relationship hasn't developed to a warm level when the mother could risk being honest about their differences.

> My father-in-law smokes. He's never smoked in the same room as G. But every time he comes, he asks to hold her, and every time he gives her back she smells of tobacco. I'm not sure what to do or what to say. Maybe I'm being fussy. [G, 4 weeks]

> My mother-in-law is visiting all week. B cries a lot, because he can only sleep when he is upright in his sling, and, even then, only when he consents to sleep. So B cries and I try to calm him, and she says, 'He *needs* to cry. It's *good* for him to cry.' I just don't know what to say to that. [B, 4 months]

It's hard to know the line between help and interference. My in-laws come round to 'help'. That's the way they perceive what they offer

F and me. My father-in-law said he would mow our garden. I'm happy with the garden as it is. It's hard to accept the 'help', without feeling it is interfering. [B, 6 months]

The mother's parents-in-law are also the parents of her husband. Her husband is then the link between the two families. It can be easier if he supports her over any differences, and does not leave her to fend for herself. However, he may find his loyalties divided when his parents visit.

My in-laws say I am being too soft on 1B. 1B is sensitive, and he gets upset easily. My in-laws say I should say a firm 'No' to him and mean it. After they'd gone, F said [*imitating a stern hard voice*]: '1B has got to learn to do what he's told.' He just said it. There was no discussion. [1B, 4 years; 2B, 1 year]

A particular problem arises over mothers-in-law. It sounds as if several of these new grandmothers feel distanced because the baby is the child of their son's partner, rather than of their own daughter. So a noticeable pattern seems to be to respond in ways that seem overly assertive, or even surprisingly inconsiderate to the mother.

My mother-in-law is good at making insensitive remarks. Before she'd even set eyes on G, we sent her a photo, and she telephoned me and said, 'G is the spitting image of F. He looked *exactly* like G when he was a baby. I *hope* you weren't expecting something different.' She meant she hoped I wasn't expecting G to look like me. [G, 2 weeks]

I have mother-in-law issues. F's mother keeps coming in and saying, 'Now *I'll* look after B and you *must* go out.' But I don't want to. I have to laugh, because she takes a lot of photos, and then she downloads an editing programme on her computer. She cuts round all the parts of the photos which show F and me. So now she's got a lot of photos of just B. [B, 4 months]

My mother-in-law seems so worried that G won't like her. She does everything to 'prove' that G is fond of her. We arrived really late at their house, one night, after a four-hour car journey. She opened the door, just after I knocked, and reached out her arms for G. I was just starting to say, 'I know you are longing to play with G, but she's very tired and I think it would be better to wait till morning.' But she just reached into my arms and snatched G off me. [G, 15 months]

These mothers-in-law don't seem to recognise their own important role in the new family. It surely isn't necessary to assert their presence. Their daughters-in-law could benefit greatly from all their experience and support. But these need to be given in ways which respect the wishes and indeed the existence of the mother.

Some daughters-in-law manage to improve the relationship themselves.

I took B to my in-laws, and B obviously reminded my mother-in-law of F. I overheard her saying to B, 'Shall I show you to Daddikins? Oops, I mean *Grand*-daddy.' I thought, Do I think this is kinky? No. I'm too tired. Just let her get on with it. [B, 2 months]

M: My mother-in-law is very intense. The first time she visited, she wanted to be holding B the whole time. After an hour of it, I really needed B. It was a physical sensation. But I didn't like to ask for him back. Then, after she left, I felt all those things associated with depression: drained, no energy, wanting to cry all the time, getting angry with B.

Me: How long did that last?

M: Oh, several days. Then I decided I'd telephone my mother-in-law. I said, 'I know you love holding B. But when you were holding him, I really needed him back.' And she said, 'Well, next time, you must *ask* for him.' And after that my energy came back. [B, 8 months]

G used to cry when my mother-in-law held her. I think she was responding to *my* feelings. Because my mother-in-law has just retired, and now she looks after G while I work – and as soon as I'd decided to ask her to look after G, my attitude to my mother-in-law changed, and G's changed too. [G, 13 months]

Sometimes, the new mother has married into a family which holds completely different values from hers. The issues are complex. With time and goodwill on both sides, a good relationship can evolve in which everyone is respected for their choices. But often, when the first grandchild has been born, these differences have hardly been recognised.

My in-laws are more religious than I'd realised. My mum told me recently that my mother-in-law was disappointed that we didn't get married in church. I don't believe in any of that. My mother-in-law obviously did her best not to tell me. But I feel quite funny about it, now I've found out. [B, 3 months]

My husband comes from a family where feelings are never talked about. I knew his mother wasn't happy about the way I was mothering B. But she suddenly lost it, one mealtime at her home. The whole family was sitting with us round her table. B wasn't making a lot of noise, but she suddenly stood up and shouted: 'It's all about him, him, him, him, him, *him!*' Then she said she shouldn't have let herself get angry. But afterwards, she must have had a rethink. She told F some weeks later that she thought I was a much better mother than she had ever been. [B, 7 months]

Sometimes, the father comes from a different culture. It may not be easy for the mother to build a relationship with *his* mother.

I hadn't met my mother-in-law before G was born. I kept saying I didn't want to meet the baby and my husband's mother at the same time. But literally three hours after we got home from the hospital [*after G's birth*], she turned up and stayed with us for a month. She was not a bad woman, nothing like that. It was just that I didn't know her. She was born in a tiny African village. She didn't cook for me. I think she thought I wouldn't like to eat her food. It was six months ago. It's strange what *strong* feelings I still have about that time. [G, 7 months]

More rarely, the mother in a lesbian relationship wants to relate to the parents of the biological father of her child.

My partner's a woman. I've had a baby through artificial insemination, and the father, F, keeps coming round to visit. But my partner's G's other carer. My parents aren't alive any more. But F's are. My partner and I have been to visit them several times because they are G's only living grandparents. They never talk to us. They never want to know anything about us. Yet they are G's grandparents. It's all very odd. [G, 11 months]

One useful prerequisite for creating good relationships with grandparents on either side is having had grandparents oneself, and to see one's parents relating to them.

We had the first grandchild on both sides. So 1B got a lot of attention. I don't know if it was entirely good for him. I'm not sure what is normal. Because I never knew *either* of my grandparents. Two of them had died before I was born. Two lived abroad, so we hardly ever saw them. So now, negotiating with the grandparents is an unknown area. I've got nothing to go on. I've never seen *my* mum with *her* mum. [1B, 6 years; G, 4 years; 2B, 8 months]

Grandparents are only one part of the family. There are also all the brothers and sisters who turn into new uncles and aunts. New mothers often describe a better understanding of sisters who had children before they did.

I saw my older sister turn into a mother. At first, I didn't see why she had to be like that. But now I can see how I'm doing *exactly* those things myself. And now I see how she's become much more confident as a mother. [B, 20 months; G, 4 months]

Having children also gives the sisters new ways of relating to one another.

I always go to B when he cries. I went to visit my sister, who has two children already, and she sighed when I jumped up. I heard her say something about 'first-time mother'. That really annoyed me. She's my *younger* sister. [B, 5 months]

I had my first baby when my older sister was just getting divorced. I remember I felt quite guilty, as if I had usurped her role [*of being the first one to reach a new phase*]. [B, 6 years; G, 4 years; B, 8 months]

For his part, the mother's brother may turn into a playful uncle.

My brother's not interested in babies. [*He was five years younger than his sister.*] When B and I reached my parents' house, my brother was there, but he couldn't be bothered to come down and greet us. But then he came down and he . . . he said, 'B's nice, isn't he? He's lovely.' And he played with B on the floor, and he really *enjoyed* being with B. When we left, he got up very early in the morning so he could say goodbye. [B, 8 weeks]

In some families, the siblings parent in opposite ways. They usually manage to sort out their differences, unless their parents favour one way and are critical of the other. 'A grandmother may be unaware', observed Sheila Kitzinger, 'that she is stimulating sibling rivalry and even exploiting it for her own ends, when she talks about her children, the partners and their children, and compares or contrasts personal appearance, behaviour, possessions, styles of parenting, or achievements. Even if she does not do this deliberately, siblings who are already competitive may take casual remarks as criticism.'[148]

There may be occasions when the whole family gets together. It might sound a good idea for everyone to gather round to 'see the new baby'. To most of the family, it might seem a celebratory moment. But the new mother is a novice, and the presence of so much family can feel overwhelming.

> I went to see my whole family, last weekend. I was so nervous, my heart was palpitating. I was sweating and felt faint. You feel under a microscope when you've had a baby. Even taking him out of the car, I felt as if everyone was watching me and had their own opinion about how I should do it. [B, 2 months]

> My mum invites us over every weekend. But I don't think I'm going this time. I find it stressful. My gran's there, and every time G cries, Gran thinks she's being naughty and spoiled. Gran says I've got to teach G to wait. I say, '*What*? Teach a child to wait who is only two months old?' [G, 2 months]

> One evening, my mother and my brother came, and then my grandmother. Then my mother-in-law with her family arrived too. It was a whole room full of people. They all wanted to hold B. They passed him from one to another, and B was getting quite distressed. I wanted to shout, 'Stop! Please go out, all of you!' It was very difficult for me. [B, 2 months]

Were this mother's feelings unreasonable? Or should she have stepped in and removed her child? Several meetings of mothers have recalled how, as children themselves, they had been made to go round, greeting all the adult members of their families. None of them seemed to have pleasant memories of this. Typical comments were:

> It depends on the culture. I used to have to *kiss* all my rela-
> tives. Ugh! All those stubbly beards and smelling breaths.
> I remember flaking face paint bearing down on me.
> Too much perfume and prickly beards.

It sounds as though the code of politeness, in which children from babyhood on are supposed to have intimate contact with members of their families, no matter how the children feel about it, can expose them to experiences which they don't enjoy and which are recalled, years later, with disgust.

Are families worth so much effort? Mothers sometimes ask this question. Yet we can't live in isolation, and no one has invented a viable alternative. Experiments to create more communal environments in which to bring up children, such as the kibbutz system in Israel, do not seem to prevail against the strong desire of many parents to be close to their own children.

Families are immensely complex and strong networks. They provide in-house working demonstrations of group dynamics to all their members. Long before anyone had formulated academic theories of family systems and studies of group behaviour, family members must have quietly worked out for themselves a rudimentary knowledge of how they all interacted.

The existential psychoanalyst R. D. Laing observed:

> The more one studies families in detail, the more it becomes apparent that patterns are spread over generations. We are acting parts in a play that we have never read and never seen, whose plot we don't know, whose existence we can glimpse, but whose beginning and end are beyond our present imagination and conception.[149]

This is beautifully put, though Laing believed in free will and that even while we were 'acting out parts in a play' we would be able to make more autonomous decisions if we had made sense of the 'plot'. Reflecting on family history often enables a mother to review the whole 'play', and this helps her to decide how to bring up a new 'actor'.

Many mothers are surprised by how much their perspective has changed once they have children. Now they can gain insights that were beyond their reach when they heard some of these stories as children. This means that their interactions with their families can become more conscious and sensitive.

These experiences should be recognised as a potential advantage when mothers return to work. A group of people who work together will often spontaneously reproduce a family structure. Some companies aspire to be 'just like one big happy family'. The author Doris Lessing describes, in *The Summer Before the Dark*, how Kate Brown, mother of a grown family, is much valued at a large international organisation for the motherly qualities she has learned. When I looked for a short quotation to illustrate this, I saw that there wasn't one. The motherly qualities are subtle, and it took Lessing several pages to build up the impression she wanted.[150]

However, employers don't seem to be aware of this. For example, one website targeted mothers specifically to return to business. It listed the qualities that mothers might contribute:

> In increasing numbers, visionary companies are turning to professional women with children to fill specific needs in their strategic employment plan. A historically under-utilized group, working moms bring to the business community key attributes prized in the corporate world – attributes like loyalty, experience, stability and commitment.[151]

These last four attributes could describe absolutely anyone. Yes, mothers who return to employed work do indeed bring invaluable experience with them. They have now learned how to relate effectively to a group of diverse family members, who feel strongly about one another. At work, on every level, they can use this experience to ease those personal tensions between people who might otherwise find it much harder to work together. Their abilities go far beyond 'loyalty, experience, stability and commitment'. Yet employers don't seem to have recognised this.

CHAPTER FOURTEEN

'Athenian' or 'Spartan'?

How can there be so many new ideas about something as ancient as parenting? New books on how to parent are published all the time. However, most of them are variants on only one of two basic approaches.

The two approaches to parenting are themselves ancient. They were identified by Pericles, the Athenian statesman, during the fifth century BC. The difference must have seemed very obvious to him. During the wars between Athens and Sparta, he made a speech in defence of his fellow Athenians. He said they made brave soldiers, even though they had not been trained in courage from babyhood, as Spartan boys were. He reminded his Athenian listeners:

> The Spartans, from their earliest boyhood, are submitted to laborious training in courage; we [*Athenians*] pass our lives without all these restrictions, and yet are just as ready to face the same dangers as they are.[152]

We sometimes talk of 'Spartan' conditions. But what were the ancient Spartans like? They seem to have been trained from babyhood not to be afraid of the dark or cold or of being alone, not to fuss over their food and not to cry. Older children were taught to endure hunger and to be punished by being whipped as a deterrent.[153]

The goal of Spartan society was to create an efficient team in which everyone was trained to co-operate for the common good. Individual desires threatened the enterprise. Part of the enterprise was to toughen up babies from the start, to enable them to grow into good soldiers, who could defend their native city.

This is one of the two approaches still evident today, though it tends to be physically gentler. True, not all mothers are trying to turn their children into soldiers from birth on. For this reason, I will use the word 'Spartan' in quotation marks. However, essentially, the ethos is similar. According to this way of thinking, mothers are urged to overrule their babies' wishes in the interests of social good. Although babies are too young to understand this and may get distressed, they are expected to learn to adjust quickly.

Babycare expert Truby King is a good example of this. He believed that mothers needed to regulate the appetites of their babies. A healthy baby needed to be breastfed by a daytime clock, he thought, at four-hourly intervals. But what if a baby were sound asleep exactly when the clock struck the breastfeeding hour? Truby King challenged what he called the 'can't be so cruel' mother who claimed that she could not upset her baby by rousing him from sleep. He said she *had* to rouse him for regular feeds.[154]

More recently, there have been books which advocate this approach on sleep-training and discipline, or which urge the mother to maintain her separate life away from her baby, and therefore require her to train her baby to get used to being in the care of other people. But modern writers no longer suggest hunger or whipping as enforcement. Instead, the baby is to be 'managed' by his mother, who uses a more subtle and psychological form of control. The British-born nurse Tracy Hogg provides a good example:

. . . you don't follow the baby; *you* take charge. You observe him carefully, tune into his cues, but *you* take the lead, gently encouraging him to follow what you know will make him thrive: eating, appropriate levels of activity, and a good sleep afterward. You are your baby's guide. You set the pace.[155]

The phrase which distinguishes the 'Spartan' mother from her 'Athenian' sister is: '. . . you don't follow the baby; *you* take charge.' The 'Spartan' mother is confident that she knows when her baby needs to eat, play or sleep. Her task is, therefore, to observe what he does and gently persuade him to adapt to the routine that she considers good for him.

'Spartan' thinking is usually clear-cut and straightforward to spell out. It lends itself to printed literature. New books continue to be published which emphasise the importance of following prescribed guidelines, and also warn mothers that if they do not follow them they will have spoiled anti-social babies. Mothers who are looking for a simple method of parenting find these books helpful.

The other approach to parenting is 'Athenian'. There isn't so much information on how Athenian children were brought up, which probably means that there wasn't a single definitive method. If there isn't a prescribed method, parents and nursemaids usually pick up the child when he cries, feed him when he is hungry and generally respond to him with compassion. Aristotle, who lived and taught in Athens for many years, thought that mothers loved their children in the same way that one friend might love another. A good friend, he wrote, is 'one who grieves and rejoices with his friend; and this too is found in mothers most of all'.[156]

The 'Athenian' approach is also still with us. It continues the Aristotelian idea of parents having friendly relationships with their children. 'Spartan' thinking strongly opposes this, and warns parents of the dangers of becoming their children's friends.

However, Athenian thinking was profoundly democratic, and this outlook must have played a role in creating a more egalitarian style of parenting. The Athenian goal was not military obedience or efficiency, but the recognition that rules were made by people, and could therefore be questioned. The basic idea is that many heads create many options, and that one has to have faith in the slower process of holding open discussion and listening to minority views in a democratic way. The 'Athenian' way means taking the child's view into account. It doesn't mean, as it is sometimes parodied, doing everything the child wants.

Obviously, there is no such thing as a completely 'Spartan' or 'Athenian' mother. I am using these terms in the interests of simplicity. We are all partly 'Spartan' because, as mothers, we depend on the social structure within which we live. We are all partly 'Athenian' because we cannot totally ignore the wishes of our children.

My sympathies have always been 'Athenian'. I have long been troubled by the 'Spartan' philosophy. Gradually, I have come to see that the 'Athenian' way, so important to me, does not appeal to everyone. Fortunately, most societies today leave mothers sufficiently free to choose. No doubt, these two ancient philosophies will continue to flourish for centuries ahead, as they have already done.

It's important to state that the Athenian way has a philosophy because 'Athenian' mothers frequently fear that they have no logic at all. From a 'Spartan' viewpoint, the 'Athenian' mother may look as if she is too frightened to take control of her child. Like Truby King, the 'Spartan' mother may think that if only this 'frightened' mother would use some firmness and discipline, she would get much better results. However, an 'Athenian' mother is *not* a failed 'Spartan' mother. She may find it hard to explain to her 'Spartan' sister her reasons for what she is doing. Nevertheless there *is* an underlying logic to her actions.

At the moment, mothers are returning to work sooner than they used to. This has led to a revival in popularity of the more structured and organised methods of 'Spartan' parenting. These methods offer hope of solving many of the problems which confront 'Athenian' mothers. Yet they counter 'Athenian' values. 'Athenian' mothers adopt 'Spartan' methods because they are effective, but feel confused, as if they are in the wrong camp. I hope that, by summarising their philosophy as 'Athenian' and by showing some of its underlying logic, I can help to clarify this whole way of mothering.

Many mothers are initiated into the nature of 'Athenian' mothering when they breastfeed. Breastfeeding is democratic. It works well when mother and baby co-operate. Co-operative decisions are pragmatic and do not require rules, nor even the help of a clock. Babies make it clear how often they feel hungry, when their mothers are holding them in a good position for breastfeeding and when they have fed enough. On the other hand, breastfeeding can easily fail if the mother is taught to 'know better' and to control the intervals between feeds and the duration of each one. A small baby, terrified by acute hunger, is often too distressed to relax enough to breastfeed when at last his mother wants him to. Breast milk is created on a supply/demand basis, which means that the baby's sucking decides how much milk his mother will produce. If they act in harmony, mother and baby make a good team to establish and maintain breastfeeding.

The mothers who founded La Leche League, the international breastfeeding organisation, began to collect information about breastfeeding. They discovered that four-hourly feeding, invented by Truby King to support breastfeeding, had actually led to widespread problems in maintaining maternal milk supply. So the authors of *The Womanly Art of Breastfeeding*, the manual published by La Leche League International, encouraged mothers to be guided by their babies: 'Don't be afraid to "give in" to your newborn.

"Giving in" to him is good parenting. Feed him according to his own time schedule. Comfort him when he is upset.'[157]

Sheila Kitzinger protested at the way some people advise mothers to 'show the baby who is master', or tell them, 'Let him see you are in command.' She quickly adds: 'But these are extraordinary words to use about this most tender and subtle form of human relationships . . . '[158]

Janet Balaskas, childbirth educator and founder of the Active Birth Centre, wrote: 'It is always best to respond to crying as soon as possible, before your baby gets too worked up and becomes really distressed. Her cries are meant to get your attention and to ensure her survival. Babies are not capable of manipulation and you will not "spoil" your baby by reacting immediately and picking her up.'[159]

It is interesting that these more 'Athenian' mothers are very aware of what 'Spartan' advocates would say. I am curious as to whether the reverse is also true. I wonder whether 'Spartan' mothers feel unsettled when they listen to their 'Athenian' sisters.

An 'Athenian' mother starts out differently from her 'Spartan' sister. She hasn't got a clear practical plan for training her baby to be obedient, but wants to befriend him.

> My parents were old-fashioned and very strict. My mother always said I was naughty. She said I was a nightmare when I was little, climbing everywhere, running away, pretty much like him [*pointing to B*] and she was embarrassed to take me anywhere. So now I am very careful not to get upset when B does those things. He doesn't *know* it's naughty. I don't want him to *feel* naughty. He's just curious, and I'd hate for him to go through what I did. [B, 15 months]

The 'Spartan' mother usually does her best, from the start, to control and regulate the behaviour of her baby. Newborns tend to adapt to their environment, so she soon gets the results she wants. Her 'Athenian' sister is not imposing order in the same way. She is trying to understand and befriend her baby. During her first weeks, she often feels lost in chaos with a baby whom she doesn't understand and who hasn't become her friend yet. So when questioned by a more confident mother, an 'Athenian' mother often sounds indecisive and apologetic.

> My mother and sister are always on at me to feed B less often. They ring up and ask, 'Have you got the feeding sorted yet?' I say, 'Sorted? In what way?' I just feed B when he cries, and it usually works. But they say, 'It's the timing. You're feeding too often.' They're just trying to be helpful. But then I start questioning myself as a mother. [B, 3 months]

> I've felt really down this week, very unsure of myself. It started when a friend said she left her baby to cry himself to sleep. Now she says he's no problem. But B keeps waking up, and I keep asking myself: 'Should I be teaching B to sleep? Am I depriving him?' [B, 6 months]

> B won't sleep through the night, and he seems late in crawling, and now my sister says I should sleep-train him. So now I've started doubting myself and questioning everything I do. I keep asking, 'Am I too soft on him?' [B, 7 months]

'Spartan' mothers use tough methods because they are orientated to the result. 'The ends justify the means.' The baby may have to suffer brief distress for the sake of the long-term outcome. Her 'Athenian' sister hasn't got such a clear-cut action plan with an obvious outcome. Some mothers feel reassured when they remember their own upbringing.

> I was brought up in a country where the children are carried. I was on my mother's back for years. I slept by her. In Britain, it is regulated. When I see a baby in a cot, it looks so *lonely*. [B, 7 weeks]

273

My mother visited [*from the Far East*] and she was asking me about routines. 'What is this "*routine*"?' she asked. 'Why do you have to do it? You *can't*. You *must* feed your baby when he needs it. It's not right, this "routine".' [B, 5 months]

M: My mother always had me up as late as I wanted. She never put me to bed. She saw it as an advantage. She used to say, 'You were much too *intelligent* to go to bed early. You liked to be up with us, and I didn't see why you shouldn't be.'

Me: So did you get tired and decide for yourself when to go to bed?

M: Yes. [B, 6 months]

However, mothers who were themselves brought up according to a 'Spartan' regime, but who switched to a more 'Athenian' way of mothering, struggle with painful self-doubts.

I was brought up to think I shouldn't have anything I wanted. So now I'm really confused about B. He likes to fall asleep at the breast. But obviously I want him to fall asleep by himself. So do I train him to do that? But then I think, B really *likes* to fall asleep at the breast. So should I let him? I mean, I just don't know. [B, 6 months]

I can't leave B to cry. No, I can't do it. I hold B in my arms, then put him in the cot, then he settles, then he wakes up. I pick him up and hold him, and we do it again. It's *hard*. I do it for about twenty minutes. And I talk to him and sing to him. I tell him night is for sleeping and for dreams. I tell him what we are going to do tomorrow and how he will need a good sleep first, to be ready to enjoy it. And I am so GLAD you do not have to use the methods of TORTURE, which you get recommended in some books, to get your child to sleep. [B, 10 months]

This mother had grown up in a central European country where the children were strictly disciplined to sleep all night. She found it hard to maintain her position, so she kept coming back to it in cycles of self-doubt followed by reaffirmation, until another incident triggered her self-doubts again.

Newborn babies do not make complex demands. After the first weeks, 'Athenian' mothers often describe their relief when they realise that their friendly style of mothering can work.

> I'm not going by the book. I didn't read any books. B was born and I just got on with it. I was the first one in my 'group' to have a baby – we were six weeks ahead. The others all went by a book. It amazed me that they were always looking at their watches and that they were too busy organising to enjoy their babies. I just *love* being with B. But I suppose they wouldn't feel comfortable mothering my way. They like organisation and control. [B, 3 months]

> Everyone's a paediatrician when you have a baby. Suddenly, everyone 'knows' what you should do. B used to wake every hour and a half at night. People said I needed to sleep-train him. But that's not the way F and I like to do things. And then, about six weeks ago, he suddenly slept straight through. I didn't do anything. [B, 4 months]

> One big decision I made was to find a circle of other like-minded mothers. You feel so vulnerable and new, you feel you only want people around you who support you. And it's been very hard, but now I'm convinced that I'm making choices that I can be happy with. It's a huge learning experience. It's the biggest learning experience that there is, having a child. And I think those parents who back away and get their rules out of books are really missing something. [G, 6 months]

I was astonished when I read through my notes to realise how frequently these mothers contrasted their approach with the more structured and organised 'Spartan' methods.

*

In time, babies develop and become more independent. Then 'Athenian' mothers discover a new difficulty. They have listened to their babies and taken seriously what they wanted. Their babies are now turning into confident and assertive small children. There is often a period when everything seems plain sailing. But their children are inexperienced. Now that they are older, they can assert clearly what they want. But now they can also see and reach things they cannot safely have. They have a lot to learn about their own physical safety and also about social niceties. How does an 'Athenian' mother convey this when she hasn't built up the obedience structure of her 'Spartan' sister? Does she suddenly start yelling '*No!*' to her child?

> The things B *can't* have are absolutely clear. But there are not too many of those. Then there are all those medium things. Things I'd *rather* he didn't have. I don't know what to do about those. [B, 16 months]

This is easier for a 'Spartan' mother. In her mind, there are clear rules governing the behaviour of children. Her method is not to explain each rule, but to state and enforce them, often with rewards and punishments. Both mothers need to teach their children about physical safety and moral social behaviour. The 'Spartan' child is expected to learn a set of rules. However, once he has mastered them, he knows just what to do. The 'Athenian' child is in the awkward position of assuming that there aren't many rules. His mother formulates her ideas as problems arise. So her child usually first discovers what he is supposed *not* to do just after he has done it. Suddenly, there can be a mass of details for her small child to learn. He shouldn't pull off a flap of loose wallpaper, he shouldn't suck the point of a biro or scrape a chair over a polished floor. Then there are more subtle social prohibitions, such as being instructed 'never' to tell lies, but then being required to say 'Thank you' to be polite, even to the point of dishonesty. His mother often tries to give her child her reason, as well as the rule, so there is a great deal for him to take in.

The difference becomes especially clear in the *way* the mother conveys a rule. The 'Spartan' way tends to be short and to the point. For example: 'Never run into the road.' That's the end of it. The 'Athenian' mother will say the same thing, but usually adds something like: 'Okay?' or 'Did you hear what Mummy said?' or 'I *mean* it.' Immediately the 'Athenian' child gets a subtext that the rule is not set in stone.

The 'Athenian' mother gradually realises that she can trust that her child has good intentions. He isn't trying to be naughty. But when should she intervene and for what reasons? In all the examples that follow, the no-nonsense 'Spartan' response would have been obvious.

Things are changing. B can crawl now. The other day, I was cleaning my teeth in the bathroom, and I suddenly realised that B had got our toilet brush, which was really disgusting. I don't want to keep telling him *not* to have things. But he definitely *couldn't* have the toilet brush. Suddenly I have to start telling him about dangers. [B, 6 months]

B has nightmares. I sat up all night with him because he was scared to fall asleep. I don't know if I should be doing things like that, or if I'm crazy. I feel lost. [B, 19 months]

What do you do when another child hits yours? I don't want my child to hit back, but I've read that it's good for them to express their aggression. [B, 2 years]

Tensions arise between mothers from their differences.

There isn't only *one* set of social rules. Each group of friends is different. Some are like: 'Fine. Fine.' But others are: 'We don't behave

like that *here.*' Part of being a mother is the anxiety. I feel it in my
whole body. [B, 6 years; B, 4 years; B, 7 weeks]

To listen to 'Athenian' mothers talking, it can sound as though
'Spartan' mothers are clear and organised, while they are chaotic
and have no boundaries. But this isn't true. It is impossible to have
no boundaries. The difficulty is that the 'Athenian' mother is questioning her boundaries in order to be fair to her child.

1B is not allowed to have felt pens. But this morning he asked me
for one. He wanted it so badly. Suddenly I could see that he really
needed it. So I gave one to him. He fell asleep with it in his hand,
saying '*Pen!*' I could tell it was desperately important. [1B, 2 years;
2B, 3 months]

This boundary change depends on the mother being able to
explain her logic ('If B *desperately* wants something, I should recon-
sider whether he can have it,') and, if her child is old enough,
explaining her logic to him. The 'Athenian' child can then expect
boundaries to make sense.

If the 'Spartan' child breaks a rule, his mother simply says, 'I
don't want to hear any excuses. You know perfectly well that you
are not allowed to play with Mummy's laptop.' The 'Athenian' child
gets a much longer dialogue. But at least he gets a voice. His mother
wants to hear what went wrong. Accidents and mistakes then
become explainable and, often, forgivable.

Both mothers may overestimate their child's experience. Being
adults, they both have a rough idea of what will break easily, what
will be too expensive to buy and which remarks will sound offen-
sive. If an 'Athenian' mother tells her child not to do something,
she usually explains her reasons. However, some good reasons seem
so obvious to her that she assumes that her child must know them.
She then gets exasperated with him because he doesn't.

For the 'Spartan' mother, it's the behaviour that counts. It doesn't matter *why* the child did the wrong thing. Explanation doesn't excuse it. Wrong is wrong, which can be simple and clear for the child. The 'Spartan' child may be punished for doing wrong. The 'Athenian' child will be questioned and taught the missing logic to help him understand how to do right.

At what stage do children need understanding and explanations? 'Athenian' mothers say they try to explain their logic, even when their children are babies, because, so they reason, their babies will imbibe a message from their tone of voice. However, even then, a thoughtful child will not always accept his mother's logic.

> B knows the oven is hot. But he reaches out to touch it and he gives me this look, as if to say, 'I've got to feel it for myself.' [B, 10 months]

This is often mistaken for deliberate 'naughtiness', especially if the child is disobeying his mother. How many children have been punished for being 'naughty' when, if only they were old enough to explain themselves, they could have told us that their motives were experimental? One mother, who later became a professional researcher, recalled:

> I can remember thinking – I must have been about three – 'I wonder what happens if I pull my mother's hair?' I remember feeling puzzled that I really didn't know the answer. So I pulled her hair very hard with both hands, because it was an experiment. And she yelled, and was very angry with me, and shut me in my room. And I can clearly remember thinking, Oh, I see. *That's* what happens. [B, 6 months]

If, however, a child is experimenting with something really dangerous, then both 'Athenian' and 'Spartan' mothers will cry out in alarm. Children seem to recognise this high-pitched cry by instinct. The most assertive child seems to know that this is the moment to be obedient.

The drawback is that, in a non-urgent situation, when a mother tries to understand what her child is doing, the whole process takes a long time. Her 'Spartan' sister simply says a firm 'No', and that is sufficient. Shouldn't the 'Athenian' one do the same?

A typical situation arises over physical dangers. One day, a toddler tries something that looks to him like just one more everyday experiment. He turns on a gas tap at the cooker, which is at the perfect height for him. It turns easily, and there doesn't seem much else to do with it, so he walks off to try something else. He is surprised to hear his mother shout, '*Oh, no!*' She turns off the tap, and tells him, for no obvious reason, that he must never touch it. Why is she upset? Why does she act as if he has done something terrible? Some toddlers will withdraw, and not-touching-the-gas-taps will be another of those unexplained injunctions which they teach themselves to obey. But others are doggedly experimental, turning the tap back on at the first opportunity. There is no obvious change to the gas tap, but again the mother gets very upset.

The mother may take her child out of the kitchen and close the door. Next day, they are both in the kitchen, her back is turned, and the toddler immediately makes for the cooker. Why does this intelligent child keep playing with the gas taps, when his mother has asked him not to? She has always listened to him with respect. Why won't he take a turn at listening to her? She thought she could trust him. Now she wonders if she has been raising a delinquent and has failed as a mother. Suddenly, he has changed in her eyes from being her loved and trusted son into a potential monster.

It is easy for a mother to convey by her tone of voice that her child was at fault for not immediately understanding about the risks of gas. So her child will be wrong-footed, in addition to being mystified by his mother's anxiety. This is much too complicated for him to explain, so he tries to solve the problem by doing. He keeps returning to the gas tap, not to drive her insane, but (so I believe from listening to many mothers describing this kind of situation) to get a better reaction from her. He seems to want her to acknowledge that he is not a monster but her lovable son – even if he plays with the gas tap. But his mother is perplexed. She has heard 'Spartan' criticisms that she is being too lenient with her child. She suddenly wonders if his repeated actions express *deliberate* disobedience. 'Spartan' guidelines come to mind very readily: 'He knows perfectly well what I'm asking'; 'He just likes pushing my buttons'; 'He's asking for a firm hand.'

A 'Spartan' mother would oblige with a very firm hand. However, what the child needs is for his mother to disentangle the confusion. The gas taps *are* dangerous, even though nothing shows. They have to be kept in the 'off' position unless they are in use. But the child is not at fault for not realising this, nor for finding it extremely difficult to understand. Most dangers are more obvious. A water tap, for example, can be turned on and immediately the water is clearly visible. Gas taps belong to a new category. In this kind of situation, a mother may find that it takes a long time to work out what the child doesn't understand. Then, if she spells out the danger in simple language, not just once, but repeatedly, perhaps in 'story' form so that her child can take in this difficult piece of new information, she can restore their friendship.

> *First mother*: I find it helps to say, 'I know you want to play with whatever it is, but I don't want you to because . . . ' And give a reason. [G, 4 years; B, 12 months]

> *Second mother*: I think that's right. B doesn't like it if I only tell him *not* to do something. He wants to be sure I understand his reason for *wanting* to do it. [B, 14 months]

> *Third mother* [*slowly*]: Maybe that's what G wants: for me to understand her reasons. When I get angry with her for doing something – I mean, when I've told her and *told* her not to do it – she throws

herself onto the floor and has a mini tantrum, and then she comes running to me for a cuddle. [G, 18 months]

Children need to learn. This can mean repeating experimental behaviour, even when it is exasperating to their mothers.

First mother: B likes to be in the toilet with me. He likes to lift the lid and tear off toilet paper and wipe me with it, and pull the chain. I find that *so* irritating. [B, 15 months]

Second mother: G is just the same. And does B try to push the whole toilet roll into the water? [G, 16 months]

First mother: He used to. Now he tries pushing me off the seat. Does G do that to you?

Third mother: B used to do *all* the things you've both been describing. I remember it so well. I think, just before he was two, he mastered everything he needed to know about going to the toilet. And then he stopped. [B, 3 years]

Do 'Athenian' mothers have to suffer so much personal inconvenience? Although they sometimes worry that they are becoming martyrs to their children's whims, they feel more relaxed once they have worked out the reasons for what their children were doing.

A similar difference arises over feelings. 'Spartan' children are perceived as naughty if they get angry or cry for a long time.

I've got a thing in my head that says that B shouldn't be angry. If he gets angry, that means I'm a bad mother. But I've been thinking. I don't want B to be afraid of his temper. So I shouldn't be afraid either. I need to let B be angry. But I find that very hard. [B, 18 months]

G is so emotional. She expresses all her emotions *totally*, in a way I was not allowed to [*as a child*]. She pushes all my buttons to get my attention. So I have to make my boundaries. I have to think on the spot what my limits are, and explain them to her with love.

And that can be very difficult. But I am learning to find a middle place, between my normal calm and my anger. [G, 3 years; B, 11 months]

First mother: I always used to bounce B on one of those blue birthing balls to stop him crying. I can't even *look* at one now, because I spent so long on them. And then, one night, it must have been six months ago, I decided I wouldn't. It was a real turning point. I lay down and I held B on my chest and I thought, I'm not going to be afraid of your crying. I'm being here for you. I'll just *absorb* it. [B, 17 months]

This was clearly the mother's individual decision, based on her knowledge of her child. But another mother, listening to her account, drew the following conclusion:

Second mother: That means that I have to let G be sad. But I can't bear it. When she's sad, I feel I have to do something about it. But, from what you're saying, I should let her be sad and just accept it. [B, 3 years; G, 9 months]

This isn't logical. The second mother might be impressed by the first one's discovery. But these solutions are personal.

'Spartan' mothers seem much calmer at this under-five stage, and their children are impressively well behaved in public. The 'Athenian' mother is struggling to be patient with her child. But he screams at her in the playground, won't play with her friend's child and keeps fiddling with things, scribbling on and breaking them. Most mothers then struggle with the temptation to be furious.

Why shouldn't a mother shout in fury at her child? Surely then he will understand that he did something wrong. The problem with expressing fury is that the 'Athenian' mother (and possibly the 'Spartan' mother too) has encouraged her child to think for himself, and so he does. This means that when he does something which she had previously asked him not to do, and gave him the reason why not, his action might look to her like straightforward defiance.

But her child might have had several other ideas on the go. From his own perspective, his independent thinking seemed reasonable. So he feels confused. Wasn't he supposed to think for himself? He is too young to articulate this, so typically he is silent. His mother supposes that he hasn't understood yet, so she repeats her case in a more exasperated way. Within seconds, the two can be embroiled in argument. Each finds the other one unreasonable. But if a mother can avoid resorting to fury (although can any mother keep calm every time?), she can avoid the unnecessary pain to both their feelings, and see that her child was being reasonable, after all.

> I've had a completely different week. It's taken me six months to get here and I wish I'd done it earlier. I have shouted at B, and it doesn't make any difference anyway because B never listens. So this week, I decided to do what I like: I go with B. It's no use having expectations of him. He is what he is. And when I accept him as he is, he's a different person. I see a little face emerging from the *shell* he puts on to protect himself from *me*. [B, 17 months]

The 'Athenian' way requires a good deal of self-control and patience from mothers. But in time it does bear fruit.

> I'm sorry I ever pushed B into doing anything. He does it all himself, and it's so *lovely*. I just have to wait for him to be ready. [B, 2 years]

As children grow older and go to pre-school and then primary school, social problems arise. The 'Athenian' child is likely to feel well-mothered enough to confide in his mother. He may complain bitterly one evening, so she worries about him all next day. Yet he may then turn down all her offers of help. In that case, he must only have wanted to spell out the difficulty to her. He is independent enough to want to cope with it himself.

His 'Athenian' mother can now see that, despite all her early self-doubts, her child has turned into a friendly person who is well on the way to independence. Like Pericles in the observation quoted at the start of this chapter, she may question the virtue of training. She feels especially pleased because her 'Spartan' sister had always sounded so confident about training and doubt-free. However, in my experience, all mothers question themselves. Perhaps mothers of both philosophies study one another and enable one another to ask themselves valuable questions about their mothering.

CHAPTER FIFTEEN

Mothers together

Mothers today are struggling in a culture which has minimal respect for them.

You don't think so? Then come and look with me at a busy city street. There's a mother slowly walking along, with her baby in a pram or sling. Her baby has just fallen asleep and she is trying not to joggle him awake. Passers-by hurry past her. They don't notice the mother's pale face and shadowed eyes. They are unlikely to realise that she must be exhausted because she has been waking up for her baby several times during the night. They certainly don't realise why she is walking slower than they are. No, what they perceive is a woman who has *time* to walk slowly. Obviously, she isn't 'working'.

> A friend of mine said to me: 'Are you enjoying your time off?' I thought that was quite funny. I know I'm not at work but I've never worked as hard as this in my life. [B, 15 months]

The friend and the busy people in the city street are part of a broader social attitude. Is it right for anyone to ignore mothers, or to define their work as 'time off'? It's hard for mothers to give their love generously. It's much harder when surrounded by people who don't value them.

There is another way in which the prevailing disrespect affects mothers. Most of them enter the 'mother culture' from a 'work culture'. There, they have already created their individual identities. Many are contracted to resume work after a few months. This makes it possible for a mother to see her work identity as her 'real' self, while the motherly one can seem an anomaly. The psycho-analytic psychotherapist Sue Gerhardt gives a personal description of this at the end of her book, *Why Love Matters*:

> I found that in this Baby World no one knows or cares what you think, what you have done, whom you have loved. You are simply the 'mum with the baby'. This role subsumes all other selves you have been or want to be. For many women, this is intolerable.[160]

A number of mothers who take short maternity breaks do not see the point of creating identities as mothers. What respect would they gain if they did? It must be the first time that a whole generation of mothers has been faced with such an acute identity dilemma.

You might think that, in the face of the existing social disrespect, dedicated mothers would support one another. But the journalist Lucy Cavendish points out how many mothers do the opposite:

> I find it impossible to talk to mothers without that unspoken element of competition creeping in from both sides. Whether it's about choices around education, feeding, sleeping or even something as simple as the name you have given your child, we are all playing a desperate game of one-upmanship. For if our children are successful, or deemed by our peer group to be 'successful', then all the pain and heartache and sleepless nights and worry will have been worth it.[161]

Other journalists who are mothers confirm this same intense amount of competition.[162] Work can be competitive, and success-driven. But is competition meaningful for *mothers*? Can we truly love our children for the persons they are if we set them up to appear 'successful', and as potential exhibits to impress our peer groups? Is this the best we can do?

Motherhood covers many possibilities. None of us can be good at more than a fraction of them. In this vast terrain, it seems cruel to compete. If we notice another mother doing something better than we could, this need not diminish ourselves. She is simply doing her personal fraction of what is possible.

Mothers in competition have lost sight of all that connects us. There are fundamental changes that many mothers undergo, or at least understand. These all connect to a mother's love for her child. We probably don't make all these changes ourselves. But at least we can understand where other mothers are 'coming from'.

For example, many mothers develop a new alertness and sensitivity to other people's opinions of their mothering. This sensitivity is valuable because mothers are bringing up new members of our society. However, new mothers aren't used to it, and often interpret other people's looks or comments as signs that they are being criticised. Perhaps an experienced mother notices a new mother struggling in a shop with money, shopping basket and her baby, and asks: 'Can I help?' The experienced mother probably feels warm sympathy for the new mother who reminds her of how she used to be. But the newer mother hears this question as a criticism. After all, at work, a person who needs help would be seen as incompetent. So she replies, 'I'm fine, thanks,' sounding cool and defensive. The experienced mother might well feel snubbed, until she remembers how defensive she used to feel herself.

Another common change is a new appreciation of patience. Mothers discover that patience 'works'. But that doesn't make it easy. Many mothers compare themselves to other mothers who, they say, are 'much more patient'.

One can usually be patient over anything that seems important. But different mothers regard different situations as important. So one mother might be especially patient when her child is learning to walk or talk. Another mother might get impatient at anything so ordinary, but find ample patience if her child shows a particular interest in, for example, sport or music. Some mothers find it hard to be patient when their child is ill, while others discover infinite resources of patience exactly then.

> B kept waking at night, crying and very upset. It would take about three hours to calm him and it was very unlike him. I was like, 'I don't know if I can *do* this. I didn't sign up for all of this.' I was exhausted. I needed my sleep. I felt I was running on empty. And then, one night, B puked really badly, and I realised, 'Oh, my God, he's ILL!' And suddenly, I wasn't running on empty. There was a whole extra tank that I could use. [B, 6 months]

Some mothers can be patient with young babies, but find it harder when they grow.

> B and I do things together, and it's like driving a car in first gear. There's a part of me that's longing to move up gears and go *faster*. I feel very impatient and sometimes it bursts out. [B, 2 years]

Children give us many opportunities to learn patience. Yet none of us could possibly be patient in every situation. Perhaps another mother was patient when we are sure we wouldn't have been. But she might well think the same about us.

However, mothers aren't always patient. Even a gentle woman can change to being a determined mother. This is another area where mothers may be able to understand one another. The sheer single-minded persistence of a mother can be difficult for other people to tolerate. A mother usually wants life and health for her child – much more intensely than other people may realise. Medical practitioners must be very familiar with this form of motherly strength. Many mothers become worried or distressed when their child is ill. Some doctors are extremely informative and sympathetic.

Others are the opposite, dismissive of the mother and irritated with her.

G has thrush. I thought something was wrong and I took her to the doctor when she was ten days old. But my doctor said, 'Oh, new mother, don't worry!' *Now* he tells me it is thrush. It's interesting because last week our cat died. The day before he died, I took him to our vet. I said, 'He's not behaving like his usual self.' The vet really *listened* to me. He assumed I knew what I was talking about. Whereas with G, my doctor assumed that *he* knew. [G, 2 months]

I took 2G to the doctor who was very handsome, so I thought he'd be nice. I said who I was, I told him my name, and he said: 'Right, Mum, well, you take a seat and . . .' I wanted to say: 'But I've just told you my *name*. Why won't you use it?' [*Other mothers replied that they too had been called 'Mum' or 'G's mum' or 'B's mum', which they found disrespectful.*] [1G, 4 years; B, 2 years; 2G, 3 months]

Many doctors and health workers seem to perceive mothers as 'worrying too much' or even being obsessional. They must see mothers at their most anxious moments. Perhaps it then becomes hard to respect them. Mothers seem to get *so* upset over ailments which, for doctors, are common medical events.

M: When G is ill, I have this fear that she will die. [G, 7 months]

Me: Has any other mother here had that fear? ['Oh, yes!' 'All the time.' 'Definitely.' *All the other mothers sounded relieved to acknowledge their fear.*]

G vomited for *ten* days. It was awful. I mean, it was just a bug. When I say that, it sounds like nothing. My sister is a doctor and she was very reassuring. But we were terrified, and we sat up with G for several nights. I can't explain; it's over now, but then it seemed for ever. I kept feeling terrified we were losing her. [G, 9 months]

Yet would any of us, doctors or lay people, be alive today if our foremothers hadn't worried about the minutiae of the health of our ancestors, and nursed them vigilantly till they recovered? We surely each owe our lives to a long history of mothers who have noticed and worried 'too much'.

If her child is more seriously ill, the mother may feel herself going beyond worry. People react differently. Some mothers find extraordinary energy to learn about the options facing their child. Others reach a state of almost insane terror. The most difficult part is coping with the uncertainty as to whether the child will survive. The whole ordinary world seems to recede, and to close around the mother, her child and the doctors. Little else matters. People have to remind the mother not to neglect herself. The doctors may not immediately know how to treat the child, so each day can feel eternal, filled with terrifying possibilities.

> B has been very ill. At one stage, we feared for his life. I think I suffered a kind of breakdown. I'm ashamed because I wasn't a proper mother to B. I wanted to die myself. I honestly wanted to *die*. I couldn't help B, and I didn't know what else to do. [B, 16 months]

Has any other person the experience to compare with that of the mother of her own seriously ill child? She alone connected to him before his birth. She shared their early history, knew what he liked, and what frightened him. To see his familiar face suffering pain or struggling for life is harrowing. No wonder she feels desperate. This is the risk she takes when she lets herself love her child. She is deeply connected. If her child suffers, so will she. It can feel like a loss of connection when her child is in the hands of doctors, or simply of time, and she feels helpless. But on the most basic level, she is clinging on. A mother who has lived through this frightening experience, even if she feels she survived it badly, has something special to communicate.

The mother who felt she wanted to die when her child was so ill was speaking after her son had recovered a little. She received warm and generous comfort from the mothers who heard her. She returned the following week and thanked them. But, she explained, this wasn't what she really wanted.

I'm very grateful for all the compassion that everyone gave me. But I do want it known that I failed B as a mother. I want my failure to be *honoured*. [B, 16 months]

This is an important statement. Often, mothers get stuck in protecting one another from a sense of failure. The mother who felt she had failed at a critical moment wanted what she saw as the truth of her experience to be recognised so that she could be genuinely restored to the 'community' of mothers.

She, in turn, had helped the other mothers by trusting them with the heavy burden of her helplessness and times of despair. Often, mothers feel they should not burden one another with their troubles. It can feel too heavy to share. But surely the burden can be too heavy for one mother to bear alone. People who are not mothers simply cannot imagine what it is like. Surely all mothers share the dread that their children, whom they bore, might die before they do. However difficult it can be, it strengthens us to listen to another mother who pours out her anxiety, bitterness and grief.

Every time a little circle of us listens like this, we become part of a larger international community of mothers who are able to understand and absorb an acute level of distress to the point of near-insanity. As individual mothers, we may sometimes need a dose of this resilient compassion for ourselves. Collectively, mothers can offer a realistic acceptance of distraught people. From those moments of our greatest weakness, we can generate a special tender strength.

Apart from illness, can mothers connect over other issues? Some questions seem divisive. Yet they don't have to be. One question much debated today is whether mothers are 'damaging' their children by returning to work while their children are very young. There are reports of research claiming to provide the definitive answer. However, research reports disagree with one another.[163] This may be because of the different ways in which 'damage' can be defined and measured. In any case, the whole question is surely too many-sided and individual to be settled by research results.

Here again, we don't need to argue for one solution for everyone. We can unite over a more basic position. Mothers need flexible options, especially options that allow them to change their minds if they can see that one way isn't working. Many women sign contracts with their employers before their babies are born, committing themselves to short maternity breaks. Yet no woman can be sure either of how she will feel as a mother, or of how her child is going to develop. Mothers should not have to be chained to decisions they took in such unavoidable ignorance.

> With my second baby, I understand the situation better. It's as if everything to do with babyhood has to be rushed. People talk as if the baby is the 'problem' that has to be solved so we can all go back to the all-important world of work. But to me, 2B is much more important. The real problem is what to do about my work. [1B, 12 years; 2B, 3 months]

Maternal flexibility isn't convenient for everyone else. We therefore depend on employers and others to understand and respect the importance of what we are doing as mothers. At the moment, many people pay 'lip service' to us. This is another issue that connects many of us. Mothers keep noticing signs that they are not valued for being mothers.

Most of my examples are from mothers on maternity leave, because they have time to come to meetings. But I have heard employed mothers complain that their work colleagues roll their eyes whenever they pack away work on the stroke of five-thirty. The colleagues do not appreciate that a mother's childcare might end at six-thirty. Mothers on maternity leave meet similar everyday disrespect.

> My local pharmacist talks down to me. I don't go there any more. He doesn't seem to reflect that a mother with a baby might have a degree in nuclear physics. So he doesn't address me like an intelligent person. [G, 3 months]

> As soon as you have a baby, people treat you as if your IQ has gone down several notches. [1B, 2 years; 2B, 5 months]

> I have a very nice job and, when I'm at work, people look at me as if they respect me. But when I go out with B people seem to look right through me. [B, 5 months]

People who lack respect for mothers are usually unaware of how much mothers are doing.

> *M*: No one at my work has had a baby. A woman at my office was really annoyed at me for wanting to work only three days a week. She said, 'Well, I could take time off to do what *I* want. Why should I pick up your phone just because you are at home with your baby? You should be working.'

> *Me*: Did she say what *she* would be doing if she took time off?

> *M*: She makes hats. [B, 5 months]

In the hat-maker's defence, it is only fair to add that many mothers, including myself, admit that we had very little understanding of how much mothers were doing before we had babies ourselves. Now we know only too well why hats are different from babies. A hat cannot grow into a viable member of our society. Nor can hats collectively form a new generation which will affect us all as it comes of age. The feminist economist Nancy Folbre used a different analogy, explaining that many people compare having a baby to having a pet.[164] In making hats or caring for a pet, there may be some overlap. But there are major differences.

However, a mother who wants to work part-time when she has a child may feel misunderstood by the 'working community'. Her work as a mother is to prepare a social member of the next generation. Despite this, she is often treated as a person on the outer fringes of our society. Social respect seems to be reserved for people perceived as 'working'.

Mothers don't only encounter disrespect for apparently not working. People talk about a 'mumsy look', meaning a frumpy, unappealing appearance. The features writer Kira Cochrane tried to explain why many women today feel so depressed when they become mothers. She suggests that many women feel compelled to possess the latest luxuries in order to take pride in themselves.[165] From this perspective, it might seem hard to respect some mothers. Haven't they 'let themselves go'?

My godmother has just given me a cheque for my birthday. She said, 'Make sure you spend it on yourself, not on G.' But what in the world does she think I'll spend it on? [*Hugging G.*] I have everything I need. [G, 3 months]

Before G was born, I worked in the City. If I heard that a new style of Gucci shoes had arrived in London, I'd be off and I'd have a pair of those latest shoes, on the same *day*. That's how important I thought it was. Then, when I had G, I sort of . . . [*This was at an evening meeting. G was curled up in her lap, unable to sleep because she kept coughing. M was stroking G's long hair, and the rest of her sentence had to speak for itself.*] [G, 3 years; B, 13 months]

I've spent *so* much time and energy trying to get my home nice. It's my nest. But now we've been burgled and there are tiny shards of broken glass everywhere. And that's made me realise something. I used to think that the most important thing was the state of my home. But it's not. The *most* important thing is my relationship with my children. That's something that burglars can't take away from me. [B, 4 years; B, 9 months]

Women react differently to being mothers. Some mothers care very much about material values. They may not sympathise with a mother who has changed her priorities after having a child. Nevertheless, they may well understand her.

Three-quarters of British mothers return to work within the first eighteen months of having a baby.[166] Aren't they 'voting with their feet'? Aren't they telling us that only a minority of women can be satisfied by motherhood, whereas the majority prefers to be back at work? Surely most women feel trapped at home?

But appearances don't tell the whole story. Just because mothers *are* back at work doesn't mean that this is what they all wanted. Most mothers need the money, and many enjoy the stimulus of work. If they are in a competitive profession, they fear that they will fall behind if they don't resume promptly. Besides, many are contracted to return to work at a particular time. At the point of signing the contract, the timing must have seemed reasonable. But that was before discovering how much they loved their babies.

If I don't go back to work, I'll have to repay my maternity leave, and I can't. But I don't want to go back [*tears*]. It's a complete surprise. I love B so much. I want to go on looking after him. [B, 8 months]

The thought of returning to work when G is one year is *poisoning* my last months with her. People keep telling me, 'You'll manage when the time comes.' I feel quite violent when they say that. [G, 8 months]

B learned to clap on Monday. I wouldn't want a childminder to see his first clap. [B, 9 months]

Because returning to work promptly has become the norm, it creates a group pressure on mothers to fit in.

I didn't miss my work. I loved being at home with G and B. But I was worried about how I'd be seen. My work in law is very competitive. It would be held against me if I hadn't gone back. [G, 2 years; B, 3 months]

I could easily stay at home with G till she's five. I don't miss my job. It seems far away. On the other hand, all my friends are back at work. I don't want to be the only one who's missing the party. I'd feel odd if I was the only one at home with G. [G, 8 months]

So not every mother feels trapped at home. Some feel just as trapped by being contracted to go back to work before their children are ready. This can be so painful that many mothers only acknowledge it when the pressure is off them.

I was feeling quite depressed, and I thought it was because I was missing my work and feeling trapped with G at home. Then G got a place at a nursery and we went to visit it several times. But the last time we visited I thought, I can't *do* this. G's not ready. It's not the right place for her at the moment. So I talked to F and we decided I'd work at weekends when he could look after G. And the minute we'd decided, I felt . . . My depression lifted. I *love* being at home with G. I don't feel trapped. It *expands* my whole life. I'm learning a lot. I could easily be at home with G for another year. [G, 12 months]

Before I had my first child, I worked in the City and it never occurred to me that I wouldn't return to work three months after having a baby. I enjoyed my work and I thought having a baby wouldn't make any difference. I wasn't prepared for how completely different

I'd feel when G was born. After six months, I talked to F and we agreed that I wouldn't go back to work at all. And the *moment* we'd made that decision, I felt my love for G burst out at double the strength. I think I was afraid to love her properly when I thought I'd have to leave her to go back to work. [G, 3 years; B, 13 months]

This is not the reaction of every mother. Some depend on their income, while others are thankful to resume their jobs, for emotional as well as financial reasons. However, there must be many who are swayed by social expectation. If a mother is expected to experience 'cabin fever' unless she returns to work promptly, it might take a good deal of self-confidence to ask herself if this is what she really wants. Perhaps the image of a despised 'mumsy' woman discourages some mothers who then *think* they couldn't bear it. But if social expectations shifted, then surely more women would discover that they could 'bear' to look after their children for longer than they thought.

If a mother does stay at home with her child for longer – for how long should she stay? Children develop at individual rates. Some children seem to aim for a very high level of independence, and then it can be puzzling that they need their mothers for a long time before they reach it. To an outsider, a child may appear perfectly happy and confident. However, if the mother keeps breaking down in tears at the prospect of sending him to a form of daycare, it suggests that, even though her work with her child might look secure, she *knows* that her child needs longer with her.

B was offered a place at a very nice nursery. It starts in six weeks, though I was expecting to start months later. I think we'll take it. [*Sudden burst of tears.*] I'm sorry I'm crying. I never thought I'd cry saying this. It's just that I've had an idyllic two years looking after B. But now we can't afford for me to [*unable to finish*] ... [B, 24 months]

I went back to work when 1G was twelve months, and it was too early for her. I felt terrible, and felt like punching people at work. By fifteen months, 1G was ready, and it was completely different. [1G, 2 years; 2G, 5 months]

When mother and child are genuinely ready, they both have a great deal to offer nursery and workplace. Here is the first harvest of the mother's work. Her child is excited to make friends and to become part of a larger society. Once he has got used to it, his mother finds that he can manage, so she can relax and focus more on her work.

Mothers make reliable and practical employees. Bringing up a child is so responsible and so thought-stimulating that mothers often say that they now find it easy to stay calm in a mere work crisis. They feel more grounded and able to distinguish the important issues from the trivial.

A colleague was going to tell me something. Then she said, 'But that wouldn't interest you. You're only interested in your baby.' I felt insulted. It's hard to explain, but G helps me to see the relevance of work. Issues *mean* more. I care about them passionately. [G, 6 months]

Yet one newspaper showed a large photo of a baby with a speech bubble coming out of its mouth saying, 'Say bye-bye to your career, Mummy!'[167] This idea is absurd. It must be a great loss to employers if they do not appreciate how much experience mothers are bringing back to their work.

But is every woman capable of being a mother for several years? What about those who really seem unable to cope with being mothers at all? Most of their difficulties are beyond the scope of this book. One aspect is relevant here, though. We need to remind ourselves that a mother is essential, not an add-on. She is in a relationship with her child. (So is the father, but I want to focus here on the essential role of the mother.) If a mother is evidently unable to care for her child, we have legal procedures which enable social workers to intervene 'in the interests of the child'. In extreme cases, it might be necessary to take the child away from his mother. But this means cutting into the relationship with a hidden cost to the child. Even if a mother has failed her child in many ways, it might be possible to intervene sensitively in order to find ways to understand and support the vitality of the relationship.

However, if social workers, medical practitioners, employers, and other people are going to give more support to mothers, they all need a much better understanding of what mothers are doing. Many people seem to think that the role of a mother is overrated. After all, babyhood and even childhood are soon over. They both disappear behind the curtain of 'the past' and are quickly forgotten.

These people see a mother's love for her baby as a sentimental extra, like the sugar icing over a cake. The mother has a job to do, according to the 'cake' theorists, keeping the baby fed and warm. If a baby looks contented, people assume he must be a 'good' baby. If a baby is crying, this is counted as a black mark against his mother. Some people won't notice more than that.

But whether a child looks contented or is crying is not the most important indicator. If a baby or child is being well mothered, that child will look very much alive. The mother's love will be the crucial element. Her love is an active and voluntary process. It doesn't mysteriously happen. It can't. It is a true giving. It isn't her child's reward for good behaviour, nor can it be withdrawn at the mother's whim. It takes time for her to learn how to love each child. Once she does this, her love seems to flow, through her actions, for a lifetime. True, we all tell our children stupid things that we don't really mean – things like, 'If you don't come now, I'm going home without you' – especially when we are tired or annoyed with ourselves. But on a deeper level, our love is constant.

When children arrive with their mothers for a Mothers Talking meeting, I can see how alive they look. One toddler may come running in, laughing and excited. Another is more tentative and I see him emphatically shaking his head, backing away from the open doorway. His mother cannot persuade him to walk in, but eventually, he allows her to carry him. A third child is miserable and I can hear him, a long way off, complaining to his mother. A fourth is asleep in his pushchair and wakes up halfway through the meeting, sitting up immediately, startled to be missing everything.

None of these children is apathetic. Each looks intensely present, glowing with the wonder of being alive. They radiate a kind of warmth, which expresses their joy in life and in their mothers' love. With this love, they are learning to weather difficulties. Even in their short lives, these children have all encountered pain. A mother's love cannot protect her child from that. Instead, the child seems to convert her love into his own bright energy.

This is not to claim that all mothers are generous in loving. Some ways of mothering could definitely be better. Children who have gone short of a warm relationship tend to withdraw. For example, one morning, I was walking up a hill when I noticed a toddler in his buggy, coming down towards me. Something made me really look at him. He seemed to have sunk into himself. His head was down. His hands lay limp in his lap. His legs were splayed. He didn't look tired or sulky. He looked resigned. Then I saw his caregiver, who was pushing his buggy down the hill. She was animated, laughing on her mobile. For a moment, I was tempted to scream at her: 'Don't let your toddler look like that! Get off the mobile! *Talk* to him! *Cuddle* him!' But I wouldn't like a passer-by to scream at me, so I said nothing.

Besides, what's wrong with being on a mobile? Surely mobiles are a part of ordinary life. Surely it's good for a child to learn to wait for attention. Yes, but it's a question of degree. This child's body language showed how disconnected he felt from his caregiver.

He seemed to have withdrawn, not just from her, but from feeling alive.

In this instance, the caregiver may not have been the toddler's mother. However, some mothers *are* uncaring and sometimes cruel. I know some people assert that every mother is doing the best she can 'in her own way'. Yet I'm not sure if this is true. Some women might be insulted to hear that we think their mothering is the best they could do. They *know* they are mothering poorly, but it's from a kind of despair. They may tell themselves that it doesn't matter. But on another level, it must be difficult for a mother to see her withdrawn child and convince herself that her mothering *really* doesn't matter.

Mothering certainly matters. But that doesn't mean all mothering has to be the same. Unfortunately, the media seem to debate mothering issues as if there could only be one 'right' choice for all – one sleep method, one kind of sling or whatever the issue. This often persuades mothers to take sides against others who have chosen differently. But do we need to divide against one another? We would do better to agree that, however we differ in practice, we are united in asserting our basic right to make our own autonomous mothering choices.

Our choices are often influenced by contemporary ideas. This isn't at all a recent development. For millennia, 'experts' have produced handwritten scrolls and printed books in which they claimed to have superior knowledge of babies and children. In centuries when many women couldn't read, this 'expertise' must have been intimidating.

However, today many of us have received excellent educations. We can read books that might have been too technical for our great-grandmothers. Many of us have been taught how to question what we read rather than just to accept it. Better still, we have been encouraged to formulate our own views, so that, when we become mothers, we can articulate those many existential questions that arise when we are responsible for our babies.

If we can do all this, we can surely question some of the theories that today's 'experts' have published. Besides, after the first few years of being mothers, aren't we in a position to *give* information instead of only receiving it? We could then show how widely mothers vary. This would surely help us to feel stronger and more connected to one another.

One reason why many mothers today feel competitive with one another, and also complain that they feel so guilty about being inadequate mothers, seems to be that they are constantly oppressed by the weight of values that are not their own. Measured by these alien values, most mothers fail. But couldn't we find our own words to define our own values?

We first need to see which theories surround us today. These theories *shape* our idea of motherhood. But should we allow them to? Who first thought of them? Were the theorists mothers themselves?

Psychoanalysts, even while intending to liberate us, have been surprisingly prescriptive about mothers. The only way we can free ourselves is by looking at what these psychoanalysts, and later psychotherapists and psychology researchers have written about mothers.

I am going to select a few examples to show how we need not feel overawed into accepting theories because we are 'only mothers'. Quite the opposite. It is only as mothers that we can truly question them.

The psychoanalyst Margaret Mahler was a pioneer in systematic mother-and-baby observation. She set up a children's centre in New York where she was able to observe mother-and-baby couples daily. Her theoretical starting point was to assume that most babies had a 'symbiotic' relationship with their mothers. She was curious to find out how babies first learned how to distinguish their separate identities. Her own theory was to call the baby's moment of discovery the 'rapprochement crisis'.

Mahler wanted her staff to notice 'the way the mother brought her child to the Center; removed his wraps; put him down; whether or not, on arriving, she left the child alone; and so on'.[168] With great attention to detail, she began to collect impressions of how mothers and babies interacted. She began to coin unfussy terms such as 'melting' or 'stiffening' to describe the way babies responded to being held by their mothers.

From this promising start, she could have gone further. She could easily have sat down with the mothers at her centre. She could have explained her theories of 'symbiosis' and 'the rapprochement crisis', and asked mothers for their views. However, this wasn't at all the way she saw it. She considered that her role was to teach them. 'We must educate parents as to the pitfalls and landmarks of vulnerability throughout the process [*of the rapprochement crisis*],' she wrote.[169] She didn't seem to consider that parents might have significant insights to teach her.

She went to great trouble to ensure that mothers felt at ease at the children's centre. Yet how easy do people feel when they know they are being observed? She instructed her staff to be 'as passive as the situation permitted'.[170] But did she imagine that the observer would be unobserved? One of Mahler's biographers described being taken to lunch with Mahler and feeling too overawed to eat. 'As I tried to eat, she gave me a typical Mahler look, a quiet look, an unostentatious look, and I knew she had taken in the situation.'[171] So although this look is described as 'unostentatious', the word 'look' is repeated three times, and the episode remembered decades later.

How much can an observer learn from looking? She can see behaviour, but not the reasons for it. Can she really be sure what babies are doing? Mothers themselves make tentative hypotheses, based on earlier observations, because they have to. They need to guess when their babies are too hot, too tired, too hungry and so on. Over these simple daily guesses, mothers find that they can often be wrong.

Mahler was an energetic researcher. She would notice children '. . . everywhere – on the street, in the subway, and in the super-market . . . ', she wrote.[172] The one aspect of the relationship that she couldn't see was the sheer number of unspoken interactions between children and their mothers. Here, we, as mothers, have a unique perspective. We don't need to go out of our way to look at our children. We don't need to watch them intently. We are interacting with them.

Mahler herself wasn't a mother. Her book, *The Psychological Birth of the Human Infant*, offers some clear observations which Mahler thought revealed how babies develop. The 'rapprochement crisis' depends on the earlier 'symbiotic phase'. However, neither of these theories has been discussed or evaluated by mothers *as* mothers.

The American researcher Dr Allan Schore used several of Mahler's theories, including that of 'symbiosis', in his own work on early brain development. However, his magnum opus might well seem daunting to any reader: *Affect Regulation and the Origin on the Self* has over five hundred pages of text, followed by no fewer than one hundred pages of references. Dr Schore has synthesised an impressive amount of research on early brain development. Yet his subject connects to *our* subject: how babies develop.

Mothers, Schore wrote, are crucial to the development of their children's brains.[173] In order to explain this, Schore has to move from brain development to behaviour. Here his theories intersect with mothers' experience. For example:

> At 18 months children begin to imitate what it would be like to be someone other than their own self – role taking – in pretending to be the mother.[174]

Schore's source for this observation is Dr Andrew Meltzoff, an American psychologist. Schore is scrupulous about quoting sources. It's not his fault that he hasn't used maternal ones. We haven't given him enough. But surely we *could*. This observation is about everyday child behaviour. Which of us hasn't seen a child pretending to telephone? At a young age, they lift something to their ear – a teaspoon, a toy brick, anything. Then they chatter, as they hear us do, and laugh exactly as we do. I've seen toddlers do this long before eighteen months.

Schore's book has been a respected resource for over a decade. It may teach us about babies' brains, but should we allow it to speak for our experiences as mothers? Muriel Winch, who wrote a book on mothers as early as 1924, said: 'You can talk of a baby in scientific terms, and think you have described him and labelled his characteristics, but it is only the mother who can tell you what her baby really is.'[175] If 'it is only the mother who can tell you' – why don't we?

Like so many, Schore believed he was in a position to define what mothers should be doing. He wrote: 'The essential task of the first year of human life is the creation of a secure attachment bond between the infant and his/her primary caregiver.'[176] We may be used to this terminology, but does 'secure attachment bond' really reflect how we both keep our children safe and help them to develop beyond ourselves?

The psychoanalyst Peter Fonagy has given similar definitions of what he believes is the mother's role. For example:

> What is critical is the mother's capacity mentally to contain the baby and respond, in terms of physical care, in a manner that shows awareness of the child's mental state, yet reflect coping (mirroring distress while communicating an incompatible affect).[177]

Fonagy is describing a mother's role in language that she would be unlikely to use. But are his terms better? What does he mean by a mother 'mirroring distress' of a baby? Does the image of a mirror really convey any of the aliveness of a compassionate mother? And what does Fonagy mean by 'communicating an incompatible affect'? His use of the word 'incompatible' seems illogical. Wouldn't the mother want, while not in any way denying her baby's distress, to convey a sense of hope? In that case, these two communications would be compatible. Also, 'affect' indicates the mother's feeling. But a mother would want to go beyond feeling, and reassure her baby that there was reason to be hopeful. So by considering Fonagy's terms in simpler English, we can begin to see that they are alienated and inaccurate.

Throughout this genre of psychology books on motherhood, mothers sound a constant hazard. Mahler, Schore, Fonagy and others set out clearly what they see as some of the essential tasks of mothering. This is usually followed by examples of 'types' of mothers who fail to measure up. The impression one gets is how *many* mothers must fail. Yet, it is vital for us to notice that, even when they succeed, they don't sound like real mothers. They seem two-dimensional, shadowy facilitators of their babies' development. So, even when mothers are shown to 'succeed', this genre hardly does justice to our experience.

Can we afford to let 'experts' define what we are 'supposed' to do, and then complain how badly most of us do it? If we want respect, especially from employers, or family members, or the government, we ourselves need to spell out what we do. Together, mothers are a vast and widespread international group. Nevertheless, with the Internet linking so many of us, we can hold genuine discussions. After millennia of theorists defining our role, we are, at last, in a position to define it for ourselves.

The political role of mothers is also changing. Every society owes a great deal to the work of its mothers. We could exert an even stronger and more conscious social and political influence than we have recently started to do. I often wonder if people are afraid that we might. Perhaps this is why so many 'experts' have wanted to advise us.

> Being a mother really matters. It's big. It's huge. It's *political*. The values you use to bring up your child are a political statement. [G, 7 months]

This is an important message. However, we would be stronger and more effective if we could agree together on the reasons why our work as mothers is so crucial. It's still quite usual today to hear a woman introduce herself as 'only a mother'. Yet without a mother's love, it is difficult for a child to grow into an adult who can negotiate the complexities of adult relationships. Civilised life depends on enough adults being able to read one another's many-sided signals.

We might need to find some better words. I like the medieval word 'motherful'. It has fallen out of use because 'motherly' seemed as good. But 'motherly' now means *like* a mother. We could do with a few more motherful words.

Our love seems integral to being motherful. Thank goodness it can't mean following someone else's recipe. We don't need to ask other people how to love. Often, people seem both to desire love and to fear it, because many of us have been hurt in childhood and dread being hurt in the same way again. Love is what we do when we are less afraid. It is *there*.

People sometimes say that loving a baby is hard. However, not-loving seems much harder. The eyes of a newborn have a quality of soft, numinous wonder – a look of alert sensitivity. It is hard to put into words. Dante, whose own mother had died when he was young, wrote how his words failed when he tried to describe love. The end of Dante's *Divine Comedy* describes love at the centre of Paradise.

> Now shall my speech fall farther short even of
>   what I can remember, than an infant's who
>   still bathes his tongue at the breast.[178]

Dante's image of a baby at the breast adds a new dimension to his disclaimer. Perhaps he intuitively knew that an infant at the breast would understand about love best of all. A newborn seems whole and in touch with that love which, as Dante wrote, is *'l'amor che move il sole e l'altre stelle'*, 'the love which moves the sun and the other stars'.

Too many accounts of mothers' love either idealise or denigrate it. But the reality of this love is simple. One afternoon, I was chatting to a couple while their baby slept upstairs. Then the mother said she could hear her baby stirring through the baby monitor and stood up with a tired sigh. I immediately remembered how tired I used to feel, and couldn't help feeling thankful that I was no longer on call as a new mother. Soon she came back with her baby, and I stood up to say something comforting. But I didn't say anything. For a moment, I couldn't speak. Mother and baby looked indescribably tender together. Her husband got up to kiss his daughter, and then we began discussing practical questions. But I knew I had just seen a moment of intimate love.

Notes

Every effort has been made to credit titles correctly and to acknowledge the copyright owner wherever possible. In case of any omissions, the copyright owner concerned should get in touch with Naomi Stadlen immediately.

1   Monika Abels, 'Field Observations from Rural Gujarat' in *Researching Families and Children*, ed. S. Anandalakshamy et al., New Delhi: Sage, 2008, p. 221.
2   Joni Nichols, in *International Doula*, vol. 10, issue 4, 2008.
3   Vicki Culling and Claire Wright, 'Am I Still a Mother? Making Meaning of Motherhood After the Death of a Baby', at the Meaning of Motherhood Conference, Auckland, 28 November 2008.
4   Kate Hilpern, 'Unfit to be a mother?', *Guardian,* 'G2' section, 15 January 2008. © Hilpern/Guardian News & Media Ltd 2008.
5   In her poem, Alice Meynell (1847–1922) uses the simplest words to explain how mothers feel:

Maternity
One wept whose only child was dead,
New-born, ten years ago.
'Weep not; he is in bliss,' they said.
She answered, 'Even so,

'Ten years ago was born in pain
A child, not now forlorn.
But oh, ten years ago, in vain,
A mother, a mother was born.'

The cadences at the end of each short line tell us how deeply the mother felt about the untimely death of her child. Inwardly, she had made a deep preparation, heartroom, for a living child. This loving preparation does not seem to be tidily disposable.

A social question arises when older or adult children die young. If a mother's children die before she does, is she still a mother? If her husband dies, she becomes a widow, a role which tells everyone that she had been married. No one would call her a spinster. But for a mother whose children have died there is no specific word to give dignity to the painful change, and to warn other people to be sensitive, as the word 'widow' would do. She certainly remains a mother, and there should be a word to safeguard her position. A similar word is needed for a father who no longer has a child.

6   Mary Wollstonecraft Godwin, later to become Mary Shelley, 1797–1851.

7   C. Kegan Paul, *William Godwin: his Friends and Contemporarie*, London: H. S. King, 1876, vol. 2, Chapter 1.

8   The same image was used by Brenda Hunter. When her daughter announced that she was pregnant, Dr Hunter whispered, 'Yes, and in the not too distant future your little baby will have a mother who has made room in her heart for him.' Brenda Hunter, *The Power of Mother Love*. Colorado Springs: Waterbrook Press, 1997, p. 1.

9   Leo Tolstoy, *War and Peace*, translated by Louise and Aylmer Maude, Oxford: Oxford University Press, 1954, book 4, Chapter 8.

10   Sheila Kitzinger, *A Celebration of Birth*, Seattle, Washington: Pennypress, 1986, p. 16.

11   Anne Enright, *Making Babies*. London: Jonathan Cape, 2004, p. 96. I emailed the author to ask how she had found this

image, and she replied, 'I have always been attracted to the image of the self as a house.'

12   Mariella Frostrup, *Observer* magazine, 16 November 2008. © Frostrup/Guardian News & Media Ltd 2008.

13   Søren Kierkegaard, *Kjerlighedens Gjerninger*, Copenhagen: Gyldendals Bogklubber, 1962, p. 207; *Works of Love*, translated by Howard and Edna Hong, London: Collins, 1962, p. 203.

14   Tess Stimson, *Sunday Telegraph*, 'Stella' section, 25 January 2009.

15   Anne Perkins, 'Clijsters' victory has rebooted the debate about what our culture says mothers are', *Guardian*, 15 September 2009, p. 11. © Perkins/Guardian News & Media Ltd 2009.

16   Stephanie Merritt, *The Devil Within: A Memoir of Depression*, London: Vermilion, 2008, p. 173. Reprinted by permission of The Random House Group.

17   Letter in *Breastfeeding Matters* #179, Nottingham: La Leche League GB, September–October 2010, p. 19.

18   Stephanie Merritt, *The Devil Within: A Memoir of Depression*, London: Vermilion, 2008, p. 174.

19   Harriet Lane, 'First Person' report in *Observer* magazine, 12 February 2006. © Lane/Guardian News & Media Ltd 2006.

20   OUP Material: Hopkins, G.M., *The Poems of Gerard Manley Hopkins*, 4th edition edited by W.H. Gardner, N.H. MacKenzie (1976), 3 lines from 'No worst, there is none. Pitched past pitch of grief', (1948). By permission of Oxford University Press on behalf of the British Province of the Society of Jesus.

21   Hazel Douglas and Mary Rheeston in *Keeping the Baby in Mind*, ed. Jane Barlow and P. O. Svanberg, London and New York: Routledge, 2009, pp. 33–4.

22   Carol Davis, 'A big push', *Guardian*, 'G2' section, 2 November 2010. © Davis/Guardian News & Media Ltd 2010.

23   Glenda Cooper, 'I thought my baby was a monster', report on the documentary, 'Help Me Love My Baby' (Channel 4), *Daily Telegraph*, 3 December 2007.

24   Lucy Atkins, 'I felt completely out of control', *Guardian*, 29 January 2008. © Atkins/Guardian News & Media Ltd 2008.

25   Ingrid Biery in *New Beginnings*, La Leche League International Inc., issue 6, 2008–09, p. 16.

26   Stephanie Merritt, *The Devil Within: A Memoir of Depression*, London: Vermilion, 2008, p. 264.

27   Neil Rhodes (ed.), *John Donne: Selected Prose*, London: Penguin, 1987, p. 126.

28   The mothers who refer to their babies as 'like a tyrant' have got into this position.

29   Elizabeth Cleghorn Gaskell, *My Diary*, privately printed by Clement Shorter, London, 1923, p. 20.

30   'Apology' in *Portrait of Socrates*, translated by R. W. Livingstone, Oxford: Oxford University Press, 1938, 1961, pp. 11–12.

31   Ina May Gaskin gives a moving example in *Spiritual Midwifery*, Summertown: Tennessee Book Publishing, 1978, p. 457. In *Babies, Breastfeeding and Bonding*, she describes the illness and death of her first child, aged twenty.

32   Tillie Olsen describes this sense of her baby being 'a miracle to me' in 'I Stand Here Ironing' in *Tell Me a Riddle* (1960), London: Virago, 1986, p. 12.

33   Alessandra Piontelli, *From Fetus to Child*, London: Tavistock/Routledge, 1992, p. 78.

34   J.-P. Laurenceau and B. M. Kleinman, 'Intimacy in Personal Relationships' in *The Cambridge Handbook of Personal Relationships*, ed. A. L. Vangelisti and D. Perlman, Cambridge, New York: Cambridge University Press, 2006, pp. 645–6.

35   Samuel Taylor Coleridge, *Opus Maximum*. Princeton, New Jersey: Princeton University Press, 2002, p. 132.

36   John Bowlby, *Attachment* (1969), Harmondsworth: Penguin, 1971, pp. 380–81.

37   Patreascu Peberdy, quoted in a report in the *Daily Telegraph*, 10 November 2006, p. 7.

38   Virginia Ironside, *Janey and Me – Growing Up With My Mother*, London: Harper Perennial/HarperCollins, 2004. She also describes wanting not sex but 'the buzz of closeness'.

39   D. W. Winnicott, *The Maturational Processes and the Facilitating Environment*, London: Hogarth Press, 1972, p. 49. Winnicott also pointed out that not all mothers can hold their babies in a safe way.

40   D. W. Winnicott, *The Child, the Family and the Outside World*, Harmondsworth: Penguin, 1963, p. 86.

41   Julia Hollander, *When the Bough Breaks, a Mother's Story*, London: John Murray, 2008, extract in the *Guardian*, 'Family' section, 8 March 2008. © Hollander/Guardian News & Media Ltd 2008.

42   Ibid.

43   F. Truby King, *Feeding and Care of Baby*, Oxford: Oxford University Press, 1913, p. 259.

44   Ibid., p. 42.

45   Personal communication with a one-time member of the staff.

46   Sigmund Freud, *The Standard Edition of the Complete Psychological Works of Sigmund Freud*, translated and edited by James Strachey, published by The Hogarth Press. Reprinted by permission of The Random House Group Ltd. Henceforth abbreviated as *SE*, vol. VII, p. 156.

47   Sigmund Freud, *SE*, vol. VII, p. 223.

48   Sigmund Freud, *SE*, vol. XXIII, p. 188.

49   Sigmund Freud, *SE*, vol. VII, p. 223.

50   Ibid.

51   Ibid.

52   Sigmund Freud, *SE*, vol. XVI, p. 314.

53   Sigmund Freud, *SE*, vol. XXIII, p. 154.

54   Sigmund Freud, *SE*, vol. XVI, p. 313.

55   Ibid.

56   Sigmund Freud, *SE*, vol. XVI, p. 314.

57   Sigmund Freud, *SE*, vol. IV, p. 252.

58   Sigmund Freud, *SE*, vol. X, p. 6.

59   His son, Martin Freud, comments helpfully in his autobiography, *Glory Reflected*: '. . . my mother would never expect father to act as a nursemaid.' Martin Freud, *Glory Reflected*, London: Angus & Robertson, 1957, p. 55.

60   Sigmund Freud, *SE*, vol. XVI, p. 313.

61   J. M. Masson (ed.), *The Complete Letters of Sigmund Freud to Wilhelm Fliess*, Cambridge, Massachusetts and London: Belknap Press/Harvard University Press, 1985, p. 67.

62   Sigmund Freud, *SE*, vol. XVI, p. 314.

63   Sigmund Freud, *SE*, vol. XXIII, p. 189.

64   Sigmund Freud, *SE*, vol. XXII, p. 122.

65   Diane Bengson, *How Weaning Happens*, Schaumburg, Illinois: La Leche League International, 1999.

66   Alexander Solzhenitsyn, *One Day in the Life of Ivan Denisovich*, translated by Ralph Parker, Harmondsworth: Penguin, 1963, pp. 23 and 98.

67   *Holy Bible, Book of Isaiah*, chapter 49, verse 15.

68   Peter Fonagy, *Attachment Theory and Psychoanalysis*, New York: Other Press, 2001, p. 166.

69   Mariella Doumanis, *Mothering in Greece: From Collectivism to Individualism*, London: Academic Press, 1983, p.44.

70   Kate Hilpern, 'Umbilical cords just got longer', on 'helicopter' parents, *Guardian*, 10 September 2008. © Hilpern/Guardian News & Media Ltd 2008.

71   Lyn Craig, *Contemporary Motherhood: The Impact of Children on Adult Time*, Aldershot, Hampshire: Ashgate, 2007, p. 137.

72   Bernard Law Montgomery, *The Memoirs of Field-Marshal the Viscount Montgomery of Alamein K.G.*, Watford, Hertfordshire: Odhams Press, 1958, p. 13.

73   Ibid., p. 77.

74   From an unpublished, unsigned and undated essay written

for my Birkbeck course, 'The Psychology of Motherly Love'.

75 Dorothy Rowe, Preface to *Death of a Mother, Daughters' stories*, ed. Rosa Ainley, London: Pandora/HarperCollins, 1994, p. xi.

76 Rosa Ainley, 'My Mother was a Footballer' in *Death of a Mother*, ed. Rosa Ainley, London: Pandora/HarperCollins, 1994, pp. 197–8.

77 Camila Batmanghelidjh, *Shattered Lives: Children who live with courage and dignity*, London: Jessica Kingsley, 2006, p. 94.

78 Decca Aitkenhead, 'They have our minds opened up, dissected and put back together again', article on Grendon Prison, *Guardian*, 'Weekend' section, 14 July 2007. © Aitkenhead/ Guardian News & Media Ltd 2007.

79 Thomas Szasz makes this point in *The Meaning of Mind*, Westport, Connecticut: Greenwood Press, 1996, especially Chapter 5.

80 The psychoanalyst Donald Winnicott said that if a mother could 'feel herself into her infant's place' her infant would get a sense of 'going on being'. Unfortunately, he seemed to think mothers only did this towards the end of pregnancy and for 'a few weeks after the birth of the child'. That sounds a very short time. *Through Paediatrics to Psychoanalysis*, London: Tavistock, 1958, pp. 303–4.

81 Alison Gopnik, Andrew Meltzoff and Patricia Kuhl, *How Babies Think*, London: Weidenfeld & Nicolson, 1999, p. 53.

82 John Clare, 'I Am'. This poem is in many collections.

83 Judith Woods, 'A pushy mum knows best', *Daily Telegraph*, 21 September 2010.

84 René Spitz, *The First Year of Life*, New York: International Universities Press, 1965, p. 123.

85 Margot Sunderland, *The Science of Parenting*, London: Dorling Kindersley/Penguin, 2006, p. 224.

86 D. W. Winnicott, *The Child, the Family and the Outside World*, Harmondsworth: Penguin, 1964, p. 78.

87 Alison Gopnik, *The Philosophical Baby: What children's minds tell us about truth, love and the meaning of life*, London: Bodley Head, 2009, p. 245.

88 Anne Manne, *Motherhood: How should we care for our Children?* Crows Nest, NSW: Allen & Unwin, 2005, p. 312.

89 *Daily Telegraph*, 1 March 2007, p. 4.

90 *Cassandra, an essay by Florence Nightingale*, introduced by Myra Stark. New York: The Feminist Press, 1979, p. 52.

91 Mary Kenny, 'The party's always over when motherhood begins', *Daily Telegraph*, 26 September 2000.

92 James B. Pritchard (ed.), *The Ancient Near East, An Anthology of Texts and Pictures*, Princeton, New Jersey: Princeton University Press, 1975, vol. II, p. 216.

93 D. W. Winnicott, *The Child, the Family and the Outside World*, Harmondsworth: Penguin, 1964, p. 27.

94 W. M. Brody, 1959, quoted by R. D. Laing in *Self and Others*, London: Tavistock, 1969, p. 85.

95 R. D. Laing, *Self and Others*, London: Tavistock, 1969, p. 67.

96 Phil Daoust, 'Aah! Alone at last', *Guardian*, 'G2' section, 2 February 2010. © Daoust/Guardian News & Media Ltd 2010.

97 Ibid.

98 V. Groskop, 'Private: keep out', interview with Kate Atkinson, *Daily Telegraph* magazine, August 2006.

99 David Elkind, *The Hurried Child: Growing Up Too Fast Too Soon*, Reading, Massachusetts: Perseus Books, [1981] 1988, p. 3.

100 Anne Manne, *Motherhood: How should we care for our Children?* Crows Nest, NSW: Allen & Unwin, 2005.

101 Brenda Hunter, *The Power of Mother Love*. Colorado Springs: Waterbrook Press, [1973] 1999, p. 56.

102 'Man can become whole not in virtue of a relation to himself but only in virtue of a relation to another self', Martin Buber, *Between Man and Man*, [1947] London & Glasgow: Fontana edition, 1961, p. 204.

103 René Spitz, a psychoanalyst, put it starkly: 'Man, when he is deprived of dialogue from infancy, turns into an empty asocial husk ... Life, as we conceive of it, is achieved through dialogue.' René A. Spitz, *Dialogues from Infancy: Selected Papers*, edited by Robert N. Emde, New York: International Universities Press, 1983, p. 159.

104 Michele Roberts, herself a twin, tried to recapture the experience in the womb in *The Visitation*, London: Women's Press, 1983, p. 3.

105 Sheila Kitzinger, *A Celebration of Birth*, Seattle, Washington: Pennypress, 1986, p. 20.

106 Sheila Kitzinger, *The Experience of Breastfeeding*, Harmondsworth: Penguin, 1979, p. 46.

107 Frederick Leboyer, *Birth Without Violence* [French original, 1974], London: Wildwood House, 1975, p. 68.

108 Lynne Murray and Liz Andrews, *The Social Baby*, Richmond, Surrey: The Children's Project, 2000, pp. 26–7.

109 The poet William Wordsworth traced his poetic genius back to early experiences of studying his mother's face. William Wordsworth, *The Prelude*, 1805–6 version, edited by J. C. Maxwell, Harmondsworth: Penguin, 1971, p. 84.

110 Alessandra Piontelli, *From Fetus to Child*, London: Tavistock/Routledge, 1991, p. 9.

111 John Locke, *An Essay Concerning Human Understanding*, 1690, Book II, Chapter 1.

112 Examples can be found in '"Yum, yum! Delicious Babies!"', an article on 'parentlit' in poetry and prose by Jenny Turner, *Guardian*, 'Review' section, 1 August 2009. © Turner/Guardian News & Media Ltd 2009.

113 This point is well introduced by the Catholic-existential theologian Dietrich von Hildebrand, in *The Nature of Love*, translated by John F. Crosby with John Henry Crosby, South Bend, Indiana: St Augustine's Press, 2009, pp. 196–9.

114 René A. Spitz, *The First Year of Life*, New York: International Universities Press, 1965, p. 127.

115 Lynne Murray and Liz Andrews, *The Social Baby*, Richmond, Surrey: The Children's Project, 2000, pp. 56–7.

116 'The degree of connectedness that may exist across interactions in an intimate relationship may wax and wane.' Jean-Philippe Laurenceau and Brighid M. Kleinman, 'Intimacy in Personal Relationships' in *The Cambridge Handbook of Personal Relationsips*, edited by Anita L. Vangelisti and Daniel Perlman, Cambridge: Cambridge University Press, 2006, p. 640. 'Wax and wane' seem good words to describe the way that mothers adjust.

117 Geraldine Bell, *Observer*, 14 December 2008. © Bell/Guardian News & Media 2008.

118 Alison Gopnik, *The Philosophical Baby: what children's minds tell us about truth, love & the meaning of life*, London: Bodley Head, 2009, p. 242.

119 Martin Buber, *I and Thou*, translated by Walter Kaufmann. Edinburgh: T. & T. Clark, 1970, p. 79. 'In the drive for contact (originally, a drive for tactile contact, then also for optical contact with another being) the innate You comes to the fore quite soon, and it becomes ever clearer that the drive aims at reciprocity, at "tenderness".'

120 Virginia Woolf, *Moments of Being*, London: Grafton Books, 1989, p. 107.

121 'First Person: "Fran Broadwood"', *Guardian*, 'Family' section, 16 September 2006. © Broadwood/Guardian News & Media Ltd 2006.

122 Aldous Huxley, *Brave New World*, 1932. Many editions. Citations taken from Chapter 3.

123 Quoted by Patricia Morgan, *Who Needs Parents?* London: The Institute of Economic Affairs, Health and Welfare Unit, 1996, p. 39.

124 'Research suggests', reports a government Green Paper, 'that only a minority of parents find that having a child actually improves their relationship with their partner in the short-term, often because of practical issues.' *Support For All: the Families and Relationships Green Paper*, London: HMSO, 2010, pp. 56–7.

125 See Ina May Gaskin, *Ina May's Guide to Childbirth*, New York: Bantam Books, 2003, p. 239 for an account of the husband's role during birth, especially in minimalising medical intervention. She gives examples of birth stories in which the husband's participation made a significant difference (see p. 137, for example).

126 Adrienne Burgess, Head of Research at the Fatherhood Institute, personal communication.

127 Scott Coltrane, *Family Man: Fatherhood, Housework and Gender Equity*, Oxford: Oxford University Press, 1996.

128 David Code, *To Raise Happy Kids, Put Your Marriage First*, New York: Crossroad Publishing, 2008. This is misleading. Parents are not facing an either/or choice between prioritising one another or their children. They are creating a family relationship to which they all belong. It's a complex situation and no overall ruling is the answer for every occasion.

129 Marc and Amy Vachon, *Equally Shared Parenting, Rewriting the rules for a new generation of parents*, New York: Penguin, 2010.

130 Adrienne Burgess, Head of Research at the Fatherhood Institute, personal communication.

131 Daniel N. and Nadia Bruschweiler-Stern, *The Birth of a Mother*, London: Bloomsbury, 1998, pp. 64–5.

132 Dr Jack Newman, 'The medicalisation of motherhood, implications for psychotherapy'. Anthony Stadlen, Inner Circle Seminars no. 151, London, 9 May 2010. http://anthonystadlen.blogspot.com.

133   Jaber F. Gubrium and James A. Holstein, *Analyzing Narrative Reality*, London: Sage, 2009, p. 130 on *nomos*, the 'we' of marriages.

134   For example, Carl Rogers, founder of Person-Centred Therapy, explains how it felt to be the fourth child out of six. Carl R. Rogers, *A Way of Being*. Boston: Houghton Mifflin, 1980, p. 55. See also Godfrey T. Barrett-Lennard, *Steps on a Mindful Journey*, Ross-on-Wye: PCCS Books, 2003, especially Part 2.

135   Rebecca Abrams, *Three Shoes, One Sock and No Hairbrush, Everything you need to know about having your second child*, London, Cassell [1988], 2001, pp. 9 and 17.

136   Judy Dunn and Carol Kendrick, *Siblings: Love, Envy and Understanding*, London: Grant McIntyre, 1982, p. 220.

137   Rachel Cusk, *A Life's Work, on becoming a mother*, London: Fourth Estate, 2001, p. 2.

138   Rebecca Abrams, *Three Shoes, One Sock and No Hairbrush, Everything you need to know about having your second child*, London: Cassell [1988], 2001, p. 61.

139   Jane Patricia Barrett, 'Mother-Sibling Triads', unpublished PhD thesis, 1992, p. 209, microfilm in British Library.

140   Judy Dunn, *Sisters and Brothers*, Cambridge, Massachusetts: Harvard University Press, 1985, p. 98.

141   Sigmund Freud, *SE*, vol. IV, pp. 251 and 255.

142   Judy Dunn and Carol Kendrick, *Siblings: Love, Envy and Understanding*, London: Grant McIntyre, 1982, p. 219.

143   Adele Faber and Elaine Mazlish, *Siblings Without Rivalry*, New York: Avon Books, 1987, pp. 16–17.

144   Max Scheler, *The Nature of Sympathy*, translated by Peter Heath, London: Routledge, 1954, p. 247.

145   Sheila Kitzinger, *Becoming a Grandmother: a Life Transition*, London: Simon and Schuster, 1997, p. 184.

146   Truby King's concept of mothering is quoted on p. 76.

147 'One in six grandparents now babysitting 40 hours a week', research from Saga Insurance in www.maturetimes.co.uk, 3 April 2010.

148 Sheila Kitzinger, *Becoming a Grandmother: a Life Transition*, London: Simon and Schuster, 1997, p. 156.

149 R. D. Laing, 'Family Scenarios' in *The Politics of the Family*, London: Tavistock, 1971, pp. 86–7.

150 See Doris Lessing, *The Summer Before the Dark*, Chapter 2, 'Global Food', London: Jonathan Cape, 1973.

151 www.WorkLifeInitiative.com.

152 Thucydides, *The Peloponnesian War*, translated by Rex Warner, Harmondsworth: Penguin, 1954, p. 118.

153 Plutarch, 'Lycurgus' in *Greek Lives*, translated by Robin Waterfield, Oxford: Oxford University Press, 1998, p. 25. See also A. Powell, *Athens and Sparta*, London: Routledge, 1988, 2001, p. 235.

154 F. Truby King, *Feeding and Care of Baby*, Oxford: Oxford University Press, 1913, p. 70.

155 Tracy Hogg and Melinda Blau, *The Baby Whisperer Solves All Your Problems: Sleeping, Feeding and Behaviour – Beyond the Babies from Infancy through Toddlerhood*, London: Vermilion, 2005, p. 16.

156 Aristotle, *The Nichomachean Ethics*, Oxford: Oxford University Press, 1971, vol. IX, p. 4. See also vol. VIII, p. 7.

157 La Leche League International, *The Womanly Art of Breastfeeding*, Seventh Revised Edition, Schaumberg, Illinois: LLLI, 2004, p. 69.

158 Sheila Kitzinger, *The Experience of Childbirth*. Harmondsworth: Penguin, 1971, p. 219.

159 Janet Balaskas, *Natural Baby*, London: Gaia Books, 2001, p. 74.

160 Sue Gerhardt, *Why Love Matters*, London: Brunner-Routledge, 2004, p. 208.

161 Lucy Cavendish, 'The war at home', *Observer* magazine, 28 March 2010 (other title: 'Motherhood: stay-at-home or back-to-work? The battle continues'). © Cavendish/Guardian News & Media 2010.

162 For example, Sali Hughes, 'I'll never be a Proper Mum', *Guardian*, 'Family' section, 27 March 2010. © Hughes/ Guardian News & Media Ltd 2010.

163 Amelia Gentleman, 'The Great Nursery Debate', *Guardian*, 'Family' section, 1 October 2010. © Gentleman/Guardian News & Media Ltd 2010.

164 Nancy Folbre, *The Invisible Heart*, New York: New Press, 2001, p. 109.

165 Kira Cochrane, 'All too much', *Guardian*, 'G2' section, 29 April 2010. © Cochrane/Guardian News & Media Ltd 2010.

166 Amelia Gentleman, 'The Great Nursery Debate', *Guardian*, 'Family' section, 1 October 2010. © Gentleman/Guardian News & Media Ltd 2010.

167 Illustration to Madeleine Bunting, 'Baby, this just isn't working for me,' *Guardian*, 1 March 2007.

168 Paul E. Stepansky (ed.), *The Memoirs of Margaret Mahler*, New York: Macmillan, Free Press, 1988, p. 140.

169 Ibid., p. 151.

170 Margaret S. Mahler, Fred Pine, Anni Bergman, *The Psychological Birth of the Human Infant*, London: Hutchinson, 1975, p. 26.

171 Alma Halbert Bond, *Margaret Mahler: a biography of the psychoanalyst*, Jefferson, North Carolina: McFarland, 2008, p. 131.

172 Paul E. Stepansky (ed.), *The Memoirs of Margaret Mahler*, New York: Macmillan, Free Press, 1988, pp. 149–50.

173 Schore wrote, 'In the first Chapter I asserted that a number of disciplines are now converging on the centrality of the basic principle that the growth of the brain is dependent

upon and influenced by the socioemotional environment, and that for the developing infant the mother essentially *is* the environment', Allan N. Schore, *Affect Regulation and the Origin of the Self*, Hillsdale, New Jersey/Hove: Laurence Erlbaum, 1994, p. 78.

174 Allan N. Schore, *Affect Regulation and the Origin of the Self*, Hillsdale, New Jersey/Hove: Laurence Erlbaum, 1994, p. 492.

175 Muriel Wrinch (Mrs H. H. Schultz) and H. H. Schultz, *Mothers and Babies, A Practical Book about the Everyday Life of the Baby from Birth to Four Years Old*, London: T. C. and E. C. Jack, 1924, p. 4.

176 Allan N. Schore, 'Attachment Trauma and the Developing Right Brain: Origins of Pathological Dissociation' in *Dissociation and the Dissociative Disorders*, edited by Paul F. Dell and John A. O'Neal, New York/Abingdon: Routledge, 2009, p. 109.

177 Peter Fonagy, *Attachment Theory and Psychoanalysis*, New York: Other Press, 2001, p. 166.

178 Dante Alighieri, *Paradiso*, translator unknown, London: J. M. Dent, 1900, p. 407, canto 33, ll.106–8. Dante's poetry abounds with beautiful images of mothers.

Bibliography

Abels, Monika, 'The expression of Emotional Warmth: Ethno-theories of Rural and Urban Indian Mothers and Grandmothers', unpublished dissertation, Universität Osnabrück.

Abrams, Rebecca (1988), *Three Shoes, One Sock and No Hairbrush*, London: Cassell.

Ainley, Rosa, ed. (1994), *Death of a Mother*, London: Pandora/HarperCollins.

Anandalakshmy, S., Chaudary, Nandita, Sharma, Neerja, eds (2008), *Researching Families and Children*, New Delhi: Sage.

Aristotle (1971), *The Nichomachean Ethics* [350BC], Oxford: Oxford University Press.

Balaskas, Janet (2001), *Natural Baby*, London: Gaia Books.

Barlow, Jane and Svanberg, P. O., eds (2009), *Keeping the Baby in Mind, Infant Mental Health in Practice*, London and New York: Routledge.

Batmanghelidjh, Camila (2006), *Shattered Lives: Children who live with courage and dignity*, London and Philadelphia: Jessica Kingsley.

Bengson, Diane (1999), *How Weaning Happens*, Schaumburg, Illinois: La Leche League International.

Bond, Alma H. (2008), *Margaret Mahler: A Biography of the Psychoanalyst*, Jefferson, North Carolina: McFarland.

Bowlby, John (1971), *Attachment*, Harmondsworth: Penguin.

Bradish, Prudence (1919), *Mother-Love in Action*, New York and London: Harper.

Buber, Martin (1961), *Between Man and Man* [1947], London & Glasgow, Fontana edition.

Buber, Martin (1970), *I and Thou* [1923], Edinburgh: T. & T. Clark.

Burgess, Adrienne (1997), *Fatherhood Reclaimed*, London: Vermilion.

Code, David (2008), *To Raise Happy Kids, Put Your Marriage First*, New York: Crossroad Publishing.

Coleridge, Samuel Taylor (2002), *Opus Maximum* [c. 1819–23], ed. Thomas McFarland, Princeton, New Jersey: Princeton University Press.

Coltrane, Scott (1996), *Family Man: Fatherhood, Housework and Gender Equity*, Oxford: Oxford University Press.

Craig, Lyn (2007), *Contemporary Motherhood: The impact of children on adult time*, Aldershot, Hampshire: Ashgate.

Cusk, Rachel (2001), *A Life's Work, on becoming a mother*, London: Fourth Estate.

Dante Alighieri (1900), *Paradiso* [c. 1308–21], London: J. M. Dent.

Derrida, Jacques (2005), *On Touching – Jean-Luc Nancy*, Stanford, California: Stanford University Press.

Doumanis, Mariella (1983), *Mothering in Greece: From Collectivism to Individualism*, London: Academic Press.

Dunn, Judy (1985), *Sisters and Brothers*, Cambridge, Massachusetts: Harvard University Press.

Dunn, Judy and Kendrick, Carol (1982), *Siblings: Love, Envy and Understanding*, London: Grant McIntyre.

Elkind, David (1981), *The Hurried Child, Growing Up Too Fast Too Soon*, Reading, Massachusetts: Perseus Books.

Enright, Anne (2004), *Making Babies, Stumbling into Motherhood*, London: Jonathan Cape.

Faber, Adele and Mazlish, Elaine (1987), *Siblings Without Rivalry*, New York: Avon Books.

Folbre, Nancy (2001), *The Invisible Heart*, New York: New Press.

Folbre, Nancy (2008), *Valuing Children, Rethinking the Economics of the Family*, Cambridge, Massachusetts: Harvard University Press.

Fonagy, Peter (2001), *Attachment Theory and Psychoanalysis*, New York: Other Press.

Gaskell, Elizabeth Cleghorn (1923), *My Diary (1835–38)*, London: Clement Shorter.

Gaskin, Ina May (1987), *Babies, Breastfeeding and Bonding*, South Hadley, Massachusetts: Bergin & Garvey.

Gaskin, Ina May (2003), *Ina May's Guide to Childbirth*, New York: Bantam.

Gaskin, Ina May (1978), *Spiritual Midwifery*, Summertown, Tennessee: Book Publishing.

Gerhardt, S. (2004), *Why Love Matters, How Affection Shapes a Baby's Brain*, Hove and New York: Brunner-Routledge.

Gopnik, Alison (2009), *The Philosophical Baby: what children's minds tell us about truth, love & the meaning of life*, London: Bodley Head.

Gubrium, J. F. and Holstein, J. A. (2009), *Analyzing Narrative Reality*, London: Sage.

Hewlett, Sylvia Ann (1993), *Child Neglect in Rich Nations*, New York: United Nations Children's Fund.

Hicks, Jennifer, ed. (2006), *Hirkani's Daughters: Women who scale mountains to combine breastfeeding and working*, Schaumburg, Illinois: La Leche League International.

Hogg, Tracy with Blau, Melinda (2005), *The Baby Whisperer Solves All Your Problems*, London: Vermilion.

Hollander, Julia (2008), *When the Bough Breaks, a Mother's Story*, London: John Murray.

Hunter, Brenda (1997), *The Power of Mother Love*, Colorado Springs: Waterbrook Press.

Inness, Julie C. (1992), *Privacy, Intimacy and Isolation*, Oxford: Oxford University Press.

Ironside, Virginia (2004), *Janey and Me – Growing Up With My Mother*, London: Harper Perennial/HarperCollins.

Kierkegaard, Søren (1962), *Kjerlighedens Gjerninger* [1847],

Copenhagen: Gyldendals Bogklubber; *Works of Love*, London: Collins.

Kitzinger, Sheila (1997), *Becoming a Grandmother, a Life Transition*, London: Simon & Schuster.

Kitzinger, Sheila (1986), *A Celebration of Birth*, Seattle, Washington: Pennypress.

Kitzinger, Sheila (1979), *The Experience of Breastfeeding*, Harmondsworth: Penguin.

Laing, R. D. (1969), *The Politics of the Family*, London: Tavistock.

Laing, R. D. (1969), *Self and Others*, London: Tavistock.

Laing, R. D. and Esterson, Aaron (1964), *Sanity, Madness and the Family*, London: Tavistock.

La Leche League International (2010), *The Womanly Art of Breastfeeding*, completely revised and updated 8th edition, Diane Wiessinger, Diana West, Teresa Pitman, London: Pinter & Martin.

Leboyer, Frederick (1975), *Birth Without Violence*, London: Wildwood House.

Lerner, Harriet Goldhor (1989), *The Dance of Intimacy*, Wellingborough, Northamptonshire: Thorsons.

Lessing, Doris (1973), *The Summer Before the Dark*, London: Jonathan Cape.

Livingstone, R. W. (1938), *Portrait of Socrates*, Oxford: Oxford University Press.

Lomas, P. ed. (1967), *The Predicament of the Family*, London: Hogarth Press.

Magagna, Jeanne, et al., eds (2005), *Intimate Transformation: Babies with their Families*, London: Karnac.

Mahler, Margaret S. (1988), *The Memoirs of Margaret S. Mahler*, ed. Paul E. Stepansky, New York: Macmillan, Free Press.

Mahler, Margaret S., et al. (1975), *The Psychological Birth of the Human Infant*, London: Hutchinson.

Manne, Anne (2005), *Motherhood: How should we care for our children?* Crows Nest, NSW: Allen & Unwin.

McDougall, Joyce (1989), *Theatres of the Body*, London: Free Association.

Merrill, Barbara and West, Linden (2009), *Using Biographical Methods in Social Research*, Los Angeles/London: Sage.

Merritt, Stephanie (2008), *The Devil Within, a memoir of depression*, London: Vermilion.

Minturn, L. and Lambert, W. W. (1964) *Mothers of Six Cultures*, New York: Wiley.

Morgan, Patricia (1996), *Who Needs Parents?* London: The Institute of Economic Affairs, Health and Welfare Unit.

Murray, Lynne and Andrews, Liz (2000), *The Social Baby: Understanding Babies' Communication from Birth*, Richmond, Surrey: The Children's Project, CP Publishing.

Nightingale, Florence (1979), *Cassandra* [1852], introduction by Myra Stark, New York: Feminist Press.

Odent, Michel (1999), *The Scientification of Love*, London/New York: Free Association Books.

Olsen, Tillie (1986), *Tell Me a Riddle*, London: Virago.

Piontelli, Alessandra (1992), *From Fetus to Child*, London/New York: Tavistock/Routledge.

Plutarch (1998), *Greek Lives* [late first century BC], Oxford: Oxford University Press.

Powell, A. (1988), *Athens and Sparta*, London: Routledge.

Pritchard, James B., ed. (1975), *The Ancient Near East, An Anthology of Texts and Pictures*, Princeton, New Jersey: Princeton University Press.

Scheler, Max (1954), *The Nature of Sympathy*, London: Routledge.

Schore, Allan N. (1994), *Affect Regulation and the Origin of the Self*, Hillsdale, New Jersey/Hove: Erlbaum.

Schore, Allan N. (2009), 'Attachment Trauma and the Developing Right Brain' in *Disassociation and Dissociative Disorders*, Dell, Paul F., ed., New York/Abingdon: Routledge.

Solzhenitsyn, Alexander (1963), *One Day in the Life of Ivan Denisovich*, Harmondsworth: Penguin.

Spitz, René A. (1983), *Dialogues from Infancy*, New York: International Universities Press.

Spitz, René A. (1957), *No and Yes, On the genesis of human communication*, New York: International Universities Press.

Spitz, René A. (1965), *The First Year of Life*, New York: International Universities Press.

Stadlen, Anthony and Naomi (2005), 'Families' in *Existential Perspectives on Human Issues*, van Deurzen, Emmy and Arnold-Baker, Claire, eds, Basingstoke, Hampshire and New York: Palgrave Macmillan.

Stadlen, Naomi (2004), *What Mothers Do – even when it looks like nothing*, London: Piatkus.

Stern, Daniel N. and Bruschweiler-Stern, Nadia (1998), *The Birth of a Mother*, London: Bloomsbury.

Stern, Daniel N. (1995) *The Motherhood Constellation, a Unified View of Parent-Infant Psychology*, New York: Basic Books.

Sunderland, Margot (2006), *The Science of Parenting*, London: Dorling Kindersley/Penguin.

Szasz, Thomas (1996), *The Meaning of Mind*, Westport, Connecticut: Praeger.

Szasz, Thomas (1961), *The Myth of Mental Illness*, New York: Harper & Row.

Thucydides (1954), *The Peloponnesian War*, Harmondsworth: Penguin.

Tolstoy, Leo (1954), *War and Peace*, Oxford: Oxford University Press.

Truby King, F. (1913), *Feeding and Care of Baby*, Oxford: Oxford University Press.

Vachon, Marc and Amy (2010), *Equally Shared Parenting, Rewriting the rules for a new generation of parents*, New York: Penguin.

Vangelisti, A. L. and Perlman, D., eds (2006), *The Cambridge Handbook of Personal Relationships*, Cambridge and New York: Cambridge University Press.

Von Hildebrand, Dietrich (2009), *The Nature of Love*, translated by Crosby, John F. with Crosby, John Henry, South Bend, Indiana: St Augustine's Press.

Winnicott, D. W. (1963), *The Child, the Family and the Outside World*, Harmondsworth: Penguin.

Winnicott, D. W. (1972), *The Maturational Processes and the Facilitating Environment*, London: Hogarth Press.

Winnicott, D. W. (1971), *Playing and Reality*, London: Tavistock.

Woolf, Virginia (1989), *Moments of Being*, London: Grafton Books.

Wrinch, Muriel (Mrs H. H. Schultz) and Schultz, H. H. (1924), *Mothers and Babies*, London: T. C. and E. C. Jack.

Index

Abels, Monika 4

Abrams, Rebecca 220, 223-4

activities with babies and toddlers 122-34
    allowing child to choose 144-5
    educational 123, 132-3, 144
    experimentation 126, 133, 279, 280, 282
    independence of child 128-9, 131
    nurseries and playgroups 128, 129-30, 132
    organised 122, 128, 129

adoption 12, 64, 68

advice 8, 34, 117, 233
    unwanted 43, 118-19

Ainley, Rosa 101

Aitkenhead, Decca 103

anger
    child's 282, 289
    mother's 35-7, 70-1, 107, 112, 145, 181,
        260, 279, 283-4

anxiety 25, 32-5, 115-16, 122, 278, 290

appearance
    father's 215
    mother's 214-15, 295

appetite, mother's 31

arguments *see* quarrels

Aristotle 269

'Athenian' (democratic) *vs.* 'Spartan'
        (authoritarian) approach 267-85
    boundaries 278
    and breastfeeding 271-3
    and child's safety 276, 277, 279-81
    explaining to child 278-9, 281
    mother's anger 283-4
    'naughtiness' 279, 282-3
    and school problems 284-5
    sleep-training 268-9, 273, 274
    teaching social rules 276-8

Athens, ancient 46, 267, 269

Atkinson, Kate 153

'attachment parenting' 68, 69, 77,
    117

attention 85-110
    baby's demand for 18, 23
    benefits to child 106-8
    breaks from 95-6, 103-4, 172
    divided 98-9
    effect of death of mother 100-1
    father's role 104, 105
    forgetfulness 87-8
    lack of 101-3
    as lifetime commitment 108-9
    nanny's 105-6
    negative 99-100, 102
    and second child 104
    of working mother 104-5
    worrying 96-8

aunt 261-2

authoritarian philosophy 23
    see also 'Athenian' *vs.* 'Spartan'
        approach

baby
    communication with 5, 41-2, 44, 53
    demand for attention 18, 23
    as guest 3, 13-14, 15
    like an intruder 29-30
    learning about 40-53

muscles 56
need for heat 65
newborn behaviour 69, 140, 159, 162-7, 168-9
sensitivity of 25-6, 44
uniqueness 43-4, 45, 46-8
see also specific topics
baby shower 15
'baby-wearing' 68
babycare education 46
'back-seat drivers' 118-19
Balaskas, Janet 272
Barrett, Jane Patricia 224
bath or shower time
child's 230
mother's 114, 137, 139, 146, 179, 195
Batmanghelidjh, Camila 101-2
bedtime 58, 178-9, 274
see also sleep
Bell, Geraldine 172
birth
as disappointing experience 34, 161
father and 190-1
feelings of love after 17-18
loss of child 11, 12-13
mother's feelings during 16
of second child 222-5
as start of intimacy 161-3
books, instruction 68, 275, 302-3
boredom
of child 127, 170
of mother 20, 142, 172, 183
boundaries 278
Bowlby, John 62, 66
Bradish, Prudence 2
brain
child's 125, 305-6
mother's 2
breastfeeding 57, 85-6, 90, 137, 146, 166-7, 194, 247-8, 255
effect on father 191-2

Freud on 78-84
night-time 140
regulation of 76, 268, 271-3
second child 225
sucking reflex 56
Truby King on 76, 268, 271
weaning 82, 83
Bruschweiler-Stern, Nadia 214-15
Buber, Martin 180, 318
Burgess, Adrienne 193, 209
Byrd, Richard 153

career *see* work
Cavendish, Lucy 287
cerebral palsy 71-2
Charcot, Jean-Martin 77
chastisement, physical 70-1
choices
child's 144-5
mother's 98, 136, 302
Clare, John 108
clothes
baby 15
mother's 215, 295
Cochrane, Kira 295
Coleridge, Samuel Taylor 13-14, 60
commitment, mother's 18, 21
communication with child 5, 41-2, 53, 147, 165-6, 167-8
conversation 2, 44, 59, 106, 125, 133, 165, 179
development of speech 73
face-to-face 125
negotiation 42-4, 139-40
reading each other's signals 169
taking turns 143-4
see also touch and holding
competition
among mothers 287-8, 302, 303
with father 205-6
conception 11-12

confidence
    child's 45, 60, 130, 148, 152, 276, 298
    mother's 118, 119-21, 123, 160, 214,
        251-2, 257, 273
'continuum concept' 68
conversation 2, 44, 59, 106, 133, 165, 179
    face-to-face 125
'core' 29-30, 31
Craig, Lyn 98
crèches 61, 129
criticism
    dealing with 118-19
    by family 35, 58
    of father (by mother) 201-3, 205, 206
    by grandmother 19, 249-50, 251, 255,
        257, 258, 260, 263
    self-criticism 112-21
crying 19, 41, 44-5, 65-7, 115, 116, 137,
        140, 172, 174
    'Athenian' vs. 'Spartan' approach to 272,
        273, 274, 283
    mother's 114
    second child's 228
cuddling
    by father 196, 197-8, 207
    inability to 62, 66-9
    Truby King on 76-8, 84, 248
    see also touch and holding
cultures, different 4, 260-1, 273-5
curiosity, baby's 27, 72-3, 272
Cusk, Rachel 221-2

Dante Alighieri 308-9
death
    of child 11, 12-13, 311-12
    of grandmother 251
    of mother 100-1, 184-5
decision making
    by child 144-5
    by mother 112
depression 297

father's 192, 212
    postnatal 30-8, 198, 295
diary 118
disability
    of child 71-2
    of mother 66-8
disapproval, mother's 133
doctors 289-91, 300
Donne, John 38
Doumanis, Mariella 96
'down' times 20, 22, 23-5, 114
Dunn, Judy 221, 229

education
    in babycare 46
    pressure to introduce 123
    spontaneous 132-3, 144
Einstein, Albert 5
Elkind, David 155
'emotional health' (as term) 8
energy
    changing 24-5
    low 113-14
    recovering 35-6, 118
Enright, Anne 21
Equally Shared Parenting 201
Expectations, mother's 26-7, 195, 220, 284
experimentation, child's 126, 133, 279, 280,
        282
'experts' 75-84, 302-8
eye contact 139, 142, 162-3

Faber, Adele 233
facial expressions, reading 163
failure, feelings of 48-9, 112-21, 292
family, extended
    aunts and uncles 261-2
    complexity and interaction 264-5
    criticisms by 35, 58
    gatherings 58, 263-4
    influence of background on mother 35-6

family, extended (*cont.*)
    relationships 243-66
    see also grandfathers; grandmothers;
        grandparents; in-laws; mother of
        mother
father-in-law 257-8
fathers 27, 185, 189-217
    appearance 215
    arguments 212-14
    attention of 104, 105
    and the birth 36, 190-1
    and breastfeeding 191-2
    as chief carer 196
    compared to mothers 13
    in competition with mother 205-6
    and consistency of parenting 210-11
    contribution of 198, 201-5, 207-11
    and couple relationship difficulties
        196-7, 199, 200-1, 204-7, 212-17
    demands on 194-6
    depression 192, 212
    divided loyalties to wife and parents 258
    feelings of exclusion 192-4, 212
    holding baby 190-1, 196, 197-8
    importance to child 208-10
    mothers' criticisms of 201-3, 205, 206
    pride 215-16
    reluctance of 211-12
    and second child 226-7
    sex life 196-7, 214-15
    and slings 63
    supportiveness 198-9
    and work 194, 195, 196, 199, 211
fears
    child's 132
    mother's 35
    prisoners' 102-3
feelings, child's expression of 131-2
feminists 135
Folbre, Nancy 295
Fonagy, Peter 92, 306-7

forgetfulness 87-8, 114
Freud, Sigmund 77-84, 231-2
Froehlich, Edwina 109

Gaskell, Mrs 45
Gerhardt, Sue 287
Godwin, William 13-14
Gopnik, Alison 106, 126, 175
grandfathers 253-5
grandmothers 244-53
    compare children's parenting skills 262-3
    criticisms by 19, 249-50, 251, 255, 257,
        258, 260, 263
    difficult relationships with 251-3,
        258-61, 272
    help of 211, 226, 246, 255, 260
    influence of their childhood 248
    lack of interest 250
    learning process of 245-6
    misguided involvement 146, 171, 259, 260-1
    mother's own 263
    review their own mothering 247-8
    see also mother-in-law; mother of
        mother
grandparents 243, 244, 246, 261
    as carers 255-6
    see also grandfathers; grandmothers
growing up, pace of 155-6
guilt 31, 33, 303

heartroom 14-28
    difficulties maintaining 22-5
    difficulty developing 29-39, 54
    expansion of 26-7
    giving too much 25
    as long-term commitment 18
    as two-way process 18-19
    uses of term 14, 22
heat, baby's need for 65
'Help Me Love My Baby'
    (documentary) 35

helpers 20-1, 67-8
helpfulness of child 147-8
Hogg, Tracy 268-9
holding *see* touch and holding
Hollander, Julia 71-2
honesty 167
Hopkins, Gerard Manley 33
house-room, creating 14-15, 18
housework 52
humility 47
humour *see* laughter
Hunter, Brenda 156
Huxley, Aldous 185-6

'I-you' and 'I-it' relationships 180-1
identity
    linked with career 30-1, 136, 176-7,
      287, 297
    loss of 29-30
illness, child's 23, 50-1, 236, 289-92
impatience *see* patience
independence
    of child 128-9, 131, 164, 177-8, 298
    of mother 29-31, 38, 135-43, 172, 183-4,
      235-6
India 4
individuality
    of child 169, 186-7, 241-2, 244
    of mother 43-4, 45, 287
    see also independence; person, child as
injections 64
in-laws 19, 146, 171, 249, 256-61
interdependence 38
Internet 113, 307
intimacy 158-88
    baby as person 164-7
    baby's withdrawal from 168-9
    betrayal of 180-1
    continuity as crucial 171
    of couple 199, 200-1, 204-7, 212-17
    and death of mother 184-5

    definition 166
    difficulty with 181-2, 184, 185-8
    excessive 182-4
    extended to other children 177-8
    honesty and 167
    importance of 158-60
    increasing complexity 167-8, 177-80
    intensity 173-7
    misunderstandings 170-2
    and other adults 185, 186
    reading each other's signals 169-70
    start of 161-3
    unexpectedness 172-4
Ironside, Virginia 65
irritability 20
Isaiah, prophet 86-7

'kangaroo care' 77
Kenny, Mary 136
kibbutz system 264
Kids Company 101
Kierkegaard, Søren 22
Kitzinger, Sheila 16, 161, 162, 245, 262-3, 272
knowledge, mother's lack of 46-7
Kuhl, Patricia 106

La Leche League 6, 109, 271-2
Laing, R. D. 152, 264-5
Lane, Harriet 33
laughter
    first 174, 230
    in mothers' group 115
    sharing with child 23, 170, 208
layettes 15
learning
    by child 91, 126
    by mother 46-8, 52-3, 90-3
Leboyer, Frederick 162
lesbian couples 261
Lessing, Doris 265
Liddiard, Mabel 77

Liedlof, Jean 68
Locke, John 164-5
love, mother's
    at birth of child 17-18
    courageous nature 2-3
    defined 1-7
    importance of 53, 300-2, 308
    link with learning 47-8
    for second child 21-2, 36, 223-4
    unconditional nature 19
    'upbuilding' quality 22
    see also heartroom; intimacy
lullaby, Sumerian 141

Mahler, Margaret 303-5, 307
Manne, Anne 126
    maternity leave 122-3, 171, 198, 287,
        293-4, 296
Mazlish, Elaine 233
Meltzoff, Andrew 106, 306
'mental health' (as term) 8, 31
'mentalisation' 92
Merritt, Stephanie 30-1, 32, 38-9
Meynell, Alice 12-13, 311-12
Montgomery, Bernard Law, Field-Marshal
        99
mother-in-law 19, 146, 171, 249, 256-61
mother of mother
    admired for mothering skills 244-5
    criticisms by 249-50, 251, 255
    death of 251
    difficult relationship with 251-3, 272
    as helper 211, 226, 246, 255
    influence of childhood relationship
        with 35, 36, 68, 246
    lack of interest 250
    need to be independent of 246-8
    pride in daughter 247
    see also grandmothers
mothering, nature of 25-6
mother's presence, importance of 126-7

Mothers Talking 5-6
multiple births 16
Murray, Lynne 162

nannies 105-6, 156, 160
nappy-changing, help with 195, 225
'naughtiness' 279, 282-3
needs of mother 135-43
negotiation 42-4, 139-40
newborn behaviour 69, 140, 159, 162-7,
        168-9
Nichols, Joni 7
Nightingale, Florence 135
nurseries 129-30, 132, 298-9

observation *see* attention
Odent, Michel 2
orphanages 64
oxytocin 2

patience 133, 140-1, 288-9
Peberdy, Patreascu 64
peers, child's interaction with 148-51, 177-8
Pericles 267, 285
person, child as 37, 43, 45, 46, 48, 106,
        116, 128, 129, 164-7, 173
    definition of 'person' 164
    first eye contact 162
    new sibling 221
    see also individuality
'personal choice' 136
phenomenology 4-5
Piontelli, Alessandra 55, 164
play 4, 126, 127, 147
    and siblings 150-1
playgroups 128, 129-30
postnatal depression 30-8, 198, 295
pregnancy 13, 16-17, 55-6, 161-2, 190
    second 220-1, 223
prisoners 102-3
Pritchard, James 141

problems, articulating 34
psychoanalysts 303-7
   see also Freud, Sigmund

quarrels
   children's 151, 240
   parents' 212-14

'rapprochement crisis' 304, 305
relationships
   adult 152-3, 158-9, 167-8, 184
   child's 126-7, 153
   couple 189-90, 196-7, 199, 200-1, 204-7,
     212-17
   'I-you' and 'I-it' 180-1
reluctant mothers 153-4
research, inadequacies of 3-4, 5
role playing 305-6
routines, appropriateness of 44
   breastfeeding 76, 268, 271-3
   sleep-training 76, 117, 197, 208, 268-9,
     273, 274-5
   see also 'Athenian' *vs.* 'Spartan'
     approach
Rowe, Dorothy 100-1

safety, child's 10-11, 93-4, 234, 276, 277,
   279-81
scans 55, 164
Scheler, Max 244
Schore, Allan 305-6, 307
second child 104, 218-42
   behaviour of older child 236-39
   birth of 222-3
   contrast in mother's attitude to 228-9
   effect on mother's relationship with
     first child 224-5, 226-8, 220
   mother's love for 21-2, 36, 223-4
   preparing first child for 221
   protecting two children 234
   response of older child 225-6

and tiredness 234-6, 239-40
   see also siblings
separation, mother and child 128-9, 173,
   180
self-doubt, mother's 17, 45-6, 49-50,
   273-5, 285
self-sacrifice, mother's 135-8
sex life 73, 196-7, 214-15
sexual abuse 181
sexuality, Freud on 78-84
sharing, mother and child 142-4, 148-9
shopping 124
showers *see* bath or shower time
siblings
   behaviour of older child 236-40
   comparisons and differences 232, 241
   disputes 239–40
   effect of new baby 226-7
   family awareness of 244
   helpfulness of older child 225-6
   interaction of 229-31
   mother's 261-2
   rivalry 231-4
   significance of birth order 220
   taking turns 150-1
   see also second child
sister, mother's 261-2
sleep
   bed-sharing 196, 248
   child's refusal to 23, 24, 34, 47-9, 56, 91,
     115, 140-1, 178-9, 219, 248, 277, 289
   in cot 58, 77
   father and baby 196, 207, 208, 211
   Freud on 79, 80, 81
   mother's lack of 31, 98, 117, 133, 140,
     141-2, 200
   newborns and 140, 164
   training 76, 117, 197, 208, 268-9, 273,
     274-5
slings 63, 72, 117, 128-9
smacking 70-1

smell 161
smiling 152, 174, 208
Social Baby, The 162, 168
social disrespect 286-8, 290, 293-5, 298, 299
social life
    adult 144, 153
    of child 142, 149
social workers 300
Socrates 46
Solzhenitsyn, Alexander 85-6, 109-10
'Spartan' approach see 'Athenian' vs.
       'Spartan' approach
speech 73, 131-2, 178-9
Spitz, René 124, 165-6
Stern, Daniel 214-15
stimulation 122-8
stress (of child), research into 131
'success' and 'failure' 48
sucking 78-84
Sumer, ancient 141
Sunderland, Margot 125
support groups 113-21, 275, 292
swimming 26-7
'symbiosis', theory of 303-4, 305

'tabula rasa', theory of 164-5
teamwork (of mother and baby) 138-40,
      143, 171
timing 48-9
tiredness, mother's 6-7, 19-20, 88, 93,
      113-14, 133-4, 169
    effect on relationship with partner 200,
      213
    family concern for 249
    lack of sleep 31, 98, 117, 133, 140,
      141-2, 200
    mental fatigue 89-90, 94-5
    after newborn phase 45
    and two children 234-6, 239
toddlers 22
Tolstoy, Leo 16

touch and holding 54-74
    adults' sex life 73, 196-7, 214-15
    art of picking up and putting down
      69-70
    'attachment parenting' 68, 69, 77, 117
    calming effect 60
    chastisement 70-1
    communication through 58-9
    co-operation of baby 69, 71-2
    curiosity 72-3
    deprivation behaviour 64
    development of distance 73
    family members and 146
    by father 190-1, 196, 197-8, 207
    grasping reflex 72
    importance of 60-2, 74
    inability to cuddle 62, 66-9
    as protective yet sensitive 166
    reasons for benefits of 64-6
    sexual abuse 181
    slings 63, 72, 117, 128-9
    theories of 68
    Truby King on 75-8, 83-4, 248
    work environment creates
      desensitisation to 57
toys 123, 124, 127, 143-4, 149
trapped, feeling of being 153-4, 167, 172
    father's 212
    by need to return to work 297
Truby King, Frederic 75-8, 83-4, 248, 268,
      270, 271
trust
    child's, for mother 71, 103
    mother's, for child 49, 277
turns, taking
    adult difficulties with 152-4
    copying behaviour 151
    generosity of mother 154-5
    by mother and child 143-8, 156-7
    with other children 148-51
    by parents 154

quarrels 151
social pressures 155-6
unfairness 152, 153

uncertainty, mother's 45-6, 49-50
uncle 262
understanding, mother's 11, 47, 48, 85-6,
    90-5

Vachon, Amy and Marc 201

weaning 82, 83
What Mothers Do 7-8
Winch, Muriel 306
Winnicott, Donald 66, 69, 126, 142,
    317
Wollstonecraft, Mary 13-14
Woolf, Virginia 183
Wordsworth, William 319
work
    benefits of mothering experience to
        employer 265-6, 299

daycare 60, 298
desensitisation at 57
divided attention of mother 104-5
early return to 187-8, 271, 293, 296
father as chief carer 196
grandparents as carers 256
maternity leave 122-3, 171, 198, 287,
    293-4, 296
nannies 105-6, 156, 160
nurseries and playgroups 128, 129-30,
    132, 298-9
pressures on father 194, 195, 196, 199,
    211
reluctance to return to 52, 61, 156,
    296-9
and sense of identity 30-1, 136, 176-7,
    287, 297
and social disrespect to mothers 286-8,
    293-5, 298, 299
standards of competency translated to
    motherhood 203
worrying 96-8, 290-1